David Alb

The Other

A Historical Introduction to Philosophy

Universo de Palabras
Universe of Words

4000 N. 7th St.-Suite 102
Phoenix, Arizona 85014. U.S.A.
Phone (602) 264-5011. Fax (419) 821-5046
editor@orbispress.com
www.orbispress.com

To **Know More** Series **2**

The Other / David Alberto Muñoz

The Other

A Historical Introduction to Philosophy

David Alberto Muñoz

To Know More Series
N° 2

Editorial *Orbis* Press
2003

The Other / David Alberto Muñoz

We cannot say anything absurd,
a philosopher has not said before.
Cicero

A mi padre..

Acknowledgments

As I attempt to write a list of all the people who helped in the production of *The Other*, I discover that it would be impossible to thank every single person who has contributed one way or another to this project. Throughout my life and my years of teaching, I have encountered a great number of people who willingly or unwillingly have helped me develop this venture, professors, students, colleagues, family, friends and acquaintances, among many others. It is to all of them, that I wish to express my personal gratitude.

Yet, I do want to convey my appreciation to several people who assisted and supported me throughout this undertaking. First of all, I wish to thank those professors who guided me, taught me, and even today continue to help me in the challenging endeavor of intellectual research, Dr. David Meyer, professor of Philosophy and History at Trinity Theological Seminary; Dr. Michael Baird and Dr. Clark Youngblood, both professors of Christian Studies at Grand Canyon University; Dr. Clyde Wilton from Bryan, Texas, whose scholarship I have never forgotten. Dr. Wilton inspired me to learn the Greek language. His careful methodological approach taught me to be careful as well as analytical on every premise I make. Dr. David William Foster, Emeritus Professor at Arizona State University, his teaching showed me the value of the "other," the one who just happens to be different.

Thanks as well, to my friends and colleagues, who helped as editors for this book, Yolanda De La Cruz, Associate Professor of Education at Arizona State University West Campus; Pamela Davenport, Division Chair of Language and Humanities at Chandler-Gilbert Community College, Caryl Terrell-Bamiro, Residential English Faculty, Chuck Neely and Blair Gadsby, professors of Philosophy and Religious Studies all of these at Chandler Gilbert Community College, thank you all for proofreading the text and for helpful insights and suggestions.

Also, I wish to say thanks to Dr. Manuel Murrieta Saldivar, General Editor and President of Editorial Orbis Press. His encouragement and the full collaboration of the Editorial made a big difference as I was writing this book; his literary vision lent a hand in the construction of the pages before the reader.

Accompanying these individuals, I want to express my infinite appreciation to my father, Dr. Alfonso Victor Muñoz, who literally threw me the novel *Nausea* by Jean Paul

Sartre when I was fifteen years of age. This piece of work written in the 20th century changed my life. With it, my father taught me to challenge even my own belief. His open mind opened new spaces for me as I continued to live, to experience, and of course, to study. ¡Gracias Padre!

Special thanks to the people who helped in the typing of this manuscript, Anna Muñoz, Iris Verdugo, Clara Priester and especially David Castañena; without their help, this project would have taken longer to complete.

This list would not be complete without a word of thanks to my beloved wife Mireya Muñoz, and my daughter Mirita, thank you both for your loving patience, allowing me to work night after night, for understanding that Dad had to work. Sometimes we get caught on the intellectual web and forget about the world of sense experience, where emotions seem to come from. I love you both very much!

Last but not least, I want to say thank you to all my students of philosophy, every one of you who through the years, has disputed ideas from Socrates to Sartre. Thank you for all your insights, all your questions, all your challenges, and all your interest in a field that is not very popular in our society at the beginning of the XXI century.

Thank you all!

Sincerely,
David Alberto Muñoz, Ph.D.
Phoenix, Arizona
January, 2003

Contents

Chapter 1
Brief Introduction to Philosophy

Chapter 1
Brief Introduction to Philosophy

Many students have asked me, why should we study **philosophy?** Why should we learn the name of those guys who lived long time ago? Why should we bother with a discipline that can be extremely boring and in some instances, has no benefit at all? Who cares about **Socrates**, **Hume** or **Camus** anymore? Philosophy sometimes appears to be a never-ending set of questions without answers.

For the society of the 21st century, to talk about premises and conclusions is to waste our time in a very ancient field of study. As one glances at the enrollment in colleges and universities, it is very evident that most people choose a major with some kind of mathematical, scientific or technical inclination. Math, biology, chemistry, computer science, business, or engineering, are some of the most popular subjects in our colleges and universities today. As the new millennium begins, philosophy has been kept to a simple **humanities** credit one has to take as a freshman. In all my years of teaching, I have encountered less than one percent of the college population who wants to major in philosophy.

Nevertheless, it is very important to understand the real meaning behind the **art** and/or **science** of creating philosophy. As we merely glance upon society, we realize that our contemporary civilization does not have a sense of reflection. We live in the United States of America at a very fast pace, especially those of us who live in big cities. We never have time to stop and think. We have to work, study and raise a family all at the same time. In this context, we want everything fast, in a split second. A good example of these predispositions would be what this writer calls the "**fast-food syndrome**." In almost every aspect of today's society, we find elements that help us speed up life, ATM machines, online billing, crash courses on how to manage time, family and friends, and of course, fast food restaurants, to name only a few. Sometimes we find that all these, are not fast enough for us.

For this reason we are always seeking new ways of saving time, for "time is money." We want our college degree in the shortest period of time. In today's world, we can even get a graduate degree on the Internet. Therefore, any analytical or reflective exercise that is suggested to us is immediately thrown aside, for we simply do not have the time to think. A common sentence I have heard my students speak, in relation to the ancient philosophers is, "These guys had a lot of time on their hands."

Chapter 1
Brief Introduction to Philosophy

The thinking process has been diluted through the complex mass media production we see in our world today. With the help of computers, the Internet, DVD's, satellite systems etc., we have lost the capacity of reflection. Everything comes to us in a manufactured package that requires no critical thinking process. By this I do not mean that the advances of technology are necessarily bad. Quite the contrary, all the resources we have available to us should be used for the improvement of the human mind, as **Plato** would put it. This statement does not intend to say that fast is bad; however, fast is not automatically always better.

As one sees the young minds in today's society, we see this generation has been raised within a **culture** of images and not letters, with virtual reality and easy access to almost every item available to human kind; no wonder we cannot see the critical thinking process taking place.

Definition of Philosophy / Why should we study it?

How can we define philosophy? Philosophy could be defined in many different ways. Sometimes one definition very easily overlaps another one. In some instances, two different definitions create a new definition; using **Hegel's** terminology, this results in a "**new synthesis.**" Furthermore, we can say that every definition of philosophy brings meaning and relevance to the word. However, first of all, we need to understand what we mean, when we speak of the word "**definition**." In its most simplistic meaning, definition is viewed as the act of defining, a statement of meaning. Yet, such meaning needs to have relevance to the person who is receiving the information. Such meaning could contain a set of different layers that would determine the real significance it is trying to convey. Things such as culture, **language** spoken or written, gender **roles**, **prejudices**, **education**, **knowledge**, personal interests, all of these items, are the ones that constitute the real meaning of the word "definition." Therefore, as one attempts to define any term in contemporary language, one needs to comprehend the different coatings of meaning behind any word. At the same time, one needs to take into consideration the changes of language through time. Language is a living phenomenon, a phenomenon that is constantly changing. If we considered this element into the construction of our definition of philosophy, we will understand that a definition only attempts to bring the student closer to the ultimate meaning, if indeed there is one.

Having this in mind, philosophy could be defined as one's own ideas, attitudes or beliefs about certain issues. This implies that the way we feel about life, death, sex, marriage, politics, and **religion** is philosophy, a philosophy that is moving from personal belief towards communal belief as a society. For example, any educational institution has a **philosophy of education**. A political party has a specific philosophy dealing with the way a nation should be ruled, this is called **political philosophy**. When a young man or woman decides to take a step in relationship to his/her own sexual orientation, such an action is the implementation of an individual **philosophy of sex**. This in turn has created the way society views sex. All of these attitudes we see in common people today, are a direct result of the philosophy our society has created. Therefore, as we attempt to make an honest analysis of the condition of our way of lives, we must take into account the many different ways people "feel" about life.

At this level philosophy implies that people have a personal perspective about life in general. The way I feel about the death penalty, abortion, euthanasia, drinking alcohol, drugs, smoking, sex before marriage, government, family, friends, community etc., would be my own philosophy about it. All of these issues will be determined by my personal philosophy on the subject. This can be illustrated with any issue in contemporary society. Therefore, philosophy means the way I see, perceive and understand life.

One of the challenges for the new millennium will be the ability to give space to the **other**. By *the Other* I mean any **ideology**, any idea, and any thought that might be in contradiction to my own personal belief. Today, we have many different philosophies; the differences among human kind are endless, ideologically, religiously, ethically and so forth. Contemporary life needs to recognize the fact that we cannot continue to ignore "the other" anymore. The "other one" needs to be recognized even though his/her recognition might create discomfort among mainstream society.

The world has become smaller with the advances of technology. I have the ability to communicate across the globe with the help of the computer. Critics speak of a new era, a new time after post-modernism, and although a name has not yet been created to identify such an age, we know there are many different ways to view life, and everyone claims to be right; everyone wants the dignity of "space."

The word used sometimes to express this tendency is **Pluralism**. The theory of pluralism might be defined as a condition marked by the multiplicity of religions, cultures, ethnic groups, and ideologies that can be adapted to live together in peace through **tol-**

eration, toleration meaning, the peaceful coexistence of "others" who fundamentally have different beliefs or values.

There are those who feel we need to draw the line at some point, for if we do not, no system of **values** would remain in place.

On the other hand, others feel we need to open out more and more, in order to give space to the circles that have been in a category of **sub-divided/hegemonic division** within the mainstream of American society. We are talking about minorities, woman homosexuals and anyone else that does not quite fit with the official discourse of our nation.

Let us look at the semantics of the word philosophy. Philosophy in a literal sense means reflection. It comes from two Greek words: Φ ι λ ο ς **(philos)** which means friendship and σ ο Φ ι α (sofia) which means **wisdom**. Therefore, philosophy means the friendship of wisdom. Since we live in such a fast paced society, we rarely stop to reflect upon the trivialities of life. Every day life continues to go without much thought; it is just a movement for the sake of movement alone. We cannot see the wisdom philosophy claims to offer. It is extremely difficult sometimes to enjoy the simple pleasures of life.

Such contemplation is viewed by contemporary American culture as a waste of time. We have more important things to do than to honestly reflect about the conditions of life. Perhaps we have created such a fast movement in order to avoid the painful reality of looking with all honesty at the society we have created. For example, when a member of society gets to be old, we don't claim this person has found wisdom; quite the contrary, elders are viewed as an inconvenience, and a bother society needs to deal with. If they have gained any wisdom through the years, who cares? They are a hindrance to the free flow of society.

This is precisely one of the reasons philosophies are so important. Socrates spoke about the importance of being honest with oneself. Honest reflection in any given group is an important element in the construction of society. Therefore, if we attempt to define philosophy and to answer the question: why should we study philosophy? We have to say, because it is an extremely important aspect of human life.

Since humanity has been creating ideas and thoughts, philosophy has been a part of human life. Without it, we would have no governments, no institutions, no traditions, and no infrastructure. It is philosophy that has created humanity's ideologies, interpretations, and viewpoints. Philosophy is at the heart of every issue, at the center of every change within society, and within every radical movement human beings have created. Philosophy seeks to understand the human experience a little bit better. Any tradition, any ideology, any religion has behind it a philosophy of life. The problem perhaps is that ordinary people in today's culture do not like complicated thoughts. The moment they see an obstacle, they scream in rage, they want the simplistic philosophy of a society that consumes and moves and moves and never stops.

However, without philosophy, without questioning, we would be condemning ourselves to spend the rest of eternity in the **limbo of conformity**. Where would we be without **Galileo** claiming the earth was round? How far could **Christianity** have spread without the revolutionary mind of **Martin Luther**? How many individuals could still be considered demon possessed without **Pasteur**? Where would the world be without the minds of **Nietzsche**, **Sartre**, **Kierkegaard** or **Marx**?

John Dewey (1859-1952), an American philosopher, was an individual very involved in the social issues of his day, especially with the reform of American schools. He believed philosophy deals with the criticism of the institutions that influence human societies. According to him, one needs to criticize society and its institutions. This helps to keep a balance within society. If nobody questions the government, the churches, the schools, this can create a very dangerous situation, a society, which is not accountable to anything or anybody. Therefore, as members of society, we must be constantly criticizing it, bringing new questions, new ideas and new dialogues.

From this perspective we can say that philosophy is a necessity within human life. In order to maintain the perfect balance of power we defend so much in the United States of America; we must be willing not only to defend our freedom, but also to exercise it, by bringing into our personal and community lives, new proposals, new submissions and compliances that will help the betterment of society.

This is a very dangerous position to take however; as mentioned above, conformity is also an element we see in society today. Many individuals in our society do not have the ability to think critically. How many times we have joked about the fact many people do not think? To a certain extent, capitalism has created a society that prefers to make money and leaves behind the reflection, the careful thinking process. Decisions are made not based on careful consideration; rather, they are made based on economic principles, on how convenient it might be for me, on what's in it for me, etc. Needless to say, this is a very narrow minded way. It is very easy to follow the majority of the people; it is very comfortable to take a passive position and never engage in the open debate of ideas. However, in order to improve life, institutions, and society, we must be willing to make a change and be critical of society, as well as its institutions and ourselves.

This writer believes that philosophy is seeking wisdom through honest reflection. We must be willing to look at ourselves with honesty and integrity. Part of the America culture is to never accept the fact that we, like all other human beings, make mistakes. We seem to have taken the cynical attitude of knowing everything there is to know, of being perfect individuals who know what to do and how to do it. When we have this kind of mentality, which can only be defined as "closed mind," there is absolutely no way we can learn from "other" people, philosophies or ideas. In this context philosophy could be defined as an art and science of being honest in the search for answers to questions we have always had: Who are we? Where are we going? What is the meaning of life? Is there life after death?

Philosophy, therefore, should be studied for the sake of discovering how we arrived at our present way of thinking. We need to study philosophy if we are serious about understanding the human condition, the complex human experience. Today's world is so diverse, there are so many different ideas about how to live one's life; one can get lost in it. However, as we approach the issues of the world with a clear understanding about where those ideas came from, we can have a clearer picture of the world we live in today. And, we might also discover what directions we might seek in the future.

Branches of Philosophy

Traditionally, philosophy encompasses a methodical, all-inclusive study of certain questions that center on meaning, interpretation, assessment, and rational consistency.

Philosophers sometimes concentrate on one of these branches or might go as far as rejecting whole areas of philosophy as unfit for study. The traditional areas of study are:

1. Metaphysics – This is the study about the nature of the world, the nature of reality. Also called, theory of existence.
2. Epistemology – This is the study of knowledge, or the justification of belief.
3. Ethics – This is the study of the conduct of life, the theory of value. This does not imply what is good or bad; it implies the limits to one's own behavior.
4. Logic - This is the principle of sound reasoning, the way of constructing good sound, logical arguments.
5. Aesthetics – This is the study of beauty, the concept of what is beautiful and how we acquire it.

There are more subdivisions within these five main branches. For example we find **axiology**, which is a subdivision of ethics and studies values. It concentrates on questions of what is worth pursing or promoting and what should be avoided, along with questions such as: What is the relation between values and facts? Can values be objective? Etc. The issue of justification arises whether or not a set of values is systematic.

What is an argument?

An argument is a group of statements, a chain of reasoning designed to prove something, one or more of which (the **premises**) support or provide evidence for another (the **conclusion**). An argument has as its aim to demonstrate the truth or falsity of a particular claim, by presenting evidence that may convince the hearer or reader to accept it. If I claim anything and do not provide any evidence for it, I am not presenting an argument; I am giving only an opinion.

What is the difference between an argument and an **opinion**? The word "argument" means evidence, proof. It comes from the Latin ***argutari*** meaning to make clear, to prove. Therefore, an argument implies the offering of reason or reasons for or against something. It refers to a discussion in which there is disagreement and suggests the use of logic and the bringing forth of facts to support or refute a point. The word "opinion" comes from the Latin ***opinari***, which means to think, to select. It is a belief not based upon absolute certainty or positive knowledge but on what seems to be true, valid, or probable to one's own mind. When we are talking about opinion, we are talking about what *seems true*, what is probable, etc.

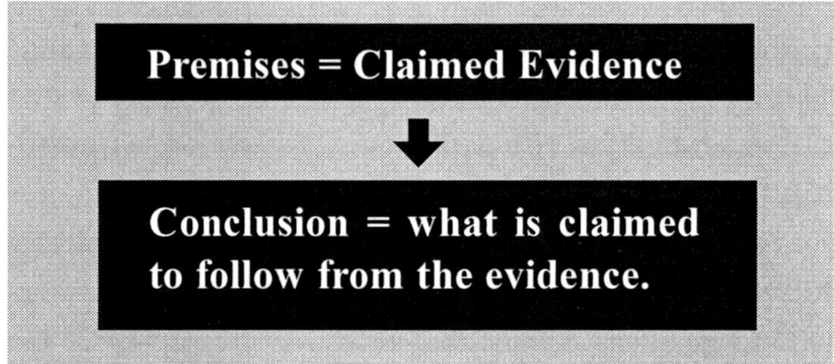

One of the issues as far as evaluating arguments is: what statement is the conclusin or what is the conclusion drawn. The conclusion of an argument should be the statement or claim that has at least one other statement in support of it.

The conclusion should not be confused with the main point in the material being examined. For example, many editorials and letters to the editor have a point to make. However, many times they do not have a good argument at all. In other words no reason is giving for the position taken; therefore, there is no conclusion. When one is not certain about whether there is a conclusion, look at a statement that is supported by at least one other statement. Sometimes in long arguments we could find more than one supporting statement. The reason might be that support is given to one or more of the argument's premises. In order to find the conclusion, it will be necessary to determine which supported statement also seems to be the primary thesis being defended in the passage.

A Small History of Logic

The person who is usually credited as the father of logic is the ancient Greek philosopher **Aristotle** (384-322 B.C.E.)[1] His predecessors had been interested in the construction of arguments, in techniques for refuting the arguments of others. However, it was Aristotle who developed systematic criteria for analyzing and evaluating arguments. Aristotle's logic is called **syllogistic logic**. The term syllogism as defined by Aristotle is: "a discourse in which, certain things being stated, something other than what is stated follows of necessity from their being so." In more simplistic terms, syllogism is a three step argument, consisting of two premises and one conclusion. We can also put it another way: three statements arranged in the form of an ***if-then proposition***.

If **A** is true and **B** is true then **C** is true of necessity and tells you something new.

The most famous syllogism is the following:

> ***If***, *All men are mortal*
> ***And if***, *Socrates is a man*
> ***Therefore***, *Socrates is mortal*

After Aristotle's death, another Greek philosopher developed a logic in which the fundamental elements were whole propositions. His name was **Chrysippus** (279-206 B.C.) He was one of the founders of the **Stoic School**. **Stoicism** is the ethical philosophy of some of the members of ancient Greek society. It emphasized the calm, undisturbed life as the highest good and thought it best reached through acceptance of the natural order of things. The stoic school was a very rigorously systematic school. Chrysippus treated every preposition as either true or false and develop rules for determining their components. In doing this he laid down the foundation for the truth functional interpretation or the notion of natural deduction. For about 1300 years after Chrysippus died no major creative work was done in logic.

It was not until the **Middle Ages** and the work of **Peter Abelard** (1079-1142) that we see new developments. Abelard reconstructed and redefined the logic of Aristotle and Chrysippus. He distinguished arguments that are valid because of their form from those that are valid because of their content; he held that only formal validity is the "perfect" or conclusive variety.

After the Middle Ages the study of logic blossomed through the work of different philosophers, such as **William of Occam** (c. 1285-1349). He was an Englishman who devoted his attention to modal logic, a kind of logic that involves such notions as possibility, necessity, belief and doubt. Toward the middle of the 15th century a reaction againts the logic of the Middle Ages was set. **Rethoric** became the central point of interest. Logic was ignored for about 200 years.

A reawakening occurred with the work of **Gottfried Wilhelm Leibniz** (1646-1716). He attempted to develop a **symbolic language** or "calculus" that could be used to settle all forms of dispute, whether in theology, philosophy or international relations. Sometimes Leibniz is credited as being the father of symbolic logic. With the arrival of **symbolic logic** and the 19th century, logic began to move ahead very rapidly and it has continued to this day.

During the 20th century much of the work in logic concentrated on the formalization of logical systems and on questions dealing with the completeness and consistency of such systems. Recently logic has made a major contribution by providing the conceptual foundation for the electronic circuitry of digital computers.

In the United States of America the **analytical school** has dominated; this tendency has been control by logical critical thinking; while in places like Latin America a different approach has been taken. The philosophers of these nations are writers of novels and short stories, who utilize their art to provide proposals about life and the way life is lived. This approach has used a more pragmatic inclination towards the application of the discipline of logic.

The Standard form of an Argument

Once we have identified a conclusion, the next step is to reconstruct the argument into what is called: a **standard form**.

We can do this either mentally or in writing. Yet, it is essential to do it, in order to make a good evaluation of the argument. This is the standard format:

Since (premise)
And (premise)
And (premise)
Therefore, (conclusion)

Usually, we do not find arguments presented this way. However, any argument can be reconstructed in this manner by orderly separation of the premises from the conclusion. The words ***since***, ***and***, ***therefore*** are indicators. One must be aware these vary from argument to argument. The number of premises also varies from one to as many as is thought to be necessary to establish the truth of the conclusion. Sometimes a statement of support and even the conclusion is not present; however, these are understood from the context.

Conclusion

As we progress in our venture into the field of philosophy, we must keep in mind these principles. For human kind, there is a tendency to argue with one another, nevertheless, at least in the Unites States of America, we feel arguing means insulting the "other." We have become a nation that has mastered rhetoric and as long as we can have the last word or insult, it makes us feel good. However, as we attempt to debate philosophical issues, we must not be fast to judge and to put aside any argument. We must weigh the evidence behind every ideology before we can make a value judgment upon it. Something we might soon discover, is the fact that the more we learn, the more ignorant we might feel. When we begin realizing, and furthermore understanding the great diversity we find in the world, we cannot help but to become humble, before the great minds of the world, the great variety of ideas. We soon discover that the truth is not an absolute. The truth lies within the human experience. And even though we have belief systems that do possess absolutes, we cannot, we must not remain closed to the possibility of change, experiences and new proposals that might give us an insight into the search for the meaning of life.

STUDY QUESTIONS & EXERCISES

I. Give the different definitions of philosophy presented in our text. Be specific!

II. According to our text, there are several reasons why we should study philosophy. What are these reasons?

III. What are some of the elements we have within today's world that make us not a very reflective society?

IV. What are the different branches of philosophy?

V. What does each of them study?

VI. What is an argument?

VII. Give a small outline of the history of logic and its main characters.

VIII. What is the standard form of an argument?

Chapter 2
Origins of philosophy

Chapter 2
Origins of Philosophy

Philosophy began between the sixth and fourth centuries B.C.E. It began all over the world, in **China**, **India**, and the **Middle East**, with thinkers who started to question the popular conception of the world in relationship with the gods and goddesses. Perhaps what can be stated is the fact that non-conformity gave rise to philosophy. Individuals who were not satisfied with the explanations given by those in power, created a challenge that through the years has given rise to a whole discipline of study.

These groups of early philosophers were **wise men**, **prophets** and **sages**. Within every society we find these types of people who somehow become leaders of thought, leaders who direct common people to understanding the ideology that produces such society. They wanted to question the notion given to human kind by popular conceptions of the world. Their minds could somehow not accept the traditional knowledge given by the **elders** or the **tradition**. In some way, they were able to see beyond their own experience and at least they tried to change human understanding, thus creating new ideologies, producing a new understanding that up to this point in history continues to bring debate, discussion and desire for improvement. These ancient thinkers were concerned with the ultimate origins as well as with the nature of things. The questions they had are perhaps the same questions all of us at one point or another have asked: What is the meaning of life? What is the origin of everything there is? Can we name the substance out of which everything comes? How can we know what lies beyond human life? Who is God? Is there a God?

In India, a man named **Siddhãrtha Guatama** (553-483 B.C.E.) was traveling across his nation searching for immortality and an answer to the suffering he saw in the world. In China, a man by the name of **Confucius** became known as a great teacher of wisdom, teaching people with the help of analogies, the way to live and to behave. Chinese philosophy concentrates in ***harmony*** as the ideal state of society and the individual. In **Persia**, a man by the name of **Zarathustra** (c. 628-551 B.C.E.)

began to shift in the direction of a comprehensive **moral monotheism**. He is the first of the world's religions prophets. **Zoroastrianism** became the ancient religion around North East **Iran**. The main idea behind this philosophy is that the very ancient Persian gods were good and evil. The leader of the ***daevas*** is the eternal opponent of the good God, **Ahura Mazda**, who according to Zarathustra taught him personally in a series of visions, that the emphasis on personal responsibility is a hallmark of the religion throughout its history. Perhaps the apparent "obsession" with a cosmic battle between the forces of good and evil was born with him and remains with the West today. Later on, the **Hebrews** were the ones that developed this idea of monotheism to the extreme, creating thus far the belief in one supreme God.

There is a tendency in today's society, to see some **ancient civilizations** as barbaric and lacking knowledge. For some strange reason, we have come to believe that somehow, we are better than ancient societies, because we have technological advances, because we can communicate in a more "effective way," etc. However, why should we

assume that these cultures were barbaric just because they were different? Why should we ignore the past just because we are the present? Once again, we must take into consideration the fact that differences should not create enemies; they should bring unity into the human picture, through a clear understanding that what makes humankind unique, is its diversity, its great variety, the great multiplicity of ideologies that compose human life.

Philosophy began with human beings questioning the establishment, individuals that were not satisfied with the answers given to them. Therefore, creating new challenges, new opportunities, a new path to follow. Human existence has been questioned since we became aware of ourselves. In order to provide a reasonable answer, philosophy and religion were created; they became a reality as an alternative, as a way to give peace, hope, or perhaps an explanation for the human experience. Since the time of **Confucius**, **Amos** and **Thales**, humans have tried to explain the so-called "meaning of life." Their explanations might not satisfy the contemporary reader; however, we must take into account their positions, their perspectives, for their ideology came out of their own human experiences and time frame. We must, therefore, make an attempt to understand the history of philosophy, the history of ideas, the history of how we become to be where we are right now.

We will concentrate on the history of philosophy in the Western World, being aware however, that human kind was also alive and searching in the Eastern region of our planet.

STUDY QUESTIONS & EXERCISES

I. Where did philosophy began and around what time?

II. What questions did the prophets and sages want to answer?

III. Give the names of the early philosophers and who they were.

IV. How does today's society view ancient civilizations?

V. How does the past have an effect in today's world?

VI. What was the main foundation of Zoroastrianism?

VII. Describe one of the main purposes of philosophy according to this chapter.

Chapter 3
Homer & The Greek Setting

Chapter 3
Homer & The Greek Setting

The literature of the ancient **Greek World** is, without doubt, the background of our present **Western Civilization**. Our institutions, attitudes, and thoughts were first written in three different languages: Hebrew, Greek, and Latin. The people who articulated these languages created their own civilizations apart from each other. However, with the development of the Mediterranean area into one economic and political force, it brought these civilizations together and produced the merging of their particular outlooks, forming the basis of all subsequent Western thought. This process of independent development, interaction, and final fusion could be described as the history of Western philosophy. When the figure of **St. Augustine** emerged, we can see the intellectual honesty and inquisitiveness of the Greeks, the social thoughtfulness and sense of order of the **Romans**, and the Hebrew's feeling of man's ineptitude and God's supreme justice. Although we believe it was at this particular time, the time of St. Augustine, when the West was born, its history can be traced back to **Homer** and the beginning of Greek civilization around the year 1400 B.C.E.

The word **civilization** is identified with the notion of citizens. When there was enough agricultural production that not everybody had to raise food, cities began to form. This happened around the year 2500 B.C.E. The inhabitants of cities are those who enjoy the rights and privileges that civilization brings. By the year 451 B.C.E., citizenship in Greece was restricted and thus its benefits desired. Specialization became possible. People could group together and trade not only goods and services but also ideas.

These, ideas however, brought **segregation**, and, in turn, subordination. Women, who up to this point had been equal to men and who in some instances dominated an agrarian economy, were now restricted to tasks of the home. Some men became full-time warriors and philosophers, while others, unfortunately, became bonded to oppression.

Each geographical area was independent of the other. In **The Tigris-Euphrates Valley**, cities flourished while ruled by powerful kings who determined the fate of the people. Greece was an area of peninsulas and islands. Separated by mountains or sea, each region was partly secluded from the others. Nevertheless, it could support more than a few million people. These people lived by trading with each other. This condition produced no great natural resources or wealth, but rather a constant flow of new ideas from one place to the next. These Greek cities organized themselves in small **democratic city-states.**

Each city owned a particular **myth**[2]. Such myths defined the inhabitants' viewpoint of the world and how it worked. These myths served to create and to enforce conformity to tradition and custom. It was believed the gods inspired **poets**; therefore, they were read as much as the Bible is read today. In order to find what was truly excellent, of value for civil and family life, the Greeks looked upon these poets as the authority who could give some picture of the world and man's place in it.

Homer & Hesiod

It is in this world that we find the figure of **Homer** (ca 800 B.C.E.) Homer was, according to tradition, a blind man, a poet, author of two masterpieces, the ***Iliad*** and the ***Odyssey***, which together with the Hebrew Scriptures, the comedies and tragedies of the Greeks **Aristophanes**, **Aeschylus**, **Sophocles**, **Euripides** and the Latin works of **Virgil**, **Horace**, **Propertius**, and **Ovid** have become the literary foundation of Western civilization. Although the dates of Homer's works are only conjectures, they were probably fixed in their final form around the year 700 B.C.E. Some scholars have suggested that Homer was not a real person, rather a group or a school whose teaching was communicated through these writings. These stories tell of the human struggles to find meaning within the human experience, an honest desire to make sense out of life. Whatever lies behind the most intriguing enigmas of life, was, and still is, the basis of any given society. By the time the classical Greek period ended around the 4th century B.C.E., the influence of Homer could still be felt within the Greek society.

A poet who further influenced Greek culture was **Hesiod** (ca 700 B.C.E.), his accounts of the origins of the cosmos and the Gods, included elements from mythologies from the **Ancient Near East**. Hesiod writes that at the beginning there was just chaos, and out of it, what materialized was the heavens and the earth as well as the underworld. He implies that the Gods are a direct result from the chaos. Also, he states that there are principles of order that explain the emergence of an orderly cosmos out of total chaos.

The *Iliad* for its part is an epic poem that recounts the story of the **Trojan War**. The goddess **Discord** requested from the god **Zeus** to choose which goddess was the most beautiful. Zeus refused to judge; instead three contenders went before the royal prince **Paris**[3], prince of Troy[4], for a decision. The contestants were **Aphrodite**, **Athena**, and **Hera**. Each made an offer to induce Paris to give her the **Apple of Discord**[5]. Athena and Hera offered military or political power, but Aphrodite proposed to give Paris the most beautiful woman in the world. He gave the apple to Aphrodite who led him to Helen, the most beautiful women in the world, the wife of the king of **Sparta**[6], **Menelaos**. The Greeks then sailed to Troy to recover Helen who later became known as Helen of Troy. The fighting between Troy and Greece continued for ten years, while **Achilles** (Akhilleus), the greatest warrior of the Greeks, refused to fight because the commander, **Agamemnon**, had offended him. Achilles finally went into battle and killed the greatest Trojan warrior, **Hector**. Having seriously weakened the Trojan defenses, the Greeks achieved final victory through the ploy of the **Trojan Horse**. The Trojans, which mistook it as a gift of surrender from the Greeks, brought inside the impenetrable walls that surrounded Troy. Once inside, the Greeks waited until nightfall before emerging from inside the belly of the wooden horse. They burned Troy to the ground and returned victorious to Greece.

The *Iliad* has as its theme: anger and revenge. At the beginning of the poem, we read the angry words of Achilles. This excessive anger brings death and destruction to many Greeks and almost cost them the war.

> Anger be now your song, immortal one,
> Akhilleus' anger, doomed and ruinous,
> that caused the Akhaians [Greeks] loss on bitter loss
> and crowded brave souls into the undergloom,
> leaving so many dead men---carrion
> for dogs and birds; and the will of Zeus was done.
>
> (*Iliad 1, 11*)[7]

We find assumptions made by Homer. He takes for granted that Zeus is king of the gods. Later on, the poem speaks about other gods. Nevertheless, Zeus seems to be the most powerful. From the beginning of the epic, the reader finds out that the world of Homer is a world of gods, kings and humans. All of these heroic figures are engaged with one another. The gods are interested in the daily affairs of human kind. In some instances, we discover that there are certain beings that are half divine and half human.

The Iliad summarizes the story of the excesses and pride of Achilles as well as his humane side. There seems to be throughout the story, a central moral teaching: reasonableness. The lack of this virtue was Achilles' downfall. At the same time, there is a celebration of heroic virtues such as courage, strength and wisdom.

Before the first *official* philosopher stepped into the human arena, the world was dominated by these moral values. This epic formed the basis of the ancient Greek society. Nobody dared to question it. Conformity to one's own destiny or what Homer called "fate" was a reality within the Greek society. Even the gods were subject to it. I believe that before any great advance in philosophy, this worldview needed to settle in. Human history is the history of thoughts that later on were transformed into more precise concepts in order to make proposals and subsequent changes within human life. Consequently, for people in the West, this is where our story begins.

STUDY QUESTIONS & EXERCISES

I. What is the setting for the history of Western philosophy?

II. How is Homer and Hesiod related to the history of Western philosophy?

III. When we find the figure of St. Augustine, we discover three different cultures fused into one. What are these cultures and what are their characteristics?

IV. Do you personally find any good reason why we should study philosophy in the 21st century? Why or why not?

V. Why are *The Iliad* and *The Odyssey* important to the West?

VI. What was the concept of the origin of the cosmos and the Gods according to Hesiod?

VII. What is the basic theme of *The Iliad*?

VIII. What are some of reasons for the creation of a civilization and its natural consequences?

IX. Aphrodite, Athena, and Hera offered certain things to Paris. What were they?

X. Before the first official philosopher came into the human arena, what was the general view of the public?

Chapter 4
Pre- Socratic Philosophers

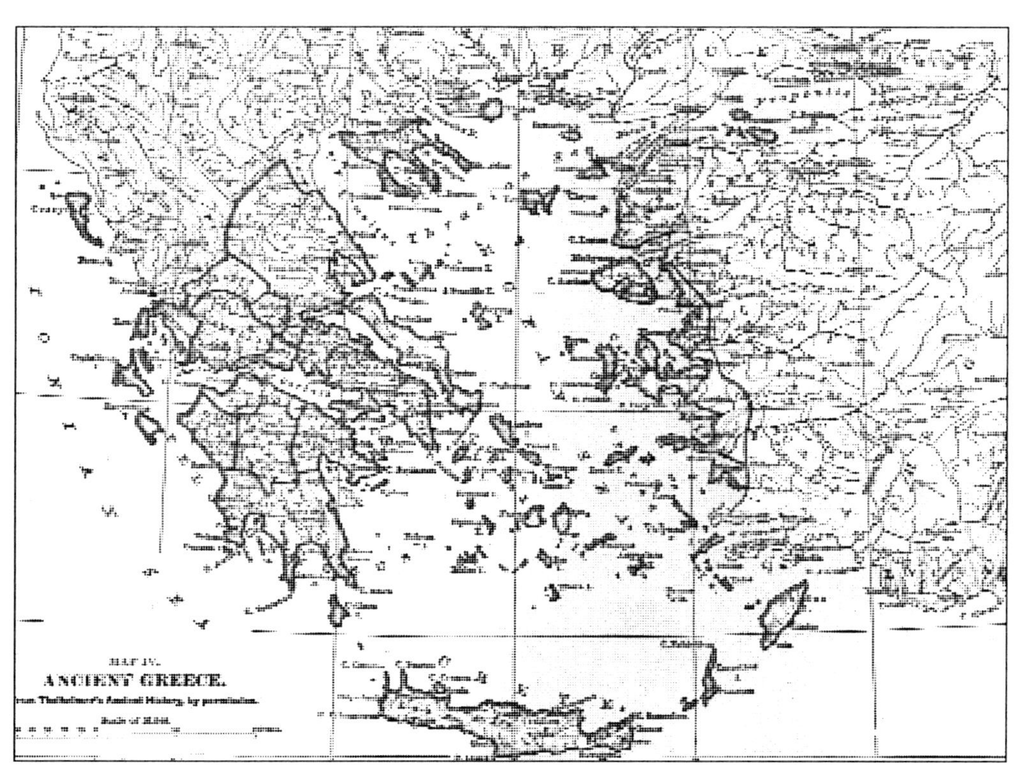

Chapter 4
Pre- Socratic Philosophers

According to tradition, philosophy in the European mold was born in the town of **Miletus**, located on the western shores of **Ionia** in Asia Minor across the **Aegean Sea** from **Athens**. Although philosophic thought began there, other sources as mentioned above eventually entered into our story (specifically Hebrew tradition). In this city, wealth made possible a life of leisure without which the arts and philosophy could not have survived. The open mind of its people created a congenial atmosphere for intellectual activity. Miletus had been an intersection for both sea commerce and cosmopolitan ideas. In later centuries, the town of Miletus would be called the "**Age of the Seven Wise Men**." In this city, a man by the name of **Thales** is born. All the information available to us is fragmentary, with references to him made by later writers such as Plato and Aristotle. The years of his life are set between the year 624 and 546 B.C.E. Even though there have been some variations as to who these Seven Wise Men were, Thales is on every list available to us today.

Thales of Miletus

Thales was an extraordinary man. He was a politician, an astronomer, a mathematician, a philosopher, and a physicist, among other things. He pushed the Greeks to unite in a federation according to **Herodotus**[8]. He predicted a solar eclipse, which must have taken place in the year 585 B.C.E. During the Persian War, he showed the army how to cross a river by building a dam, by diverting its flow into two different channels; he was also able to demonstrate how to build bridges. While traveling in Egypt, Thales worked out a way of measuring a pyramid's shadow by looking at one's own shadow at the time of day when it is equal to one's own height. His knowledge of mathematics and the laws of nature were so astounding that he is regarded by some as the first scientist. Plato writes the following anecdote in his ***Theaetetus***, when a young woman laughed at Thales for paying too much attention to the sky:

> The jest which the clever witty Thracian handmaid is said to have made about Thales, when he fell into a well as he was looking up at the stars. She said that he was so eager to know what was going on in heaven that he could not see what was before his feet . . . this is a jest which is equally applicable to all philoso phers[9].

Aristotle tells us in his *Politics*:

> There is . . . the story which is told of Thales of Miletus. It is a story about a scheme for making money, which is attached to Thales owning to his reputation for wisdom. He was reproached for his poverty, which was supposed to show the uselessness of philosophy. According to the story observing from his knowled ge of meteorology while it was yet winter that there would be great harvest of

> olives in the coming year, he gave deposits for all the olive-presses in Miletus and Chios, which he hired at a low price because no one bid against him. When the harvest time came, and there was a sudden and simultaneous demand for the olive presses, he let out the stock he had collected at any rate he chose to fix; and making a considerable fortune, he succeeded in proving that it is easy for philosophers to become rich if they like, but that their ambition lies elsewhere[10].

However, Thales is not famous for his knowledge of meteorology or his business ability. His main contribution to philosophy involves the nature of things. What is the **substance** out of which everything is made of? What kind of "***stuff***" goes into the constitution of things? Thales wanted to answer these questions and to find out what was the beginning of all things. The Greek word άρχή (arche), which means not only a beginning, but also that which begins to be something. In other words, the intention of Thales was to sketch a reasonable answer for the fact that there are so many different kinds of things, and that sometimes things seem to change from time to time into other things that resemble each other in particular ways. Thales wanted a **naturalistic** account of the origin of things. His contribution to the study of knowledge was that although there are differences between things, they all relate to each other by *the One* (a single entity). He believed this element is the *stuff* out of which everything comes into existence. This component contains its own principle of action or change; this is the άρχή that lays at the foundation of all physical reality.

According to Aristotle, for Thales, this *One*, *stuff*, or άρχή was **water**. It is not difficult to comprehend why he chose water to perform the role of being the primal stuff. No doubt he was able to notice the fact that water is essential for the nourishment of all things, including human beings, plants, and animals; the earth itself needs moisture so the seed will grow. Water changes its form, yet its essence never changes. Through other phenomena such as evaporation and freezing, Thales was able to see that water takes on different forms.

Anaximander

Anaximander, the second philosopher of the **Milesian school**, is according to Bertrand Russell[11] "much more interesting than Thales."[12] He believed that all things come from a single primal substance. However, this substance was not water as Thales hypothesized. This element is divine in nature, ceaseless, infinite. It is what Anaximander called ἀπειρου (*âpeiron*), which means ***boundless***. This boundless element is the one that governs all things. In other words, the quantity of the matter, out of which all things are created, has an origin and a cycle. It is not only the substance of the world but also the law of the world. Anaximander was the first one to present the problem of the process out of which all things come into existence. This process was for him, the process of *separation*. The birth of something is the separation of beings from the ἀπειρου (infinite substance). He held that divinities also were born and died in long intervals and that such divinities existed in worlds, which cannot be counted.

According to Anaximander there was an eternal motion; this has brought into existence the origins of worlds. The world was not created as the Hebrews believed. There seems to be an evolution even within the animal kingdom. Only the ἀπειρου can be the beginning of all things. For it has no beginning and no end. Everything must have a beginning or be the beginning. This language is familiar with the Christian belief in one God. We read in the New Testament that in God: "we live and move and have our being" (Acts 17:28).[13] Also, the statement found in the book of Revelation 22:13: "I am the Alpha and the Omega, the first and the last, the beginning and the end."

Anaximander is the first man who made a map. He maintained that the world was shaped in the form of a cylinder. There is no doubt that his mind was a scientific mind, a rationalistic way of looking at the world which favors the view that Anaximander was full of scientific curiosity.

Anaximenes

Anaximenes[14] (585-528 B.C.E.) who was associated with Anaximander is the next pre-Socratic in our survey. He believed that we ought to attach terms we know as they arise in common language instead of inventing new, abstract ones. The philosopher must not move away from ordinary jargon into an abstract one, because such terms are worthless and have no meaning. Only the expressions emanating in reference to specific things referred to in our immediate experience have real meaning. Anaximenes theorized that the use of simple language, ordinary vernacular is a much better style than the lyrical poetic prose utilized by Anaximander.

Using this language, Anaximenes considered the underlying substance to be one and infinite, just like his predecessor. However, he did not identify it with the ἀπειρου. Rather he determined it was ***air***. Our souls are the air that sustains life. The world is like a giant animal breathing, and such breathing is its soul and its life. Out of the air, all things are born, the ones that were and the ones that will be, even the gods and the divine things begin with air, which is the beginning of movement and of every change.

> Just as, he said: our soul, being air, holds together, so do breath and air encompass the whole world. . . When (air) it is dilated so as to be rarer, it becomes fire; where winds, on the other hand, are condensed Air. Cloud is formed from Air by felting; and this, still further condensed, becomes water. Water condensed still more, turns to earth; and when condensed as much as it can be, to stones.[15]

Thus according to Anaximenes, the *stuff* or primary infinite substance is not water or the *boundless*. Rather, it is *air*. It is a specific material substance, which is tangible and can be identified. The motion of the air is a far more specific process than the idea of separation given by Anaximander. Anaximenes was able to develop the concepts of "***rarefaction***" (expansion) and "**condensation**" (contraction) as the specific forms of motion, which lead to describable changes in air. Expansion of air causes warming and the transformation of air into solids by way of a gradual transition where, wings are condensed air; if this process goes on, it gives water and finally stones.

For a modern reader, these ideas might seem weird. These Milesian philosophers proceeded with scientific concerns; yet they did not develop their hypotheses the way a modern scientist would. Also, they did not offer any scientific proof of their findings. Nevertheless, we must remember that the critical question concerning nature and human limitations had not yet been raised.

Pythagoras

A man who has had a tremendous amount of influence not only in ancient times, but also in modern times is **Pythagoras**[16] (c. 572-497 B.C.E.). He was born on the small island of Samos in the Aegean Sea. **Samos** was the main commercial rival of Miletus. Pythagoras migrated to **Croton** a colony in southern Italy around the year 530 B.C.E. as a result of the excesses of the pirate king, **Polycrates**, and his totalitarian rule. It was in this city where Pythagoras cultivated his philosophy, which became eventually a religion. His character is a combination of legend and reality. His historical life has been mixed with myth and tradition. It is very possible that Pythagoras never wrote anything. The only doctrine that some scholars attribute to him is the doctrine of the eternity of the soul. According to this doctrine, later on adopted by Plato (428-348 B.C.E.), the soul is a prisoner of the human body; therefore, the soul lives on a superior world. All that we know about Pythagoras is that he founded a school in Samos and that his students practiced certain rites designed to purify the soul to free it from the "**wheel of birth**." These rites were based on mathematics and music to gain philosophical illumination.

During a short journey to **Egypt**, as a young man of 22, Thales suggested Pythagoras study in Egypt to enlarge his knowledge. Later on, he traveled to Egypt, the source of the "**Ancient Mysteries**." While traveling, he stayed for a while in the gulf of Haifa at a temple on Mount Carmel, Israel (after the destruction of the First Jewish Temple of Jerusalem). In Egypt, he remained and studied for about 22 years.

Pythagoras founded the famous **Pythagorean School** of philosophy, mathematics, and natural sciences. People from different classes came to hear his lectures, among them, women, even though the law in those days prohibited their participation in public meetings. He assembled the more talented disciples and established a brotherhood, preaching the simple life, modesty, austerity, patience, and self-control. They consumed a vegetarian dried and condensed food and unleavened bread (as the Jewish people did and still do today). It is also mentioned that they did not cut their hair, beard, and nails[17].

Pythagoras believed that things consist of numbers. Therefore, the subtance for him was the **number**. This notion might be difficult to understand. We must remember that Pythagoras became extremely interested in numbers, and he had a special conception of what numbers were. First of all, we must know that he had a conviction that the study of mathematics is the best purifier of the soul. In this context, he could be viewed as the founder of a religion as well as a school of mathematics. The Pythagoreans were concerned with the mystical problems of the purification of the soul and its immortality. Through the study of mathematics they detected a mode of life that was purer than any other. It was Pythagoras who distinguished between three different kinds of lives. The lowest class is made of those who go to the Olympics games to make a profit, to buy and sell. Next are those who go to compete, to gain honors. Last but definitely not least, the best kind according to Pythagoras are the ones that go as spectators, those who reflect and analyze what is going on. Out of these three, the spectator without any doubt reflects the Greek philosopher; one who does not involved himself with daily life and its imperfections. Rather, it is that individual who searches through mathematical thought, the liberation from the "wheel of birth." The soul must stop its migration to animal lives and other forms. Since the spectator must achieve unity with the gods, he must share their immortality as well.

Pythagoras according to tradition never allowed his novices to see him during the years of probation, he instructed them from behind a curtain. The Pythagoreans practiced mathematics and determined illiteracy; to write things down was considered a source of error. Among these teachings was the doctrine of the transmigration of souls. The soul wanders from the home of the blessed, being born into all kinds of mortal forms, passing from one laborious path of life to another.

Some of the rules of the **Pythagorean order** were:

1. To abstain from beans.
2. Not to pick up what has fallen.
3. Not to touch a white cock.
4. Not to break bread.
5. Not to step over a crossbar.
6. Not to stir the fire with iron.
7. Not to eat from a whole loaf.
8. Not to pluck a garland.
9. No to sit on a quart measure.
10. Not to eat the heart.
11. Not to walk on highways.
12. Not to let swallows share one's roof.

13. When the pot is taken off the fire, not to leave the mark of it in the ashes, but to stir them together.
14. Do not look in a mirror beside a light.
15. When you rise from the bedclothes, roll them together and smooth out the impression of the body.

Pythagoras was also one of the earliest Greek thinkers, following up hints from Anaximenes and Heraclitus (540-480), to attach ethical significance to the human soul, thus making the shift, from concentrating on the universe to human beings, where Pythagoras saw the soul as a harmonizing principle. Apart from his famous geometric theorem, Pythagoras is also credited with the discovery of the numerical ratios that determine the concordant scale. Numbers were considered somehow to have substance. Through them a divine order was imposed on the world, invisible to the eye but discernible by the mind.

Heraclitus

Heraclitus (540-480 B.C.E.) was born in **Ephesus**, in a town between Miletus and **Colophon**, on the West Coast of Ionia (today's Turkey). Heraclitus was a nobleman who was a descendent from the early kings of Ephesus. Although he was rich and of a noble descent, he rejected any right to the throne in order to become a philosopher. Unlike Thales, Anaximander, and Anaximenes, who were respectful of their societies, Heraclitus was the first of a long tradition of philosophers who openly criticized not only his society but also his fellow citizens, including other philosophers.

Heraclitus' main contribution to philosophy was his effort to answer such questions as: What is the world made of? Is it something solid or unchanging? Or can it change its shape and character? How do we account for the unity and the diversity that we experience?

These questions had troubled thoughtful people for centuries. Some studied and speculated, trying to make sense of it all. Heraclitus looked around and saw that the world seemed to be constantly changing. He began to search for some underlying unity that held it all together. Earlier philosophers had claimed that the apparently diverse reality could be reduced to some material thing, such as water (Thales) or air (Anaximenes). Others found unity in some structural principles such as pairs of opposites

(Anaximander) or numbers (Pythagoreans). But these explanations seemed inadequate in everyday life. How did one thing change into another? If water, for example, was the basic stuff of the universe, then where did dirt come from?

Heraclitus held that the basic stuff of the world was neither air, nor water, nor some fusion of opposites. It was fire. He proclaimed: "This world-order . . . was always and is and shall be: an everlasting fire."[18]

At first, this position appeared to be just another unitary "oneness" to which the "many" apparent diversities of the world could be reduced. His position seemed similar to those claiming that reality was ultimately united in earth or air or water. Actually Heraclitus also talked about fire, water, and earth, but it was the way in which these three things were constantly changing into one another that provided the clue to the "oneness" or unity of all reality. For Heraclitus, all was flux. He declared that one could not step into the same river twice.

Parmenides

While Heraclitus was working out his theory of ordered change, a young man named **Parmenides** (515-445 B.C.E.) was putting together a completely different conception of the world. Parmenides lived in **Elea**, a Greek colony in southern Italy. He saw the same change and diversity in the universe. But he did not form his opinion from what he encountered with his physical senses. Beginning with the idea that all of reality is one, he pointed to what his reason held to be two obvious ideas: "What is not is not," because it could not be thought, and "Whatever is, is."[19] These seemed on the surface like an aphorism no one would deny. But for Parmenides they had a deeper meaning.

The first premise, "Whatever is not, is not," meant that there could be no such thing as nothing. The word **nothing**, did not name anything. According to Parmenides, "you cannot know or utter what is not---that is impossible."[20] To say that "nothing exists" was unthinkable, because there was no "nothing" that could be said to exist. Yet when he asserted, "Whatever is, is," he included both objects in the world and ideas in the mind. Anything that could be thought of existed. To say of what is that it is not would be untrue. What is could not fail to exist. "What can be spoken and thought must be," Parmenides wrote: "for it is possible for it to be, but impossible for nothing to be."[21] Thus, one single, unchangeable reality existed.

As the Greeks of Parmenides' time came to see, these premises led to staggering conclusions. It followed from Parmenides' thesis that whatever is is ***uncreated***. He argued that if it had been created it would have to have been created out of nothing (***ex nihilo***). But what did not exist was unthinkable. Or it would have had to be created out of something else. But there was no something else---only what is. Similarly, what is, is *indestructible*. The destruction of a thing meant its change into *nothing*. Because there was no nothing to change into, the destruction of a thing was unthinkable. Hence, whatever is is *eternal* (uncreated and indestructible). Furthermore, whatever is is unchangeable. Nothing could change, because change required that the present state of affairs be destroyed and a new state of affairs be created. So all of reality was the same kind---unitary and indivisible. There were no degrees of being--all is one. Whereas Heraclitus had described all reality in terms of orderly change, Parmenides considered all change to be an illusion.

In the years following Heraclitus and Parmenides, the political and social situation in Greece began to deteriorate. Athens engaged in an ill-conceived and poorly executed war with Sparta. The reaction to the **Peloponnesian War** was basically negative. Civil War almost broke out in Athens. Athenians became reactionary and cynical. They trusted power rather than principle and followed expediency rather than ethics. People who had been open to new ideas became deeply suspicious of nonconformity.

Among philosophers, the views of Parmenides dominated. Several new schools of thought had developed. But all accepted Parmenides' method of beginning with reason and analysis rather than observation and experience. This along with the political changes led many people to distrust reason. If reason could deny change that seemed obvious to most people, then perhaps reason was not the tool with which to discover reality.

In this atmosphere of moral decay and distrust of reason, a new group of thinkers arose. The **Sophists** were itinerant teachers. They taught the skill of (**arete** = excellence), in the sense of bettering oneself and getting ahead. But generally they tended to deny that there was an objectively knowable world beyond the world of experience. They were either not interested in the pursuit of reason or only interested enough to help people construct theories by which to counter their opponents. The Sophist used to charge for their teaching and they became masters of **rhetoric**.

Chapter 4
Pre- Socratic Philosophers

STUDY QUESTIONS & EXERCISES

I. In what ancient Greek city does philosophy became a reality and what can you tell me about such a city?

II. Mention five things about the first official philosopher of the West, Thales.

III. What were the main differences between Anaximander and Anaximenes?

IV. What are the Pythagorean rules?

V. Who were the Sophists?

VI. Mention at least five things in relatinship to Heraclitus, Parmenides and Pytagoras.

Chapter 5
The Golen Age of Greek Philosophy
A. Socrates

The unexamined life is not worth living. ***Socrates***

Chapter 5
The Golden Age of Greek Philosophy

The **Golden Age of Greek Philosophy** is the time of maturity for the discipline of philosophy in ancient Greece. It was a time when three great individuals developed the art and/or science of philosophy to new heights, new depths, and new insights human kind had not seen before. This was a time of change, war, dispute, challenge, daring, reflective thinking, observation and so forth. **Socrates**, **Plato** and **Aristotle** became the spinal cord of philosophy. They became the center for the Golden Age of Greek Philosophy, an example that many other individuals followed in the years to come.

In this chapter, we will deal with these three men that changed human ideology forever.

Socrates's life

Socrates was born in the mid-fifth century B.C.E. He came from a middle-class Athenian family. His father was a bricklayer. His mother was a housewife. He is known for being odd looking. Yet, he was known to been brave in the battlefield. He spent most of his life dealing with philosophy.

According to Plato, one of his friends went to the official **oracle** at **Delphi**. He asked the oracle whether anyone in Athens was wiser than Socrates. The **Delphic prophetess** answered that there was no one wiser. From this point forward, Socrates' life became centered in the pursuit of knowledge and virtue. According to Plato, Socrates did not believe the oracle. He set out to prove the gods wrong. This was not viewed in a positive way by the authorities. Socrates discovered that authorities rarely like to be questioned. As one glances through the pages of human history, every time anyone questions the people in power, trouble is soon to come. Socrates also found out that authorities could answer him better than laypersons. This was because they had more education than the common citizen. However, their answers were better only to a point; after awhile they began to evade. Eventually, they refused to continue talking to him.

His method was to question his opponents, in order to make them agree with him. This is known as the **dialectical** or **Socratic method**. Through this process, Socrates was able to make his opponents say what he wanted them to say.

Socrates did not write anything. His pupil Plato immortalized his person. In His dialogues, Plato writes about Socrates as the main speaker. These four dialogues form a unit:

- ***Euthyphro***
- ***The Apology***
- ***Crito***
- ***Phaedo***

One of the most quoted sayings of Socrates is: "The unexamined life is not worth living." Socrates seems to be saying that the meaning of life is something you must discover yourself. This discovery must come through critical self-examination.

Many people did not cherish the presence of such a man like Socrates. He annoyed the authorities because he was teaching differently than the Sophist. The Sophists were a group of philosophers who used to charge for their teaching. The Sophists accused Socrates of corrupting the youth and **impiety** (creating a new religion). Socrates felt that knowledge was gained through constant self-examination. Socrates introduced the idea that the soul was immortal. He was willing to die, and he faced death with open arms. He believed the soul could perceive and have a share in truth, goodness, and beauty, which are eternal.

What troubled some and fascinated others about Socrates was his total commitment to the life of reason. He spent his life in a search for the truth through the relentless questioning of people's accepted ideas. His teaching through asking questions continues to be used in the XXI century. Living in a reactionary period of disbelief, suspicion and cynicism, the presence of a man such as Socrates was not cherished by many. He had fought with courage in the **Peloponnesian War** and lived through the friction that followed in Athens. Like the Sophists, he was dedicated to *arete=excellence*. His interest in words and arguments was well known. Yet, unlike the Sophist, he took no fees for his teaching. His intellectual standards and his pledge to metaphysical truth and moral purposes also set him apart from them.

What annoyed the authorities was the way in which Socrates' teaching differed from the Sophists. Socrates felt that he had a "**divine mission**." A friend of Socrates had asked the oracle at Delphi whether any man was wiser than Socrates. The oracle had replied, "None." Socrates knew that he was not a wise man. So he set out to find a wiser one as an excuse for going back and cross-examining the Oracle. Socrates later described the method and the results of his mission:

> Accordingly I went to one who had the reputation of wisdom, and observed him---his name I need not mention; he was a politician whom I selected for examination---and the result was as follows: When I began to talk with him, I could not help thinking that he was not really wise, although he was thought wise by many, and still wiser by himself; and thereupon I tried to explain to him that he thought himself wise, but was not really wise; and the consequence was that he hated me, and his enmity was shared by several who were present and heard me. So I left him, saying to myself, as I went away; well, although I do not suppose that either of us knows anything beautiful and good, I am better off than he is---for he knows nothing, and thinks that he knows; I neither know nor think that I know. In his latter particular then, I seem to have a slightl advantage of him.[22]

Socrates continued his mission by interviewing the poets, politicians, and craftsmen of Athens. Using his dialectic, he would enter into conversation with a person who claimed to know the meaning of certain concepts such as equality, justice, or beauty for example. Through intense questioning, Socrates would make it clear that neither he nor the person he interviewed really knew the meaning of the concept.[23] Socrates then would invite the other person to join him in a search for true knowledge of the given definition. Socrates would pose questions that could be accepted or rejected by his fellow scrutinizer. Invariably, they would fail to discover precisely what the quality was. Some, aware of their lack of knowledge, were eager to continue their search in the future.

Socrates' style of questioning reflected his theory of knowledge. He felt that knowledge was gained through constant self-examination: "The life not tested by criticism is not worth living."[24] Knowledge could not be sold like a book. It had to be discovered. Philosophy was not learning a set of answers, but the process of searching for them.

This approach was not popular among the Athenians who thought themselves well informed, being proved less than wise angered many powerful people. In 399 B.C.E., Socrates was brought to trial in the court of **King Archon** and convicted. The charges were impiety and corrupting the youth. Many felt that the real reasons for his condemnation were the questioning of his culture's "**sacred vows**," his friendship with political outcasts, his unwillingness to go along with accepted practices, and his constant criticism of the powerful.

During this time, Phaedo sat in Socrates' jail cell and listened to the condemned man's words. Many of Socrates' friends had come for one final conversation. **Apollodorus** sat in the corner sobbing uncontrollably. **Xanthippe, Socrates'** wife, had to be removed because she was so emotionally distraught. A dozen other friends fought to control their emotions as they listened to Socrates' words. **Simmias** and **Cebes** were questioning Socrates about the immortality of the soul. Socrates was about to die as an enemy of the city-state of Athens. They wanted to know what he thought and how he felt.

As the afternoon wore on and the time for Socrates' death came closer, the questioning became more intense. Was the philosophy by which Socrates had lived really worth dying for, as he apparently believed?

Socrates' friends had arrived early that morning. They knew this would be the last time they would see their beloved teacher. All of the local people who followed Socrates were there: Phaedo, **Critobulus** and his father, **Hermagenes**, **Epigenes**, **Aeschines**, **Antisthenes**, **Cresippus**, Menexenus, Crito, and others. Apollodorus, who always had a difficult time controlling himself, was also there. Only Plato, who was ill at the time, was missing. Simmias and Cebes, whose foreign accents betrayed them as visitors, added to the conversation. There were also a few other out-of-towners, such as **Euclides** and **Terpsion**. Socrates said:

> But I wish to explain to you . . . why it seems to be that a man who has really spent his life in philosophy has reason to be of good cheer when he is about to die, and may well hope after death to gain in the other world the greatest good. I will try to show you, Simmias and Cebes, how this may be. The world, perhaps, does not see that those who rightly engage in philosophy study only dying and death. And, if this is true, it would be surely strange for a man all through his life to desire only death, and then, when death comes to him, to be vexed at it, when it has been his study and his desire for so long.[25]

Then, Socrates introduced the idea that the soul was immortal because it could perceive and have a share in Truth, Goodness, and Beauty, which are eternal. As Socrates discussed this idea with his friends, he drank the hemlock poison. Slowly but surely the life of Socrates slip away. It is amazing to think that every time we have a good philosopher, a good religious leader, a good statesmen, we kill him without even thinking. Why? Why are we such a vicious kind? How can this be stopped? Where would we be without such nihilistic tendencies?

STUDY QUESTIONS & EXERCISES

I. Explain the so-called "Socratic Method." What was the main difference between Socrates and the Sophists?

II. What were the elements used to condemn Socrates to death?

III. Can we see any similar cases in contemporary society that might be similar to Socrates's case?

IV. How did Socrates face his own death?

V. What is the story about the Oracle at Delphi and Socrates?

VI. In which dialogues, written by Plato, is Socrates the main speaker?

VII. Give a cronological outline of the life of Socrates.

VIII. Go to the *Encyclopedia of Philosophy* and find the name of Socrates. Write a sum mary about his life & philosophy.

Chapter 6
The Golen Age of Greek Philosophy

B. PLATO (427-347 B.C.E.)

Love [is] between the mortal and the immortal… [It is] a grand spirit which brings together the sensible world and the eternal world merges them into one great whole. ***Plato***

Chapter 6
The Golden Age of Greek Philosophy

Plato is generally recognized as the **Father of Philosophy**. He was the first systematic **metaphysician** and **epistemologist**. He was the first philosopher to set forth a comprehensive treatment of the entire domain of philosophy.

It was him, the pupil of Socrates the one that gives us an insight not only into the mind of Socrates, but also into his own.

His Life

Plato was born to an aristocratic family in Athens. His father, **Ariston**, was believed to have descended from the early kings of Athens. **Perictione**, his mother, was distantly related to the 6th-century B.C.E. lawmaker **Solon** (the first architect of the **Athenian** constitution). When Plato was a child, his father died, and his mother married **Pyrilampes**, who was an associate of the statesman **Pericles**. Pericles (495-429 B.C.E.) was the great Athenian General and statesman. Under his leadership Athens developed into a human democracy and prospered materially and culturally. Pericles carried through a number of reforms that advanced democracy. As a result, all officials in Athens were paid salaries by the state and every office was opened to most citizens. In 451-450 he limited citizenship to those of Athenian parentage on both sides. He made an attempt, probably in 448, to call a **Panhellenic** conference, but Spartan opposition defeated his effort. He became a great patron of the arts and encouraged drama and music.

As a young man Plato had political ambitions, but he became disillusioned by the political leadership in Athens. He eventually became a disciple of Socrates, accepting his basic philosophy and dialectical style of debate: the pursuit of truth through questions, answers, and additional questions. Plato witnessed the death of Socrates at the hands of the Athenian democracy in 399 B.C.E. Perhaps fearing for his own safety, he left Athens temporarily and traveled to Italy, Sicily, and Egypt.

In the year 389 B.C.E., Plato founded the famous **Academy** in Athens. The school is often defined as the **First European University**. It provided a comprehensive curriculum, including such subjects as astronomy, biology, mathematics, political theory, and philosophy. The main purpose of the Academy was to cultivate thought to lead to a restoration of decent government in the cities of Greece. Pursuing an opportunity to combine philosophy and practical politics, Plato went to Sicily in 367 to tutor the new ruler of **Syracuse, Dionysius the Younger**, in the art of philosophical rule. The experiment failed. Plato made another trip to Syracuse in 361, but again his engagement in Sicilian affairs met with little success. The concluding years of his life were spent lecturing at the Academy and writing. He died at about the age of 80 in Athens in 347 B.C.E.

His Philosophy

Plato's goal for establishing the Academy may have been to find the ideal state. This idea is described in Book V of the ***Republic***. In this work, Plato presented the idea of philosophers ruling with justice. In the *Republic*, we also find the theory of knowledge offered by Plato, particularly in his discussion of the image of the **divided line** and the **allegory of the cave**.

In the Allegory of the Cave, Plato describes the progress of the soul as an educational journey. The soul is initially a prisoner trapped at the lowest level of Knowing and Being. This is the hellish world of sheer illusion. The soul-prisoner is then freed, and begins the long ascent up the steep and rugged road out of the cave. This ascent is not easy: it is painful and the soul is filled with dread. But eventually, the soul emerges into the daylight of the heavenly intelligible world. The soul for Plato was an immaterial principle of life and movement. The soul is divided in three parts:

1. **Reason**
2. **Spirit**
3. **Appetite**

Plato distinguishes between two levels of awareness: opinion and knowledge. Claims or assertions about the physical or visible world, including both commonsense observations and the propositions of science, are opinions only. Some of these opinions are well founded; some are not, but none of them counts as genuine knowledge. The higher level of awareness is knowledge because there reason, rather than sense experience, is involved. Reason, properly used, results in intellectual insights that are certain, and the objects of these rational insights are the abiding universals, the eternal **Forms** or substances that constitute the real world. This is known as the **theory of the forms**.

According to Plato, the soul was an immaterial principle of life and movement. As mentioned above, the soul was divided into three parts. The first, and most important, part of the soul was the reason. The reason was the thinking part of the soul, the part that could have knowledge of the Forms. The next part of the soul was the spirit. The spirit was the acting part of the soul. Finally there was the appetite. The appetite controlled the physical needs of the body.

Each of these parts of the soul had a virtue or good that corresponded to it. **Wisdom**, or the exercising of its power, was the virtue of reason. **Courage**, or the exercising of its power, was the virtue of the spirit. **Temperance**, or the exercising of its power, was the virtue of the appetite.

If the Form of the **Good** could be known, and if the good for each part of the soul consisted of pursuing the appropriate virtue, then where did **evil** come from? According to Socrates and Plato, evil was nothing more than the spirit and the appetite overwhelming the reason. Evil, therefore, was closely associated with the needs of the body. The reason did not cause evil; only those parts of the soul associated with the body caused evil. In fact, if a person really understood the situation, that is, had the virtue of wisdom, he or she would never choose to do wrong. Evil, then, was not a problem of a misdirected will, but of an unrestrained body and a weak reason. The proper way to avoid evil was for each part of the soul to fulfill its proper function in harmony and balance with other parts of the soul. This harmony and balance would promote the Good. The term, **platonic love**, comes from this idea of allowing the soul to be totally free from the needs of the body.

The state according to Plato was simply the "soul writ large." Just as there was a three-part division of the state, the ideal state was similar, in its proper make up, to the soul. Corresponding to the rational part of the soul would be a class or people known as **guardians**. These "guardians" would be the rulers of the people, using their virtue of reason. They would be few in number. As befits their emphasis on reason, these "guardians" would deny their bodies and own nothing other than the bare essentials of life. Corresponding to the spirit part of the soul would be a class of people known as **auxiliaries**. These auxiliaries would comprise the military forces and, with courage as their virtue, would defend the state. Like the "guardians," the "auxiliaries" would be few in number and would not be allow many material possessions. Corresponding to the appetitive part of the soul would be the "**craftsmen**." These "craftsmen" would make up the bulk of the state and could be allowed to accumulate private property. Just as the individual soul promoted the good by harmony and balance among its parts, so also the state would promote the Good as the different classes of people worked together harmoniously.

Was there an immortal soul that participated in the heavenly Forms? Did this theory really account for the diversity and unity of the world? Did Plato's theory of the soul really provide an adequate account of ethics and politics? Philosophy was set to continue trying to answer such questions.

REPUBLIC Book VII.

PLATO

Allegory of the Cave. (Socrates, Glaucon.) And now, I said, let me show in a figure how far our nature is enlightened or unenlightened: Behold! Human beings living in an underground den, which has a mouth open toward the light and reaching all along the den; here they have been from their childhood, and have their legs and necks chained so that they cannot move, and can only see before them, being prevented by the chains from turning round their heads. Above and behind them a fire is blazing at a distance, and between the fire and the prisoners there is a raised way; and you will see, if you look, a low wall built along the way, like the screen which marionette players have in front of them, over which they show the puppets.

I see.

And do you see, I said, men passing along the wall carrying all sorts of vessels, and statues and figures of animals made of wood and stone and various materials, which appear over the wall? Some of them are talking, others silent.

You have shown me a strange image, and they are strange prisoners.

Like ourselves, I replied; and they see only their own shadows, or the shadows of one another, which the fire throws on the opposite wall of the cave?

True, he said; how could they see anything but the shadows if they were never allowed to move their heads?

And of the objects, which are being carried in like manner, they would only see the shadows?

Yes, he said.

And if they were able to converse with one another, would they not suppose that they were naming what was actually before them?

Very true.

And suppose further that the prison had an echo which came from the other side, would they not be sure to fancy when one of the passersby spoke that the voice which they heard came from the passing shadow?

No question, he replied.

To them, I said, the truth would be literally nothing but the shadows of the images.

That is certain.

And now look again, and see what will naturally follow if the prisoners are released and disabused of their error. At first, when any of them is liberated and compelled suddenly to stand up and turn his neck round and walk and look toward the light, he will suffer sharp pains; the glare will distress him, and he will be unable to see the realities of which in his former state he had seen the shadows; and then conceive someone saying to him, that what he saw before was an illusion, but that now, when he is approaching nearer to being and his eye is turned toward more real existence, he has a clearer vision -- what will be his reply? And you may further imagine that his instructor is pointing to the objects as they pass and requiring him to name them -- will he not be perplexed? Will he not fancy that the shadows, which he formerly saw, are truer than the objects, which are now shown to him?

Far truer.

And if he is compelled to look straight at the light, will he not have a pain in his eyes that will make him turn away to take refuge in the objects of vision which he can see, and which he will conceive to be in reality clearer than the things that are now being shown to him?

True, he said.

And suppose once more, that he is reluctantly dragged up a steep and rugged ascent, and held fast until he is forced into the presence of the sun himself, is he not likely to be pained and irritated? When he approaches the light his eyes will be dazzled, and he will not be able to see anything at all of what are now called realities.

Not all in a moment, he said.

He will require growing accustomed to the sight of the upper world. And first he will see the shadows best, next the reflections of men and other objects in the water, and then the objects themselves; then he will gaze upon the light of the moon and the stars and the spangled heaven; and he will see the sky and the stars by night better than the sun or the light of the sun by day?

Certainly.

Last of all he will be able to see the sun, and not mere reflections of him in the water, but he will see him in his own proper place, and not in another; and he will contemplate him as he is.

Certainly.

He will then proceed to argue that this is he who gives the season and the years, and is the guardian of all that is in the visible world, and in a certain way the cause of all things, which he and his fellows have been accustomed to behold?

Clearly, he said, he would first see the sun and then reason about him.

And when he remembered his old habitation, and the wisdom of the den and his fellow prisoners, do you not suppose that he would felicitate himself on the change, and pity him?

Certainly, he would.

And if they were in the habit of conferring honors among themselves on those who were quickest to observe the passing shadows and to remark which of them went before, and which followed after, and which were together; and who were therefore best able to draw conclusions as to the future, do you think that he would care for such honors and glories, or envy the possessors of them? Would he not say with Homer,

"Better to be the poor servant of a poor master,"

and to endure anything, rather than think as they do and live after their manner?

Yes, he said, I think that he would rather suffer anything than entertain these false notions and live in this miserable manner.

Imagine once more, I said, such a one coming suddenly out of the sun to be replaced in his old situation; would he not be certain to have his eyes full of darkness?

To be sure, he said.

And if there were a contest, and he had to compete in measuring the shadows with the prisoners who had never moved out of the den, while his sight was still weak, and before his eyes had become steady (and the time which would be needed to acquire this new habit of sight might be very considerable), would he not be ridiculous? Men would say of him that up he went and down he came without his eyes; and that it was better not even to think of ascending; and if anyone tried to loose another and lead him up to the light, let them only catch the offender, and they would put him to death.

No question, he said.

This entire allegory, I said, you may now append, dear Glaucon, to the previous argument; the prison house is the world of sight, the light of the fire is the sun, and you will not misapprehend me if you interpret the journey upward to be the ascent of the soul into the intellectual world according to my poor belief, which, at your desire, I have expressed -- whether rightly or wrongly, God knows. But, whether true or false, my opinion is that in the world of knowledge the idea of good appears last of all, and is seen only with an effort; and, when seen, is also inferred to be the universal author of all things beautiful and right, parent of light and of the lord of light in this visible world, and the immediate source of reason and truth in the intellectual; and that this is the power upon which he who would act rationally either in public or private life must have his eye fixed.

I agree, he said, as far as I am able to understand you.

STUDY QUESTIONS & EXERCISES

I. Go to the *Encyclopedia of Philosophy* and find the name Plato. Write a summary about his life and philosophy.

II. What is the idea behind the Allegory of the Cave?

III. What are the three parts of the soul according to Plato?

IV. What are the name and the founder of the First European University?

V. What was the family background of Plato and how did it influence his philosophy?

VI. Plato believed there are parts of the state that could be compared to the parts of the soul. How do these work and what are the names of it? (Be Specific)

VII. Do you personally feel that in the Unites States of America we relate to one another in a very superficial way? Why or Why not?

VIII. How can the Allegory of the Cave be use to illustrate the view of reality according to the society we live in?

IX. Can you describe an example in which people create their own reality?

Chapter 7
The Golen Age of Greek Philosophy

C. Aristotle (384-322 B.C.E.)

Motion being eternal, the first mover, if there is but one will be eternal also. ***Aristotle***

Chapter 7
The Golden Age of Greek Philosophy

Imagine mobs forming everywhere. Athenians are celebrating the death of the emperor, **Alexander the Great**. Filled with hatred for all who had been associated with Alexander, some citizens brought accusations of impiety against his former tutor, Aristotle. At that very moment in 323 B.C.E., the courts were handing down an indictment against Aristotle. He had gotten word of the forthcoming indictment, and now he wondered what to do. Socrates had been killed in the past. Should he flee the city? How could he best live out his philosophy? Aristotle had to decide quickly.

The last philosopher that represents the Golden Age of Greek philosophy is Aristotle. He was a philosopher, logician, and scientist. Along with his teacher Plato, Aristotle is generally regarded as one of the most influential ancient thinkers in a number of philosophical fields, including **political** and **moral theory**. Aristotle's life seems to have influenced his political thought in various ways; his interest in biology seems to be expressed in the **naturalism** of his politics; his interest in comparing politics and his sympathies for democracy as well as monarchy may have been encouraged by his travels and experience of diverse political systems.

Aristotle's Early Life

Aristotle was born in the "neutral" town of **Stagira** in **Thrace** in 384 B.C.E. Had he stayed there, he might never have become involved in the struggle between the neighboring country of **Macedonia** and the city-state of Athens. But when Aristotle's father became the court physician to the king of Macedonia, the family's life was inextricably linked to politics.

Macedonia and Athens had been engaged in power plays and intrigue long before Aristotle's time. They had a common enemy in the **Persians**, but cultural differences made them suspicious of each other. Many Athenians viewed the Macedonians as uncultured, mindless brutes. Many Macedonians, in turn, saw the Athenians as weak, pampered snobs. Fortunately for Aristotle, Macedonia was strong enough to force an alliance on Athens. That made it possible for this bright, well-connected seventeen-year-old to go to Athens and study at the famous Academy of Plato.

The Academy and Plato

Sometime between 380 and 370 B.C.E., Plato had founded a school dedicated to developing Socrates's philosophy. Among Plato's philosophical tenets were the Theory of Forms, the centrality of mathematical or deductive reasoning, and the importance of political philosophy.

Plato had long held that politics should rightly come under the providence of philosophy. In the *Republic*, he declared,

> Until philosophers are kings, or the kings and princes of this world have the spirit and power of philosophy, and political greatness and wisdom meet in one . . . cities will never rest from their evils, no, nor the human race.[26]

For Plato, political philosophy was to be deductive. One should reason from **universal principles** to particular applications. For example, if one wanted to know what to include in a city's constitution, one would first try to grasp the idea or Form of "Goodness." Then, that universal principle would be applied to the particular section of the constitution being considered. This would mean that the one writing the constitution would have to be able to "grasp the Forms." The person would have to be a philosopher.

Plato did more than simply theorize about the relationship between philosophy and politics. About the time that the seventeen-year-old Aristotle arrived, the Academy became involved in political experiments in Sicily. This involvement led to a close identification of the philosophical interest of the Academy with the political interest of Athens.

During the two decades that Aristotle was associated with the Academy, he was deeply influenced by Plato. His earliest writings, intended for a popular audience, were in the style of Platonic dialogues. However, most of his works were mainly notes written by himself or members of his inner circle. This is the reason why they are very complex and at times rough texts. Unlike Plato, whose writings were written for a public audience.

Involvement with Alexander the Great

Plato died in 347 B.C.E. Aristotle left Athens and accepted the patronage of a former student, **Hermias**, who gathered a group of philosophers on the island of Assos, which he ruled. Using the resources of Hermias's court, Aristotle recorded his observations of the sea life around the small island. Following Hermias's betrayal and murder, Aristotle fled to the island of **Lesbos**. For three years, he continued his scientific studies there.

In 342 B.C.E., Aristotle moved back to Macedonia. This time he came as tutor to the king's thirteen-year-old son, Alexander. It was a different Macedonia from that which Aristotle had left as a boy twenty-five years before. The king, **Philip**, had created a powerful military machine. Macedonia now ruled the **Hellenic League** and was poised to invade Persia.

Philip saw Aristotle not only as an excellent student tutor but also as a valuable political ally with connections in the Greek cities and colonies. When Alexander reached adulthood, Aristotle accepted a political appointment in his hometown of Stagira, now under Phillip's rule. The town had been destroyed, but as a favor to Aristotle, Phillip allowed him to supervise the rebuilding of the town. After five years as a successful administrator, Aristotle was ready to return to Athens and philosophy.

The Lyceum

When he arrived in Athens, Aristotle was disappointed. He discovered that Xenocrates, whom he considered a second-rate philosopher, now headed the Academy.

Aristotle disagreed with this man's extreme emphasis on mathematics. With the good will and financial backing of the Macedonian court, Aristotle had no difficulty in establishing his own institution. He acquired the best available school property in Athens and named it the **Lyceum**. Aristotle brought with him enough teaching materials (maps, books, models, records of observations, and so on) and assistants to attract significant attention. This public awareness quickly translated into new students, and the Lyceum was an immediate success. It tended to attract the youth of the aspiring middle class. The Academy continued to be the stronghold of the more conservative aristocracy.

During the next eleven years, Aristotle concerned himself with teaching, writing, and organizing all the observations he had made in Assos, Lesbos, and Macedonia. Because of Aristotle's relationship with Alexander, the Lyceum enjoyed a privileged status. Alexander even sent records of his observations of nature and specimens of plants and animal life from the distant battlefields back to the Lyceum. As the years passed, Aristotle was able to develop his own philosophy in distinction from his mentor, Plato.

Continuity and Change

Aristotle felt dissatisfied with Plato's theory of Forms. Like Plato, he too, wanted to discover what was real. He, too, wanted to find solution to the problem of change as presented by Heraclitus and Parmenides. But, unlike Plato, Aristotle did not believe that reality was only to be found in heaven, or in the mind. It was not only immaterial, eternal ideas that were real. Particular things in this world were real. Things changed. But Aristotle's observations at the seashore had convinced him that there were patterns of continuity and stability within the changing world. Similar structures and functions could group sea animals. They reproduced their own kind with remarkable uniformity.

Actuality and Potentiality

For Aristotle, one way of understanding the continuity within change was to think of a thing's **actuality** and its **potentiality**. Xenocrates changed during his lifetime, but he always remained Xenocrates. The baby was potentially the adult. At each stage of change from infant to child to youth to adult to aged, one could recognized the continuity of the person, Xenocrates. This continuity, for Aristotle, was not because one could discern the origin from which Xenocrates came, but rather because one could recognize the goal toward which he was moving.

Nature was a realm of purpose, according to Aristotle. Each thing was developing its potential toward the actuality it could become. When Xenocrates was a baby, he had in him all of the potential to become the adult Xenocrates. His parents provided that potential. Thus, for Aristotle, actuality preceded and governed potentiality. There could be no acorns if there were no oaks first. All things grew toward the goal for which they were designed. Each entity developed according to its characteristic structure. Human babies became human adults, not donkeys. Acorns became oak trees, not orchids. Actuality and potentiality were principles that helped Aristotle understand organic change within particular things.

Form and Matter

Aristotle also needed to understand what things themselves were and how they could change into something else without destroying all continuity. Aristotle had observed that each particular thing had a certain structure or function that determined its identity. This structure was its "form." Forms were not heavenly realities, as Plato had thought, in which earthly things only partially participated. Forms were embedded in particular things. The characteristic structure of a chair was its forms. This structure was intimately related to the function that the chair performed; namely, to support a partly reclining human body. But to accomplish that purpose a chair had to be made out of some stuff, for example, wood. This stuff was the chair's "matter." Reality was a particular thing called a "substance," which was composed of both form and matter. Reality was not the concept of "chair-in general." Reality, or substance, was the particular chair on which Aristotle was sitting as he wrote. That particular chair embodied the structure or form of chairness, *and* it was made of a particular matter, wood.

According to Aristotle, form and matter were not separate things. They were paired principles which substances---real, particular things in this world---could be understood. These principles enabled Aristotle to understand the problem of **permanence** and **change**. All things passed through changes. But patterns of continuity could be observed. A chair could be broken into pieces to burn a fire. The form of the substance then changed from chair to kindling. But continuity with the former chair could be observed. The new form, kindling, had as its matter, chair. When the kindling was burned in the fire, it took on the form, ash. The matter, kindling, then provided the continuity between the new form of the substance and what it had been. Thus, for Aristotle, particular substances could take on new forms. What had been the form now became the matter or principle of continuity carried on in a new form. Or saying it in a different way, matter never disappears; it only changes its form.

Four Causes

To understand how a thing came to be what it was, Aristotle took into account four kinds of causes. The first cause was the stuff or matter of which something was made. This was its ***material* cause**. The second cause was the thing's characteristic structure or form. This was its ***formal* cause**. The third cause was the agent who acted on or affected the matter to bring it into its present form. This was the ***efficient* cause**. Lastly, and most importantly for Aristotle, was the purpose for which something was created. This purpose determined all of the other steps in the process. Aristotle called this purpose the ***final* cause**. For example, the mast on a Greek sailing ship was made from a tree trunk. Its material cause, then, was the tree from which it was made. Its formal cause was the shipbuilder's design or drawing of a straight pole of a given height and shape. The efficient cause was the work of the laborers who trimmed and smoothed the trunk according to the shipbuilders's design. The final cause, the cause which determined all of the others, was the goal or purpose of the mast, that of supporting a sail capable of carrying the ship forward in the wind.

Aristotle's Unmoved Mover

Aristotle argued that actuality preceded potentiality. There had to be something already actualized for the potential to move forward. It followed that there had to be something that was ultimately actualized. Aristotle concluded that there was an **Unmoved Mover** who actualized all of the potential movements in the universe. But, Aristotle assumed, this Unmoved Mover could not itself change. It was eternal form without matter. He identified this Unmoved Mover with divine thought or mind and did not hesitate to call it God. This God was not the creator of the material world. Matter was eternal. God was rather the energizing form of the world. God moved the world not from behind but as its goal. God moved the world as a beloved moved the lover. All things moved toward the actualization of their potential, drawn by the energy of the supremely actual one, God.

This God was not personal. It did not exercise any providential oversight of human affairs. Aristotle did not recommend praying to it. What did God do? Aristotle said: "Thought[27] thinks itself as object in virtue of its participation in what is thought." The quality of thought depended on the nature of its object. God, therefore, thought about that which was highest: the unchangeable. God was mind, thinking about its unchangeable self.

According to Aristotle, the highest function of humanity, as of God, was to think. The rational part of humanity was the divine element that separated human kind from the rest of creation. The highest kind of thought was of unchangeable ideas. Thus, Aristotle, like Plato held that theoretical wisdom was to be prized over practical. Only the active reason in humans was considered separable from the body and immortal.

But unlike Plato, in most human affairs Aristotle preferred to move from the sensible, practical, and experiential. Politics, for Aristotle, was a matter of practical knowledge. It represented the expression of another part of human nature, the desire to form groups. Aristotle contended that the human being was a social or political animal. The best kind of polis, or group, could be discovered by observations of human experiments with government.

Political Theory

Aristotle's disagreements with Plato regarding politics were rooted in his different understanding of the nature of reality (metaphysics) and how it was known (epistemology). Plato's epistemology was based on innate, abstract ideas or Forms from which conclusions could be derived. He believed that one first had to grasp the universal form and then apply it to a specific situation. He used deductive reasoning, from the universals to the particulars. Aristotle's theory of knowledge was rooted in his boyhood experience as the son of a medical doctor. His epistemology had been confirmed by his careful observations of plant and animal life. For Aristotle, most knowledge began with the observations of particular things in this world. People encountered these objects with their five senses. Then, as they gather a mass of evidence, they could reason from the particulars to generalizations that applied to them. This inductive reasoning moved from particulars to universals.

Aristotle applied his general theory of knowledge to politics. Plato had assumed that one could begin with the nature of the soul and an abstract idea about what was "good" and then embody that idea in a particular form of government. Aristotle instead believed that the "good" was that which persons sought by nature. In order to find out what people did in fact aim for, one had to begin by observing actual governments and how they worked. Then general conclusions were drawn as to which forms of government proved to be "good" for human beings. Aristotle asserted, referring to Plato:

> Now our predecessors have left the subject of legislation to us unexamined; it is perhaps best, therefore, that we should ourselves study it, and in general study the question of the constitution, in order to complete to the best of our ability our philosophy of human nature. First, then, if anything has been said well in detail by earlier thinkers, let us try to review it; then in the light of the constitutions we have collected let us study what sorts of influence preserve and destroy states, and what cause it is due that some are well and others ill administered. What these have been studied we shall perhaps be more likely to see with a comprehensive view, which constitution is best, and how each must be ordered, and what laws and customs it must be, if it is to be at its best.[27]

Aristotle acted on his theory by gathering the constitutions of 158 Greek city-states. Using these constitutions as the basis, he distinguished between three types of states: the rule of the one, the rule of the few, and the rule of the many. In each of these types of governments, Aristotle pointed out that there could be either a true or a perverted kind of rule. Aristotle did not say specifically which of these types he thought best. Instead, he pointed out that one must observe each type of state to see how well it worked. Aristotle aimed at a practical, workable state that would take into account human nature. He sought to mediate between what was desirable and what was reasonably attainable.[28]

Happiness

According to Aristotle, human beings by nature sought happiness. Happiness was the end or goal toward which all people were striving. Aristotle stated: "Everything we choose we choose for the sake of something else, except happiness, which is an end."[29]

Happiness, for Aristotle, was not simply trivial amusement or bodily pleasure. "Happiness . . . does not lie in amusement."[30] Rather, happiness was "activity in accordance with virtue."[31] When a person was acting virtuously, he or she would be happy.

Virtue consisted in avoiding extremes, in finding the middle ground or mean. For example, the moral virtue of courage was the mean between the vices of fear and foolhardiness. Courage was a balance or harmony between the two extremes.

Although Aristotle held that happiness is more than amusement and was in fact found in virtuous activities, he did not deny the importance of external influences in achieving happiness. It was not enough for a person to exercise his or her "divine element" by thinking and contemplating. A person also needed to fulfill some of the desires of the body in order to achieve happiness. Aristotle explained:

> But being a man, one will need external prosperity; for our nature is not self-sufficient for the purpose of contemplation, but our body also must be healthy and must have food and other attention.[32]

This need for some of the comforts of life was not confined to some lower class of people. Aristotle disagreed with Plato's notion that the highest class, the "guardians" or philosopher kings, should not have worldly goods. According to Aristotle: "a philosopher as well as a just man or one possessing any other virtue, needs the necessities of life."[33]

Furthermore, Aristotle believed that the things that happened to a person during his or her lifetime helped to determine whether or not that person would have a happy life. Although happiness was "acting in accordance with virtue," the fateful occurrences of life were important. Aristotle declared, "a multitude of great events if they turn out well will make life happier . . . while if they turn out ill they crush and incapacitate happiness."[34]

Aristotle concluded then that a person was happy if he or she was active in accordance with complete virtue and is sufficiently equipped with external goods, not for some chance period but throughout a complete life.

The Indictment

When Alexander the Great died (323 B.C.E.), long-suppressed feeling surfaced. The Athenians were suddenly free to vent their hatred of everything Macedonian. Throughout the city, statues that depicted Macedonians were pulled down. Orators appeared on the street corners urging a war of liberation from Macedonia, which had been identified in the popular mind with Alexander and Macedonia, and was a likely target for angry mobs.

One of the foremost anti-Macedonians, **Demophilus**, charged Aristotle with impiety. The indictment cited a hymn that Aristotle had composed in honor of his friend and former patron, **Hermias**. Demophilus asserted that the song ascribed deity to Hermias. Because Hermias had once been a slave, it was considered obvious that he could not be divine.

On the basis of this formal indictment, Aristotle was summoned to appear before the Athenian assembly. There, he would be expected to answer the charges brought against him.

The Decision

Aristotle realized that he would have to act quickly. He felt that the formal charges were fabricated. The real issue was his association with Macedonia.

Aristotle's political ideals were being tested by practical reality. Socrates had encountered a similar situation some seventy-five years before. He, too, had been indicted on fabricated charges. He has stayed and "fought" in his own way, finally choosing death over escape.

As Aristotle considered the situation, he thought about Socrates. Should he also stay and fight the charges? Or should he flee the city before some irrational mob seized him? If he left, what would become of his work, his school? How could he put his own philosophy into practice in this tense political situation? In this situation of injustice, how could he achieve happiness?

He did not have much time to decide. After careful consideration Aristotle expressed: "I will be leaving in order that the Athenians might not commit a second crime against philosophy." Such decision is viewed today as either a smart, logical decision, or as a cowardly way of dealing with danger.

This writer believes that both Socrates and Aristotle made the right decision for each of them. Socrates wanted to make a statement by staying and facing death. Besides Jesus of Nazaret, it is difficult to find another character in human history that has died in such a way. Aristotle, for his part, believed that by going away, he was not only protecting his life, but his philosophy as well; only he could preserve his influence.

Aristotle died at his mother's family state sometime after leaving Athens. His influence continues today with us, and the same questions he raised continue to be pondered by the new generation of the new millennium in the XXI century.

STUDY QUESTIONS AND EXECRSISES

I. Go to the *Encyclopedia of Philosophy* and find the name Aristotle. Write a summary about his life and philosophy.

II. How did Aristotle approach the problem of change differently from Plato?

III. Discuss Aristotle's concept of cause and effect. Define and describe the function in Aristotle philosophy of the following sets of principles:

a. Actuality and potentiality
b. Form and matter
c. Four causes

IV. Outline the elements that Plato and Aristotle shared in common as classical realists. Then contrast their views on metaphysics and epistemology.

V. What was the relationship Aristotle had with Alexander the Great?

VI. How did Aristotle consider happiness?

VII. What was Aristotle's political theory?

VIII. Explain Aristotle's concept of the Unmoved Mover.

Chapter 8
Medieval Philosophy

A. Saint Agustine of Hippò (354-430 CE)

Though philosophers disagree on the nature of things, and the mode of investigating the truth, and of the good to which all our actions ought to tend; yet on these three great general questions, all their intellectual energy is spent. ***St. Augustine***

Chapter 8
Medieval Philosophy

As **Augustine** prepared to write the letter, he was struck by the strangeness of the situation. In his youth, he had converted his friend **Honoratus** to **Manichaeism**. Now just a few years later in 391 C.E., Augustine was again trying to convert Honoratus: this time from Manichaeism to **Christianity**. Taking his pen in hand, Augustine began to write:

> Thou knowest, Honoratus, that for this reason alone did we fall into the hands of these men, namely, that they professed to free us from all error and bring us to God by pure reason alone, without that terrible principle of authority. For what else induced me to . . . follow these men for almost nine years, except their assertion that we were terrified by superstition into a faith blindly imposed upon reason, while they urged no one to believe until the truth was fully discussed and proved? Who would not be seduced by such promises: especially if he were a proud, contentious young man, thirsting for truth, such as they found me?[35]

It was true. The **Manichaeans** had appealed to both Augustine's pride and his intellect. He had been proud that the leaders of a major religion had taken an interest in him: a middle class youth from the African provinces. His intellect had found in Manichaean theology a solution to the troublesome **problem of evil**.

But Augustine had since abandoned his Manichaean beliefs. The attention of **Faustus** and the other Manichaean leaders no longer thrilled him. The clear answer to the problem of evil presented by the Manichaeans no longer seemed adequate. The certain reasonings no longer seemed so certain. **Faith** and the principle of authority were no longer abhorrent.

Sitting at his desk at the monastery in North Africa, Augustine thought about his own conversion. He remembered how he had reconciled his belief in the God of the **Old Testament** with the problem of evil. His notion of "**disordered love**" provided, for him, an adequate answer to the problem of evil. But would his arguments be convincing enough to Honoratus? How could he persuade Honoratus that faith and not reason alone led to God? How could he open his friend to the illumination that alone, it came from God?

Early Life of Augustine

Christianity had spread quickly throughout the **Roman Empire**. Despite sporadic (and often brutal) attempts to eliminate the faith, Christians had grown in numbers and power. By the early fourth century, Christianity had become the virtual state religion.

In the provinces of North Africa, towns had arisen, valleys and plains had been planted with grain, and roads had been built. In one area of North Africa an amphitheater nearly the size of the Coliseum in Rome had been built. At the same city, Christianity had spread its influence. What had begun as a Jewish heresy, soon became the dominant force in the religious and philosophical life of North Africa.

But by the year 350 C.E. much of the economic growth of the provinces had ceased. In North Africa, the Roman economy was crumbling. Wars with peoples to the north and east of the empire had drained much of the economic resources from the provinces. Corruption within the Roman government had led to swindles that further crippled the outlying areas.

In the year 354 C.E. a relatively poor but respected man named **Patricius** and his wife **Monica** had a son whom they named **Aurelius Augustinus**. Patricius was a proud man from the North Africa town of **Thagaste**. He worked hard and sacrificed much to provide for Augustine's education. Patricius died when Augustine was still young. Augustine's mother, Monica, was a Christian.

As a young boy, Augustine was anxious to be accepted and to succeed in life. Augustine enjoyed playing in the fields around Thagaste. His early days were spent stalking birds, ripping the tails off lizards, and gazing longingly at the mountains in the distance. In the early years, the light that surrounded him especially struck Augustine. He portrayed the sunlight as the queen of all colors, cascading over everything, and wrote a poem in praise of candlelight.

In 371 C.E., at the age of seventeen, Augustine went to **Carthage** to pursue his education. During his first two years in Carthage, Augustine discovered the pleasures of the big city. He took a concubine as a sort of second-class wife. She bore him a son, **Adeodatus**.

In the year 373, while reading **Cicero's *The Hortensius***, Augustine was "converted" to philosophy: the love of wisdom. Turning to the **Bible** in hopes of finding wisdom, Augustine was appalled at what he read. Being an educated young man, he was put off by the uncultivated and unpolished language of the Latin Bible of Africa. Furthermore, what Augustine found in the Bible seemed to have little to do with the love of wisdom about which Cicero had written. The Bible seemed to Augustine to be full of contradictions and inconsistencies. Finally, the God of the Old Testament seemed to be a vengeful, spiteful god who did not deserve respect or worship. How such a God who allowed evil could be considered loving completely escaped Augustine. Hence Augustine was initially drawn to a pagan position; a search for wisdom outside the bounds of any organized religion.

The Problem of Evil

The problem of evil in the world had troubled thoughtful people for centuries. They ask: "How could an all-loving, all-powerful God allow evil in the world?" The problem could be clearly seen by stating two premises or propositions---one of which had to be either denied or revised in the conclusion. These three were:

Premise 1 God is good.
Premise 2 God is all-powerful.
Conclusion There is evil in the world.

If there was evil in the world and God was *good* (in at least some sense of the word good that was understandable), then premise number 2 must be false; that is, God wanted to wipe out evil, but he could not do it. If one maintained God's powerfulness, then either God desired that evil be in the world (and thus was not good) or else one was mistaken about the apparent evil in the world. It did not seem possible to hold all three of these propositions to be true without changing at least one of them.

As a pagan, the problem of evil ceased to be a real problem for Augustine. As a pagan, Augustine denied both that God was good (sometimes the gods acted in obviously evil ways) and that God was all-powerful (there might be many conflicting gods, or no God or gods at all). So, by denying the first and second propositions, Augustine was free from the problem of evil.

Manichaeism

While in Carthage, Augustine discovered the religion of Manichaeism. Believing that this religion would lead him to wisdom, he became a "Hearer," one of the faithful, among the Manichees. He even managed to win converts (such as his friend Honoratus) for his new religion.

The Manichees were followers of the prophet **Mani**, a Persian man who called himself "t**he apostle of Jesus Christ**." In the third century, Mani had founded a new religion based loosely on the teachings of Christ. The Manichees believed that they were the "true Christians" and that they alone possessed the truth. They rejected the Old Testament and the incarnation of Jesus, holding Jesus to be a mere mortal who only seemed divine. They further rejected all authority, whether of the Bible or of the church, and accepted nothing that could not be proven by reason.

The Manichees believed that in people, as in the universe at large, two fundamental principles were struggling for dominance. One principle was evil, the other was good. Following an initiation service, the new inductees into Manichaean religion would be "illumined, filled with light." In this "illumined" state, the inductee would realize the evil at war with the good in his or her soul. The goal became to separate the darkness (or evil) from the light. The method of doing this was through denying the flesh--that is, through celibacy, poverty, and vegetarianism. But not all Manichees went through a rigorous program of self-denial, while the majority of the faithful (like Augustine) were known as Hearers and lived a normal life.

The Manichees were relieved from having any sense of guilt. Because any evil they might do arose from their evil natures, their good natures remained untouched. For Augustine, this meant that his relationship with a concubine, his fights with his mother, all of the things that seemed to be from darkness rather than from light did not affect his soul. A principle of darkness was working within him that he could no more control than he could restrain the cosmic struggle of good and evil.

The Manichees answered the problem of evil by denying the premise that God is all-powerful. God was powerful, but not powerful enough to do away with evil. Evil had an equal standing with goodness. There was no power that could do away with either one. God, therefore, was incapable of dealing with evil as Augustine found himself to be.

Neoplatonism

Augustine returned to Thagaste in the year 375 C.E. to become a teacher. When his mother, Monica, found out that he had become a Manichaean, she expelled him from her house. Finding that his hometown lacked the thrill of the city, Augustine returned to Carthage the next year. There he remained for the next seven years, teaching and continuing his own studies.

During this time, Augustine became acquainted with Faustus, Manichaeism's foremost thinker. Although Faustus was clever, Augustine was profoundly disappointed by his lack of education and his inconsistent attacks on Christianity. The more Augustine read in the standard works of academic learning, the more he began to doubt the theories of his fellow Manichees. The Manichees prided themselves on their knowledge of the heavens and the curious orbits of the planets, but Augustine found their calculations to be contradictory.

Like any young ambitious scholar, Augustine longed to be closer to the center of learning. By 382 he had grown tired of Carthage and longed to go to Rome. His students in Carthage were undisciplined and unattentive, and he had heard that in Rome the students were better behaved. As Augustine prepared to go to Rome, his mother discovered his plans. She was angry that her son had abandoned Christianity, but now he was going to leave her as well. Augustine described his departure for Rome:

I did not wish to go to Rome because of the richer fees and higher dignity which my friends promised me there . . . My principal and almost sole motive was that I had been informed that the students there studied more quietly and were better kept under control of stern disciple . . . My mother, grieved deeply over my departure, . . . followed me down to the sea. She clasped me tight in her embrace, willing either to keep me back or to go with me, but I deceived her, pretending that I had a friend whom I could not leave until he had a favorable wind to set sail. . . . That night I slipped away secretly, and she remained to pray and weep.[36]

Arriving in Rome, Augustine was very disappointed. The aristocrats whom he wanted to get to know turned out to be pompous boors. After a year Augustine left Rome for a teaching post in Milan. While in Milan, he encountered some of the writings of **Plotinus** and **Porphyry**. Plotinus was the founder of what later was called Neoplatonism. Porphyry was his disciple and popularizer. Following many of Plato's doctrines, the Neoplatonists had developed a quasi-religious doctrine of ***logos*** or "word." This doctrine became the basis for the doctrine of logos presented in the New Testament Gospel of John. In both accounts, the creative Word was understood to be immaterial, the transcendent cause of all things of flesh and blood.

The Neoplatonists had a convincing alternative to Manichaean dualism. Evil, they taught, was no substance at all, but simply a defection in substance. Evil had no being whatsoever apart from good. All things were good in so far as they existed. What constituted evil was imperfection in their existence, the corruption of their goodness. Starting from this premise, Augustine then inquired of his own experience: "what wickedness was, and . . . found that it was no substance, but perversion of the will, bent aside"[37] from God.

In terms of the three propositions that made up the problem of evil, Augustine's new position amounted to a denial of the third statement. The Neoplatonists denied that evil was a thing in the world. Evil did not exist. There was only lack of the good.

Conversion to Christianity

As Augustine continued in his Neoplatonic studies, he came under the influence of a group of Christian Neoplatonists led by **Bishop Ambrose**. In 386, Augustine was in a garden thinking about his own life when he heard the voice of a child saying: "pick it up, read it; pick it up, read it."[38] Augustine later recounted what happened:

> So I quickly returned to the bench . . . for there I had put down the apostle's book when I had left there. I snatched it up, opened it, and in silence read the paragraph on which my eyes first fell: "Not in rioting and drunkenness, not in chambering and wantonness, not in strife and envying, but put on the Lord Jesus Christ, and make no provision for the flesh to fulfill the lust thereof." I wanted to read no further, nor did I need to. For instantly, as the sentence ended, there was infused in my heart something like the light of full certainty and all my gloom of doubt vanished away.[39]

Augustine's View of Faith and Reason

At the close of the fourth century, nearly all philosophers, Christians and non-Christians alike, believed that the goal of philosophy was wisdom and blessedness. No sharp distinction was made between philosophy and theology, and non-Christian philosophies were widely used by Christians. What distinguished Christians was their view that the ultimate Truth was to be found in Jesus Christ. Thus, although other philosophies (especially Neoplatonism) contained much truth for Augustine, they could never provide what constitutes the spinal chord of the philosophy of Christianity, the heart of the Christian gospel---the life, death, and claim of the resurrection of Jesus. This was to be found only in the Scriptures and the tradition of the church. In order to find Truth, one appropriated the message of Scriptures by faith and even then sought to go from there to full understanding. Augustine put it the following way: "Believe in order that you may understand."

Augustine was far from being anti-intellectual in his emphasis on faith. Faith was the essential step to knowledge of God and salvation. But by itself faith could never satisfy the rational nature of humanity. Believing was kind of thinking---"thinking with assent"---but only of an incomplete and elementary sort. It needed to be developed further, into real understanding. The object seen through faith was always distant and obscure and therefore not intellectually satisfying. It had to be refined and brought into sharper focus---that is, to be understood---by the exercise of reason.

Two-Storied Universe

Fundamental to Augustine's thought was the duality of the universe. He asserted that there were two worlds: (1) an **intelligible** world where Truth itself dwelled and (2) this **sensible world** that people perceived by sight and touch. The sensible world was the "first" or "lower level" of the universe. This sensible world was the world of appearances. A person came to know this world of appearances by using his or her five senses. According to Augustine, this kind of knowledge, which he called ***scientia***, was clearly inferior. Although one could have knowledge of appearances, that knowledge was always changeable and incomplete. Such knowledge could never lead one to decisions about how to live one's life. Still, such knowledge could be useful if kept within bounds.

In contrast to the sensible world was the intelligible world. This world was the "second" or "upper level" of the universe. This intelligible world was the world of eternal truths, or **rationes aeternae**. These *rationes aeternae* were eternal and unchanging. They were abstract concepts rather than particular instances. Concepts such as justice, beauty, and the truths of mathematics were all *rationes aeternae*. These *rationes aeternae* were located in the mind of God.

A person could have knowledge of the intelligible world by the use of reason. When the reason was directed toward understanding the *rationes aeternae*, toward attaining knowledge of the Truth, then the reason was pursuing wisdom. This kind of knowledge Augustine called sapientia. However, for him reason never became the measure of all things, as did for the Manichees. Because of the way one came to know the *rationes aeternae*, Truth always stood in judgment over the mind in spite of the use of reason in the process of gaining understanding.

In many ways, Augustine's idea of a two-storied universe was similar to Plato's theory of Forms. Augustine agreed with Plato that the Truth, which was the foundation of all else, was immaterial and eternal. Furthermore, Augustine also agrees that this truth was perceived through reasons apart from the senses. Finally, Augustine agreed with Plato that in their present state persons were hindered from attaining a full knowledge of eternal Truth.

However, Augustine differed sharply from Plato on several key points. Augustine rejected the Platonic idea of a pre-existent soul that remembered the eternal truths from some past life. Augustine also believed that the sensible world or the world of appearances had a value. According to Augustine, God made the sensible world and was using it to bring about his eternal ends. Augustine further differed from his philosophical mentor, Plato, on why reason was hindered in its quest for Truth. According to Plato, the reason once knew the eternal truths and simply forgot them when the person was born. Augustine, however, believed that **sin** (as understood by Christianity) had cut off God's direct illumination of the Truth so that people were in darkness.

Doctrine of Illumination

In order for a person to have knowledge of the intelligible world, the *rationes aeternae* had to be given "**illumination**." Just as the physical eye needed light in order to see things of the sensible world, so also the "**eye of the mind**" needed illumination in order to "see" things of the intelligible world---the *rationes aeternae*. A person could no more "see" things of the intelligible world (such as justice, beauty, the truths of mathematics, and so on) without some illumination that one could see trees, hills, and so on without the light of the sun. This illumination of the intelligible world came from God. It was divine illumination.

In one sense, this illumination was given in some measure to all people, because all people had the image of God in their souls. Even though this image was disfigured by sin, nevertheless it always remained. This image was the receiver of the divine illumination and was affected by the light even when the person who was in God's image did not have faith in God. Augustine explained:

> But [the mind] is reminded that it should turn to the Lord as to that light by which it was touched in some way, even when it was turned away from him. For hence it is that even the godless think of eternity, and rightly condemn and rightly praise many things in the moral conduct of men.[40]

This divine illumination, available to all, explained for Augustine the common standards of justice and the common agreement on the truths of mathematics. Everyone was illumined on these matters.

But this general measure of illumination was not enough. Knowledge about God, which was the proper aim of all people, required participation by faith, a turning towards the light. Augustine explained that he had seen the *rationes aeternae* in his readings of the philosophers:

> I delighted in them, not knowing the real source of what it was in them that was true and certain. For I had my back towards the light, and my face towards the things on which the light falls, so that my face, which looked towards the illuminated things, was not itself illuminated.[41]

Augustine realized that he had been using his reason to understand some of the eternal truths in the divine light, but he had his back turned from to the light and thus came to no satisfactory knowledge of God. True wisdom, true *sapientia*, the wisdom of knowing God, was only for those who actively participated in receiving God's illumination. Augustine said:

> Let [the mind] worship the God who was not made, but by whom it was made so that it is capable of Him and can be a partaker of Him; wherefore it is written: "Behold, the worship of God is wisdom;" and not by its own light, but by participation in that highest light, will it be wise, and where the eternal light is, there it will reign in blessedness. This wisdom is so called the wisdom of man, as to be also that of God. For it is then true wisdom, since if it is only human wisdom, it is vain.[42]

Thus knowing God through faith and divine illumination was not merely an intellectual matter, but was an act of the will. One had to "believe in order to understand."

Evil as Disordered Love

As a Christian, Augustine took the Neoplatonist answer to the problem of evil and modified it. He continued to agree with Neoplatonism that evil was not a *thing*, but rather the absence of good. However, within his new Christian framework he found what he considered to be an adequate explanation of how evil (or rather, the lack of good) arose.

Everyone had the need to love. Because people were created incomplete, they needed some object of love to fulfill them. To love, for Augustine, was to focus one's attentions, emotions, and desires on an object of love. It was an act of the will. According to Augustine, there were four objects of love on which one could focus: things, other people, one's self, and God. Each of these was a proper object of love---provided that they were properly ordered. As long as one's love for things was secondary to the other three objects of love, it was proper. There was nothing wrong, for instance, with loving food when one was hungry. But if that love of food was stronger than love of another person who was also hungry and wanted to share some food, then it became evil. The highest love, the love that should be so strong as to make the others contemptible in comparison, was the love of God. People were made to love God. No finite thing or person was sufficient to fulfill the need to love God. So a properly ordered love was one where love of things, self, and others came after the love of God, which came first.

Evil, then, was simply disordered love. It was only through loving God first and foremost that people could achieve happiness. But people believed that they could achieve happiness through loving things, themselves, or other people. Although loving things, oneself, or other people were all proper objects of love, loving things, oneself, or other people was to expect too much. These objects of love were simply not capable of providing happiness. A disordered love, a love where God was not the primary object of affection, simply could not bring happiness. A disordered love took the good of loving and turned it into evil because of the absence of a proper object.

The Letter

In the year 388 C.E., Augustine left Milan and, after a short visit in Rome, returned to North Africa. He visited Carthage and finally returned to his hometown of Thagaste. In 391 he was ordained as a priest and moved to the town of Hippo in North Africa to found a monastery.

While establishing the monastery, Augustine became concerned for his friend Honoratus. Just like Augustine, Honoratus had trouble accepting the God of the Old Testament. He too had found such a God vengeful and cruel. He too had found a solution to the problem of evil in Manichaean dualism. But like Augustine, he also had some problems with Maniachaean beliefs. The Manichees believed that Christians who wanted to return to the old Jewish ways added all the references to the Old Testament in the New Testament. Honoratus, being an independent thinker, found this position hard to accept.

Still, Honoratus was troubled by the problem of evil. If God was all-powerful and all loving, how could God allow all the suffering that took place in the Old Testament or that was taking placed in the fourth century? Furthermore, Honoratus asked, why should he begin with faith in the authority of scripture and the church?

Augustine knew his friend's problems with the Christian faith. As he contemplated his own former involvement with the Manichees, he wondered what he could say that would be effective. How could he convince Honoratus that faith was not something that was to be avoided? How could he show that there was no contradiction in believing that the God of the Old Testament was not only all powerful, but also all loving? What could he say that would help Honoratus toward illumination by God?

Chapter 8
Brief Introduction to Philosophy

STUDY QUESTIONS & EXERCISES

I. Outline the logical propositions that compose the problem of evil as presented by Augustine. Indicate several methods by which people have tried to resolve this problem.

II. Describe the responses to the problem of evil by

a. The Manicheans
b. The Neoplatonists
c. Augustine

III. How was Manichaeism alike and different from the Christianity in which Augustine believed?

IV. Explain Augustine's view of the relationship of faith and reason.

V. Contrast Augustine's concepts of scientia (science) and sapientia (wisdom).

VI. Discuss Augustine's doctrines of general and divine illumination. Do these have any parallels in contemporary theory of knowledge?

VII. What would your personal solution be to the problem of evil?

VIII. Does our contemporary society care about the problem of evil? Why or Why not?

Chapter 9
Medieval Philosophy

B. Saint Anselm (1033-1109)

So truly, therefore, do you exist, O Lord, my God, that you cannot be conceived not to exist; and rightly.

St. Anselm

Chapter 9
Medieval Philosophy

In the year 452 C.E., twenty-two years after Augustine's death, the great Roman Empire fell. Following a period of conquest and chaos, a degree of order was ultimately realized through the emergence of **feudalism**. Feudalism is a method of government, a way of securing the forces necessary to preserve a regime. It is also an extreme form of decentralization. There are many centers of power. Power does not reside at a center, or at the top, even though there is a pyramidal structure in theory, with the emperor at the top and the simple knight at the bottom. This form of government initially became a system of local defense against the constant dangers and uncertainties of a rather primitive existence in northern Europe after the relative order of the Roman Empire. Feudalism could be descrive in a very simple way by presenting the following items: 1) armed forces available through private contracts; 2) division of political power; and 3) public power in private hands.

The church, which had managed to survive the social and political upheaval, gradually assumed responsibilities previously held by the civil government. This involvement in government led in turn to the secularization of the church. Bishops became ministers of the state, church dignitaries became warriors.

In the tenth and eleventh centuries, many within the church were so involved in the secular world that a movement led to the emergence of the **monastic life** as a force within the church. Those who wanted to escape the temptations of the secular world and pursue holiness were naturally drawn to the monasteries.

Thirteenth Century Europe

The thirteenth century brought more struggles to Europe. Having survived the collapse of the Roman Empire, the church was now being threatened by the **Islamic** world. As the church became more aware of the world beyond its borders, it came to see how small and limited the Christian world really was.

The predominant philosophy in the West was still the Platonism of Augustine. This philosophy put great emphasis on the world of "ideas" or "Forms." The sensible world was held to be simply a reflection of those eternal unchanging "Forms" that were in the mind of God. In order to understand the things of the sensible world, one must first know the Forms. Because these were in the mind of God and could only be known through God's illumination, faith in God was held to precede understanding.

Although the dominant philosophy of the West remained the Platonism of Augustine, the Islamic world developed a distinctly different way of thinking. Whereas the Christian church had based its thought on the works of Plato, the **Moslems** had built on the ideas of Plato's pupil, Aristotle. Aristotle had taught that the sensible world was real. In order to know reality, one must study the world around oneself, not just "contemplate" some eternal "Form."

In addition to these external pressures, there were problems within the church as well. Despite the monastic revivals, the church had become even more secularized. As the church gained more political power, it came into conflict with the secular government and, in particular, the emperor. Both the pope and the emperor involved themselves in political intrigues and military conquests.

The **Franciscan** and **Dominican** orders sought to reverse this trend toward secularization. Known as the **Medicant orders**, these groups led a life of service and lived by begging as they traveled.

Many in the church considered them spiritually excessive. The Franciscans tended to be theologically conservative, holding to the Platonism of the past. The Dominicans were innovators who used Aristotle's philosophy freely in developing their ideology. The Dominicans, in particular, put a strong emphasis on education. They established schools and had members appointed to faculty seats in all major universities. As the Dominicans took over more and more of the teaching positions, the conservative, traditional priests began to fight back. Nowhere was this conflict more visible than at the University of Paris.

St. Anslem's Life

Born to well- to-do parents in the border region of Northern Italy in 1033, Anselm was a devout studious man. After quarreling with his father on his plans to forsake the worldly life of a landowner's son and join a monastery, Anselm left home in the year 1056. Following a period of travel, he arrived at the Norman Abbey at BEC, where he took his monastic vows in 1060. Within a few years, he became prior of the abbey, and finally, in 1078, he became the abbot. In 1093, Anselm became archbishop of Canterbury. He remained in Canterbury, fighting to free the church from the power of the English kings, until his death in 1109.

Anslem was a philosophical theolgian dubbed the Father of **Scholasticism**. Scholasticism is defined as the philosophy of the "schools", this tradition arose in the medieval universities and is associated with the methods and theses of the major philosophers of the 13th and 14th centuries, namely, **Thomas Aquinas**, **Scotus** and **Ockham**.

Scholasticism remained the dominant European philosophy until the 15th century, when it gave way to the **Renaissance**, **Humanism**, **Rationalism**, and **Empiricism**. There have, however, been several revivals, and neo-scholasticism remains a feature of the philosophical landscape.

Anselm wrote important treatisies on theological subjects, these include ***Cur Deus Homo*** (Why God Became Man). In this context, Anselm was of great importance for the Christian belief.

His philosophy, largely a justification of Church practices and dogma was publicized because he felt its position needed strengthening. He was convinced that the comprehension of divine truth was the result of faith, not reason. He stated that beliving, was a necessary condition of knowledge, and that in order to believe, no proof was needed.

Anselm relationship to Augustine

Following the tradition of Augustine, Anselm held that faith precedes and leads to understanding. Like Augustine, he believed that faith is the master of reason. As he wrote in the first chapter of his ***Proslogion***:

> I do not try, Lord, to attain your lofty heights, because my understanding is in no way equal to it. But I do desire to understand your truth a little, that truth that my heart believes and loves. For I do not seek to understand so that I may believe; but I believe so that I may understand. For I believe this also, that "unless I believe, I shall not understand."[43]

In order better to understand his faith and present it more clearly to others, Anselm sought a proof of God's existence that "for its proof required no other save itself."[44] He wanted to find a proof that would not only show God existed but would also clearly show God's attributes. The notion that "perfection implies existence" seemed to him to be the key to the proof he was seeking. In 1077, after much thought, Anselm laid out his proof of God's existence in the *Proslogion*.

The Ontological Argument

The argument, which was in the form of a prayer to God, began with a description of God as "something than which nothing greater can be conceived."[45] (It was clear from the context that by "greater," Anselm pointed out even the "fool [who] has said in his heart, 'There is no God'" [46] must have such an idea.)

Anselm began the argument in the *Proslogion*, Chapter 2, by distinguishing between something existing only in the understanding (*in intellectu*) and something existing in reality (*in re*) as well. In this way, he was able to speak meaningfully of something that existed in the understanding before determining whether or not it also existed in reality.

If a being existed in reality as well as in the understanding, it must be greater (or more perfect) than one that existed only in the understanding. From this, it followed that the "something than which nothing greater can be thought" must exist in reality as well as in the understanding. If this being, existed only in the understanding, one would be left with the contradiction that it was possible to conceive of a greater being---namely, the one that existed in reality as well as in the understanding. Therefore, in order to avoid a contradiction, the greatest conceivable being must exist in reality as well as in the understanding.

Put simply, this argument stated:

First premise:
God is the greatest possible being.
Second premise:
God exists in the understanding.
Third premise:
A being that exists in reality as well as in the understanding is greater than one that exists in the understanding alone.
Conclusion:
God exists in reality as well as in the understanding.

In the *Proslogion*, Chapter 3, Anselm continued the argument. Using the same first two premises, he made a distinction between necessary existence and contingent existence. The issue was no longer just God's existence but God's uniquely necessary existence. God was defined in such a way that it was impossible to conceive of God not existing. The core of this notion of necessary being was self-existence, or aseity. Anselm later expanded on this by claiming there could never be a time when God came to exist or a time when God might cease to exist, because God was not limited by time. Therefore, God's nonexistence was simply impossible.

If the most perfect conceivable being was one that had contingent existence---that is, one whose existence was not necessary---then one could conceive of a more perfect being. A being that had necessary existence and could not be conceived not to exist would be greater. Once again, in order to avoid a contradiction, the necessary existence of the most perfect conceivable being must be affirmed. In summary form:

First premise:
God is the greatest possible being.
Second premise:
God exists in the understanding.
Third premise
A being that has necessary existence is greater than one that has contingent existence.
Conclusion:
God has necessary existence.

Chapter 9
Medieval Philosophy

Anselm's ontological argument is fascinating, since he combined the seemingly disparate roles of saint, ecclesiastical leader, and major philosopher. Theologians and such eminent philosophers as Descartes and Leibniz accepted this thesis.

Around this time, philosophy was dominated by Christianity; therefore, the natural tendencies of philosophy dealt mainly with the existence of God.

St. Anselm's Argument Point by Point:

1) God is defined as the being in which none greater is possible.
2) It is true that the notion of God exists in the understanding (your mind.)
3) And that God may exist in reality (God is a possible being.)
4) If God only exists in the mind, and may have existed, then God might have been greater than He is.
5) Then, God might have been greater than He is (if He existed in reality.)
6) Therefore, God is a being, which a greater is possible.
7) This is not possible, for God is a being in which a greater is impossible.
8) Therefore God exists in reality as well as the mind.

STUDY QUESTIONS & EXERCISES

I. Debate the following proposition: The example of medieval Europe offers a model of ordered society toward which we should strive to return.

II. Outline two forms of Anselm's ontological argument.

III. Explore the question: "Is existence a predicate (or attribute)?"

IV. Go to the Encyclopedia of Philosophy and find the name Anselm. Write a summary of his life and philosophy.

V. Anselm is known as a scholastic, why?

Chapter 10
Medieval Philosophy

C. Saint Thomas Aquinas (1225-1274)

As sacred doctrine is based on the light of faith, so is philosophy founded on the natural light of reason.

St. Thomas Aquinas

Thomas Aquinas was born of noble parents in 1225 near Naples. He was raised amidst controversy within the church. At the age of five, Thomas went to the conservative Abbey of Monte Cassino where he stayed until forced to flee because struggles between the pope and the emperor. Arriving back in Naples at age fourteen, Thomas attended the Imperial University for three years. During this time, he discovered the thought of Aristotle and the life-style of the Dominicans. At age seventeen, Thomas decided to become a Dominican novice, a decision greeted with horror by his conservative noble family. At the instigation of his mother, his brothers kidnapped him and held him captive in the family castle. After a year of reasoning, shouting, intimidating him, and tempting him with women, Thomas's family finally released him and allowed him to follow the Dominicans. Thomas went to the Dominican school in Paris where he studied under Albert the Great, an early exponent of Aristotle. Following Albert to Cologne where he was transferred in 1248, Thomas continued his studies and was ordained in the Dominican Order. In 1252, Thomas returned to Paris for graduate studies at the University.

As Thomas concluded his studies at the University of Paris, it seemed natural that he would take up a faculty chair and teach. But the antimendicant movement was strong enough to prevent this from happening immediately. In fact, it took a letter from the pope himself before Thomas was accepted into the faculty.

In addition to the controversy over the mendicant orders, Thomas became involved in the question of what to do with Aristotle. Although officially banned as heretical, Aristotle's philosophy had been taught at the university for years. With its emphasis on the sensible world, the world of sin, combined with its history of being used by Moslems, this philosophy was held to be dangerous by many in the Christian world. While not accepting Aristotle's thought uncritically, as some at the university were doing, Thomas nevertheless felt that this rediscovered philosophy could provide a solid philosophical basis for much of Christian thought as well as a possible evangelistic link to the Moslem world.

Thomas's Critique of the Ontological Argument

In many ways, Thomas Aquinas believed that it was possible to approach God from the standpoint of God's creation rather than from the standpoint of God's transcendent nature. For this reason, Aquinas was not impressed with the ontological argument. There were two fundamental problems Aquinas found with Anselm's proof.

In the first place, Thomas did not accept Anselm's notion that real things exist in the understanding. Even if the conception of God used in the argument was clearly understood, it would not prove that God really existed. It would only prove that God must be thought of as existing. Thomas said:

> Granted that everyone understands that by this name *God* is signified something than which nothing greater can be thought, nevertheless, it does not therefore follow that he understands that what the name signifies exists actually, but only that it exists mentally. Nor can it be argued that it actually exists, unless it be admitted that there actually exists something than which nothing greater can be thought; and this precisely is not admitted by those who hold that God does not exist.[47]

But for Thomas, the conception of God used in the ontological argument was *not* clearly understood. Clearly to understand any conception of God, one must know God's nature or essence. God's existence was self-evident only if one knew the essence of God. But who could know God's essence? Thomas said:

> Therefore, I say that this proposition, *God exists*, of itself is self evident, for the predicate is the same as the subject, because God is His own existence. . . Now because we do not know the essence of God, the proposition is not self-evident to us, but needs to be demonstrated by things that are more known to us, though less known in their nature---namely, by his effects.[48]

Natural and Special Revelation

Following Aristotle, Thomas held that one could discover God by examining God's effect in the sensible world. Thomas believed that the unaided human reason could know the things of this world. Reason could know the forms embedded in matter. In addition, reason could know certain things about God. Without any divine illumination, apart from the Bible and the tradition of the church, the reason could know that God existed, that God was one, and that God was perfect. This was not to say that the reason could comprehend God, but that the reason could know a few basic things about God. These truths, which all people could know apart from faith or illumination, were known through natural revelation. God was revealed through nature so that simply by using reason to examine nature, one could discover truths about God. By observing the world, one could discover certain truths about the creator in the creation. Thomas declared: "The existence of God and other like truths about God, which can be known by natural reason, are not articles of faith, but are preambles to the articles; for faith presupposes natural knowledge."[49]

This was not to say that a person must have intense reasoning powers in order to know that God existed. One could take God's existence on faith. But it *was* possible for this truth to be known by reason alone apart from faith.

There were, however, certain truths about God that the unaided reason could never discover. These truths, such as God's triune (three-part) nature and the creation of the word out of nothing *(ex nihilo*), were revealed by God through the Bible and the tradition of the church. These truths were known by faith through special revelation. Reason was not capable of knowing these truths because it was too weak---not because it was too sinful. The will, but not the reason, was affected by sin. So reason and faith were not in conflict. Natural revelation (which reason discovered) and special revelation (which faith discovered) manifested the same truth.

The Five Ways

Believing that reason was sufficient to show God's existence, Thomas set out five ways by which this could be proved. Drawing from many sources, he hoped to appeal to the Moslem world. He felt that he could not use either a preconceived conception of God or the testimony of the scriptures in the arguments. Therefore, it was necessary "to go back to natural reason, to which all are obligated to assent."[50] Using the Aristotelian method of beginning with objects in the sensible world, he argued inductively to God's existence. In all five of the arguments, he began with an observation of the sensible. Finding some feature of this world to be unexplainable in terms of the sensible world itself, he argued that there must be a God who was responsible for the given feature.

In the first argument, Thomas argued from the fact of motion to the necessity of a first mover. By motion, he meant not movement from one place to another but rather "the reduction of something from potentiality to actuality."[51] He stated:

> Whatever is moved must be moved by another. If that by which it is moved be itself moved, then this also must needs be moved by another, and that by another again. But this cannot go on to infinity. . . . Therefore, it is necessary to arrive at a first mover, moved by no other; and this everyone understands to be God.[52]

Thomas used the Aristotelian notion of efficient cause in his second argument. Pointing out "in the world of sensible things we find there is an order of efficient causes,"[53] he went on to state:

> There is no case known . . . in which a thing is found to be the efficient cause of itself; for so it would be prior to itself, which is impossible. Now in efficient causes it is nor possible to go on to infinity, because in all efficient causes follow ing in order, the first cause of the intermediate cause, and the intermediate is the cause of the ultimate cause . . . Now to take away the cause is to take away the effect. Therefore, if there be no first cause among efficient causes, there will be no ultimate, nor any immediate, cause.[54]

For this reason, "it is necessary to admit a first efficient cause, to which everyone gives the name of God."[55]

The third way turned on the notions of possibility and necessity. Because all things in the sensible world were created and decayed, it was possible for these things to be or not to be. But if all things had the possibility of not existing, "then at one time was nothing in existence."[56] This being the case, Thomas asserted:

> It would have been impossible for anything to have begun to exist; and thus even now nothing would be in existence, which is absurd. Therefore, not all beings are merely possible, but there must exist something the existence of which is necessary. But every necessary thing either has its necessity caused by another, or not. Now it is impossible to go on to infinity in necessary things which have their necessity caused by another, as has been already proved in regard to efficient causes. Therefore, we cannot but admit the existence of some being having of itself its own necessity, and . . . this all men speak of as God.[57]

The fourth way that Thomas sought to prove God's existence was by the "gradation to be found in things."[58] Because there were beings that were greater and lesser, better and worse, there must be, Thomas felt:

> Something, which is truest, something best, something noblest, and, consequently, something, which is most being . . . Therefore, there must also be some thing, which is to all beings the cause of their being, goodness, and every other perfection; and this we call God.[59]

Lastly, by examining the world, Thomas held that one could see that all natural things sought their final ends. Potentiality always sought to actualize itself. But, because objects had no knowledge, how was it that they could move toward their ends:

> Unless [they] be directed by some being endowed with knowledge and intelligence; as the arrow is directed by the archer? Therefore, some intelligent being exists by whom all natural things are directed to their end; and this being we call God.[60]

The Return to Paris

In 1259, Thomas left the University of Paris and took on a succession of tasks within the church. He was called to the papal court on several occasions over the next ten years. In 1260, he was named the preacher-general of the Dominicans. While in this office, he traveled extensively in Europe until he was made the regent master of the Dominican House of Studies at Rome in 1265. Two years later he began teaching at the University of Bologna. At this time, Thomas began writing his *Summa Theologica*. Beginning with Aristotle's philosophy, Thomas synthesized Aristotle with the traditional thinking of the church and produced a massive systematic theology.

In early 1269, Thomas was reappointed to the faculty of the University of Paris. The controversy over the Dominicans and Aristotle continued to rage. As Thomas prepared to begin teaching again, he wondered what would happen. Did his Aristotelian ideas have anything to offer the changing church? More specifically, could this emphasis on natural, unillumined reason provide a bridge between the sacred and the secular, the Christian and the Moslem? Did his five ways really prove the existence of God? Was he still operating within the tradition of the church? As he reflected on these questions, he realized how great was the task that still lay ahead of him.

STUDY QUESTIONS & EXERCISES

I. What was Thomas Aquinas' critique of Anselm's argument?

II. Describe the relationship between natural revelation and special revelation in the philosophy of Thomas Aquinas. How is this similar to or different than concepts of revelation in religious tradition with which you are familiar?

III. Briefly define the Aristotelian principle that informs each of Aquinas's five ways to know God.

a. Prime mover
b. First cause
c. Necessary being
d. Absolute value
e. Divine designer

IV. How were Anselm and Aquinas alike and how were they different in their understanding of the relationship between faith and reason? Relate each of their positions to its philosophical roots in Plato and Aristotle.

Chapter 11
The Modern Frame

Chapter 11
The Modern Frame

An Overview

In 1340, **Francis Petrarch** was named poet laureate of Rome. Petrarch's poetry had a certain quality that set it apart from previous writings. Whereas earlier poets, such as **Dante**, had rarely focused their attention on themselves, Petrarch was constantly trying to express his own passions and sufferings. Petrarch was also very interested in the writings of ancient Rome. These ancient writings, which had been preserved in medieval monasteries, seemed to him to have a richness and depth that was lacking in the literary works of the previous centuries. This emphasis on the self, combined with the appreciation of ancient culture, made Petrarch "the first writer of the **Renaissance**."[61]

The Renaissance, or "rediscovery," which began with Petrarch in Italy, slowly spread to other countries. When Constantinople fell to the Turks in 1453, trade routes to the East were cut off. This, in turn, led many countries to seek new routes to the East. The explorers who sought these new routes inadvertently discovered whole new continents. These discoveries forced rethinking of scientific theories that had been accepted for centuries. People became more interested in the world around them and less interested in the life to come.

In astronomy especially, many established ideas were being challenged. Using a model of the universe devised by Egyptian astronomer **Ptolemy**, most medieval thinkers had believed that the earth was the center of the universe. Moving outward from the earth, one encountered first the sun, then the moon, then the planets, and finally the fixed starts. All of these, including the fixed "orb" of the starts, rotated around the earth.

According to medieval theologians, when humankind fell in the Garden of Eden the entire landscape of earth "fell." Weeds, briars, mosquitoes, and other banes of humanity suddenly appeared. Instead of the perfect flat landscape of the garden, there were mountains and valleys. Mountains became the symbols of sin. People looked forward to the day when "Every valley shall be exalted and every mountain and hill made low" (Is. 40:4).

But this "fall" of earth did not extend to the heavens. The moon, the sun, the planets, and especially the fixed stars were untouched by the effects of sin. They all continued to move in the same perfect rotation as when God first created them.

In 1517, the Protestant Reformation began in Germany. Reformers such as Martin Luther and John Calvin sought to replace the authority of the hierarchy in Rome with the authority of the Bible in their hands. Luther and Calvin used Renaissance scholarship to translate and interpret the biblical texts. They used these ancient sources as the basis for a wide-ranging critique of church and culture.

The Roman Catholic Church, in response to the Reformation, began a Counter-Reformation. At the Council of Trent, many of the excesses of the church were corrected. Ideas that had previously been freely discussed were now banned and their authors punished. A group called the Society of Jesus (Jesuits) was formed to help spread the orthodox Catholic position and defend it against heresy. These Jesuits soon dominated the major Catholic centers of learning.

Despite these attempts to stem Protestant advances, by the end of the sixteenth century a significant portion of the Western world was no longer under the control of the Catholic Church, the new emphasis on the self and the natural world, the new ideas about the structures of the universe, and the rediscovery of ancient art and culture forced a radical change in Western thinking. One such new way of thinking was formulated by René Descartes.

The Renaissance and the Reformation were movements of reaction and renewal. The Renaissance of the fourteenth and fifteenth centuries was as its name indicates, a time of rediscovery and rebirth. People rediscovered the cultural heritage of ancient Greece and Rome. And, in doing so, people felt themselves to be reborn. People became interested in themselves. Human, rather than heavenly, concerns became the normal order of the day. People turned from metaphysical and theological speculations to study more practical, "worldly" matters. These studies became known as the "humanities." The ideal person was one of all-around competence, a "humanist." The norm was no longer scholarly work pursued in monastic isolation, but an active public life in which learning was applied.

The Renaissance fostered a critical use of ancient sources rather than a slavish reliance on authorities. This era was the first to identify itself as a distinct epoch. Its scholars termed the previous, medieval period "Dark Ages." Renaissance scholars felt that, for the first time in a long time, light was breaking forth from the past. Lawyers, for example, reexamined the codes of ancient Roman law. They were no longer interested in reiterating the rules. Now they examined the context and sought to understand the intent of ancient lawgivers so that their insights could be applied in appropriate ways in a new period.

Progress, in the Renaissance, was made by way of return to the classical past. Aristotle was studied for new ideas in physics, and Galen was consulted for fresh insights in medicine. Not until the Renaissance was nearly over did new ideas about the universe and humanity arise from fresh investigations done in the present. Copernicus's work on the solar system was published in 1543, and Vesalius's description of human anatomy was known in the same year.

The Reformation

The **Reformation**[61] of the sixteenth century was also a movement that attempted to recover the past in order to renew church and society in the present. **Erasmus**, **Luther**, and **Calvin** reacted against what they considered to be the decadent authority of **medieval scholasticism** and went back to earlier sources. Their model of the church was that they viewed as the pristine period of the first few centuries of the Christian era. Theologically, they went behind Thomas Aquinas to Augustine. And philosophically, they rejected the reigning Aristotelian scholasticism and adopted an earlier **Neoplatonic** style.

Most important of all the church reformers was their return to the Bible as the basic source document of their faith. They accepted its authority with personal trust. But they studied the text critically with the tools of Renaissance scholarship. Erasmus, while remaining a loyal Roman Catholic, provided Protestantism its most basic tool with his critical edition of the Greek New Testament. The Latin Vulgate, approved by the medieval church, was no longer normative. Luther took the next step by translating the Bible into German so that every burgher could read it. Calvin applied his Renaissance training in understanding law to the interpretation of the Bible. He examined the historical and cultural context and sought meaning in an empathy with intentions of the original authors.

The Bible now had new and powerful influence. The printing press had been invented. In 1454 Gutenberg produced the first printed Bible. In 1450 less than 100,000 handwritten manuscripts had been in existence. Just fifty years later there were 9 million printed books. The invention of printing thoroughly and rapidly revolutionized human life. Printed books gave people new ideas and new independence from authorities. The printed word stirred criticism of the church and society.

At the beginning of the 16th century, the Catholic Church has become extremely powerful, but internally corrupt. The clergy were unable to live according to church doctrine. The abuse of the church extends to ceremonies and practices. In the first half of the sixteenth century Western Europe experiences a wide range of social, artistic, and geo-political changes. As the result of this conflict within the Catholic Church, Reformation movement begins in 1517. A German Augustinian friar named Martin Luther posts his "*Ninety-Five Theses*" against the Roman Catholic Church. These were a list of grievances, against the Catholic Church. This is done at the church at Wittenberg. Martin Luther (1483-1546) while studying law at the University of Erfurt in Germany experiences a spiritual conversion. As mentioned above, due to the invention of the printing press, Luther's reforms are quickly spread through Europe. However, Luther is condemned as a heretic by Pope Leo X in the Edict of Worms. He is forced to escape and live for a year in hiding, but his reforms have taken root. The split in the Roman Catholic Church is now irreconcilable.

Chapter 11
The Modern Frame

Preparation for the Modern Age

The modern era really began in the seventeenth century. It was the matrix, the womb, the frame, in which the concepts that condition our contemporary thought were nurtured and finally brought to birth. In philosophy, "modern" denotes the seventeenth and eighteenth centuries, which served the scene for the "contemporary" period of the nineteenth and twentieth centuries. The modern period introduced in a rudimentary way the problems with which we still must deal.

Two discoveries near the end of the Renaissance and Reformation decisively formed the seventeenth and eighteenth centuries. The first was the development of modern mathematics, usually attributed to Christopher Clavius (1537-1612). Clavius, A Jesuit priest, was known as the "modern Euclid." He asserted the superiority of mathematical demonstrations over dialectical disputations. Mathematics, for him, was the most fundamental science. It alone gave certainty. This discovery spurred the philosophical development known as "rationalism" on the seventeenth century. Rationalism was Platonism taken to one of its extremes. The emphasis was on innate ideas and the ability to deduce all other knowledge from them.

The second discovery was the introduction of methods of observation, especially by instruments, fostered by Galileo Galilei (1564-1642). Galileo invented a telescope. Through it he saw, within his own eyes, that the earth rotated around the sun and that there were mountains on the moon. Both of those observations contradicted long and firmly held assumptions grounded in the statements of ancient authorities. The issue was method. Galileo did not consult authorities; he looked! This was a decisive break with the past. Now knowledge came from experiments in the present, which opened up new possibilities for the future. This new approach opened the philosophical possibility of eighteen-century empiricism. Empiricism developed on the side of Aristotle. Its emphasis was on sense data as the primary source of information from which all other knowledge could validly be induced.

The Scientific Revolution

The year 1543 may be taken as the beginning of the scientific revolution. It was then that Copernicus published his work entitled: *The Revolution of the Heavenly Bodies*. Within a century and a half, man's conception of himself and the universe he inhabited

was altered. The scholastic method of reasoning was replaced by new scientific methods.

In the early 1500s, the Polish astronomer **Nicolaus Copernicus** (1473-1543) presented the first major challenged to the traditional model of the universe. Using mathematical principles and a desire for simplicity, Copernicus claimed that the earth, the planets, and the fixed starts rotated around the sun. The moon was the only heavenly body that rotated around the earth. This new idea generated interest and excitement on the part of the church and the thinkers of the day. In fact, Copernicus' ideas were widely accepted--at first.

Nicholas Copernicus was born in the Polish city of Torun in 1473. While in Italy, Copernicus studied the generally accepted astronomical system of Ptolemy. This system depicted the universe as consisting of the earth and ten spheres. Copernicus had anticipated some of objections. For example, Martin Luther, the reformist remarked that: "This fool wishes to reverse the entire science of astronomy; but sacred Scripture tells us that Joshua commanded the sun to stand still, and not the earth." However, now we know these principles to be based upon reality.

Galileo

Galileo was born in Pisa of a noble Florentine family (1564-1642). His scientific successes were due to his ability to make what some historians have called "thought experiments." With mathematics, Galileo thought, there could be no mistakes. Therefore, he confidently reduced the universe to mass and motion.

Galileo answered the objections that had been offered to the Copernican system. The earth turns around the sun. He did not consult with any authorities. His work was a success. But he was summoned before the Inquisition at Rome for teaching a doctrine "contrary to Holy Scripture." He was compelled to recant.

Chapter 11
The Modern Frame

Rationalism in the Seventeenth Century

Three great thinkers of three differing nationalities developed rationalism in the seventeen-century: **Descartes** (French), **Spinoza** (Dutch), and **Leibniz** (German). The latter two built on and expanded the approach that we find developed in René Descartes.

René Descartes (1596-1650) was a scientist who made significant contributions to physics, optics, and physiology. He is considered the founder of modern analytical geometry. For Descartes, mathematics was the one language that could express scientific ideas with perfect clarity.

His most important contribution was his method. He decided to doubt everything he had ever been taught until he came to some clear and evident idea, a first principle that could not be doubted. He finally concluded that he could not doubt that he was doubting. If he was doubting, then he was thinking. And if he was thinking, then he existed as a thinking being. *Cogito ergo sum*, "I think, therefore I am," was Descartes' clear and evident first principle. Human nature was basically mind, to which a body was attached. Rationality was the key to reality.

By his mathematical method, Descartes believed that he could come to certain knowledge of everything. He began with an idea within himself that seemed obvious to his reason. Then by rational deduction he went on to demonstrate the existence of everything, including God and the world.

Baruch Spinoza (1632-1677) was a Dutch Jew who made his living grinding lenses. Descartes had left behind a significant problem, on which Spinoza worked. Mind and body seemed like two separate and incompatible substances. How did they function together? Spinoza accepted Descartes' mathematical model for synthesizing all knowledge into one system. He further tightened its systematic consistency by positing not two substances, thought and extension, but one divine substance, which he called alternately **God or Nature**. Spinoza was thus considered an atheist or "that God-intoxicated man" depending on which dimension of his system was emphasized.

Gottfried Wilhelm Leibniz (1646-1716) was the son of a university professor at Leipzig, where he was also educated. In addition to being a jurist, he was a mathematician, scientist, historian, diplomat, theologian, and philosopher; he studied the other philosophers of his day and interacted with them. He traveled widely and met leading thinkers of his day, including **Huygens**, **Newton**, **Boyle**, and Spinoza.

For an active person like Leibniz, philosophy had to be done in "odd moments," in the form of letters, memoranda, and articles. But Leibniz's dream was the same as that of Descartes and Spinoza. He hoped for a systematic organization of all conceivable knowledge. His own effort was to reform all science through the use of two instruments of his devising. First, he sought to perfect a universal scientific language that would reduce all thoughts to mathematical symbols. Second, he succeeded in developing one of the first forms of calculus. (There was later a dispute with Isaac Newton over who had first formulated what they had each apparently come too independently.) With this reasoning tool, Leibniz hoped to bring all thought under the reign of symbolic logic.

Empiricism in the Eighteenth Century

Philosophical theories are seldom rejected because they have been proved wrong. Rather, they are abandoned because they have failed to solve all the problems and people hope that a new approach will be more successful. Deduction from seemingly obvious first principles had occupied the best minds on the European continent for over a century. The mathematical side of the new science had been in focus. But not all the problems had been solved.

In Great Britain as the eighteen-century approach, a new philosophical movement was growing that emphasized the other side of the new science. The observational and experimental was in focus. The interest of philosophers in the eighteen-century shifted to an empirical and inductive approach to knowledge. The new effort among philosophers in the eighteenth-century was to develop all knowledge by intuition from sense experience alone. A philosophy was sought that would be in harmony with the developing science.

In science, the greatest name was **Isaac Newton**. He appeared as the culmination of a century of preliminary efforts to produce an experimental science. Newton was born in 1642, the year Galileo died. He elaborated the essential of calculus, apparently quite independently of Leibniz. He discovered that white light is the presence of all colors. And most important of all, he grasped the principle of gravity.

Some claim that the age of "**Enlightenment**" began with the publication of Newton's *Mathematical Principles of Natural Philosophy* in 1687. Just as the Renaissance persons felt that they had been reborn, people in the Enlightenment believed that they had grown to maturity. Humankind was now able to solve all of its problems through the use of human intelligence. A "scientific method" had been articulated by Newton. In a letter to the secretary of the Royal Society of London for the Improvement of Natural Knowledge in 1672, Newton wrote:

> The best and safest method of philosophizing seem to be, first, to inquire diligently into the properties of things and to establish those properties by experiments, and to proceed later to hypotheses for the explanation of things themselves. For hypotheses ought to be applied only in the explanation of the properties of things, and not made use of in determining them.[62]

The method of observation, experimentation, and generalization seemed to provide a new method that gave certain knowledge. The poet **Alexander Pope** expressed Newton's impact on his age:

> Nature and Nature's Laws lay hid in Night
> God said, "Let Newton be!" and all was Light.[63]

For over one hundred years in Great Britain, philosophers attempted to work out the metaphysical and epistemological implications of Newtonian science. They proposed to found all knowledge on what could be derived by induction from sense experience alone.

Three great thinkers in the British Isles developed eighteenth-century empiricism: **Locke** (English), **Berkeley** (Irish), and **Hume** (Scottish).

John Locke (1632-1704) took an approach almost exactly opposite to that of Descartes. According to Locke, at birth our minds are *tabula rasa*, blank tablets. All our ideas originate in sense experience coming to us from outside our minds. A fundamental question was "What causes sensations?" Locke's answer was to posit the existence of "matter." Matter was the stuff external to us that had power to cause the sensations received by our sight, hearing, taste, touch, and smell.

In Ireland, An Anglican bishop, **George Berkeley** (1685-1753), was disturbed by Locke's conclusions. Berkeley reasoned that if people believed that the source of all our ideas was inert, unthinking matter, they would become materialist and atheist. Berkeley did not reject Locke's method. Berkeley insisted that he too was a strict empiricist. But, Berkeley argued, on the basis of our experience we know that no ideas exist except in minds. Indeed, nothing exists, in human experience, unless it exists as perceived by some mind. The only mind capable of causing all the richness and diversity that we experience with our senses, for Berkeley, was the mind of God. Berkeley thus had an alternate empirical solution to Locke's question, "What causes our sensations?" Berkeley's answer was "God." Only God was a sufficient source and cause of all sensations and ideas everywhere.

A Scot, **David Hume** (1711-1776), inherited these arguments from Locke and Berkeley. Hume agreed with Locke that there were no innate ideas. All the ideas in our minds come originally from sense experiences. When Hume approached the question to which Locke and Berkeley gave different answers, "What causes our sensations?" Hume was honest enough to say, "We don't know!" On the basis of sense experience alone, all we know with certainty is that we have sensations. After one hundred years of empiricism, the result was skepticism. Many traditional philosophical notions had no empirical basis. According to Hume, from sense experience alone, one could not know with certainty that cause and effect were necessarily connected or, that there was an external world, a self, or God. All these ideas could be accounted for psychologically. By custom or habit, we associate ideas with experiences when there is no demonstrable connection. We may retain our beliefs for practical purposes if we wish, said Hume. But as a philosopher he had to say that empirically we know almost nothing!

Kant's Synthesis

Two opposite philosophical methods had dominated the best minds of the continent and Great Britain for a century each. Philosophers on the continent had followed rationalism during the seventeenth century. They had developed the ideal of a few innate principles from which they had attempted to deduce all knowledge. They had not been decisively proved wrong. But neither had they solved all problems. Philosophers in Great Britain had tried to be rigorously empirical during the eighteenth century. They had sought comprehensive knowledge by induction from sense experience alone. The result, finally, was David Hume's skepticism.

The person who attempted to bring order out of the chaos resulting from these two competing and inconclusive efforts was **Immanuel Kant** (1724-1804). He never traveled more than thirty miles from the sleepy university town of Königsberg, Germany, where he was born. He seemed like a stereotypical ivory-tower academician, a bachelor

who lived by a rigid routine, interested only in books. But ultimately his thought revolutionized philosophy, and we still wrestle with the problems in the context that Kant created.

His parents raised Kant in a pietistic Christian home. At Königsberg University, he was trained in the rationalism of **Christian Wolff**, who transmitted the tradition of Descartes and Leibniz. After becoming a lecturer in philosophy at the same university, Kant was redirected by his reading. He declared that studying David Hume's radical empiricism awakened him from his "dogmatic slumbers." Another new element came when he read **Rousseau**. Kant became absorbed in this new approach that for the first time in his adult life he missed his regular four o'clock afternoon walk. In Rousseau, Kant was introduced to the influenced of feelings and conscience. Here were elements not derived either from logical arguments or sensory evidence.

Kant raised the fundamental question "How is knowledge possible?" He set out to perform a "**transcendental critique**" of human knowing. The term ***transcendental***, in Kant's sense, referred to that which did not fall within experience, but that which made experience possible. His transcendental critique sought for the ***a priori*** (prior to experience) conditions in the mind itself that made knowledge possible.

Chapter 11
The Modern Frame

Kant presented a new synthesis of the conflicting methods that had been handed down to him. According to Kant, both empiricism and rationalism were partly right, but each was more limited in its scope than its proponents believed, and both had to work together. Empiricism was right in that the material of our knowledge came from the senses. If we had no sense data, we would have no knowledge. But rationalism was right in that the form of knowledge was supplied by the mind. We would have no knowledge except that certain categories in our minds gave meaningful shape to the data that the senses provided.

The knowledge humans had, was limited to the "**phenomenal world.**" It was knowledge of how things (phenomena) appeared to people. People had no knowledge of things as they are in themselves. They did not know essences, but only appearances. This meant that metaphysics in the traditional sense was impossible. Humankind could not know reality as it is but could only have a "scientific" knowledge of the way in which things appeared to human senses and minds. Epistemology had become the overriding philosophical concern. "How do we know?" Had replaced "What do we know?" As the principal question of philosophy. This was a "Copernican revolution" in philosophy, Kant contended. No longer did philosophers ask themselves how knowledge could conform to the nature of objects outside themselves. "Now," said Kant, "we make nature." Nature was understood as a system of objects manifesting an order on which predictions could be based. Kant contended that the human mind provided that order. Objects therefore, conformed to human understanding. Yet knowledge was objective, because, according to Kant, all people's minds were structured so as to order the same sense data into identical patterns.

There was also a "noumenal world" for Kant, a world outside of human sense experience. Included in that world were things-in-themselves, essences, values, **moral absolutes**. Kant wanted objective knowledge in the moral realm as much as in the scientific. Indeed, for Kant, the realm of human values was more important than the realm of nature. But Kant was convinced that one could not have knowledge of values from either the reason or from sense experience. The answer to knowledge of the noumenal world, for Kant, lay inside the individual. Morality was a postulate of the "practical reason." All people had within them, Kant believed, a sense of duty, a conscience, feelings of oughtness that rightly guided them. On the basis of this "inner sense," people could have practical certainty, what Kant called a "rational faith" that they were free and immortal and that God existed. Why? Otherwise people's inner sense of oughtness would not conform to reality outside of them. Kant could not bear that thought.

For himself, Kant had reconciled the opposing, formerly mutually exclusive, approaches to knowledge of the preceding two centuries. The mechanistic view of modern science rightly applied to the world of appearances. Empirical evidence and mathematical reasoning enabled people to understand and, to some extent, control the world as they perceived it. At the same time, Kant was able to hold to a belief in human freedom and moral responsibility that exempted humankind from being just another cog in the cause-and-effect chain of science. Human beings were citizens of two worlds, the noumenal as well as the phenomenal.

Kant synthesis did not last long in its original form. Soon after him, other philosophers emphasized one side of his thought to the exclusion of the other. Either scientific facts or human values became paramount, but rarely were they held in balance. The problems continued in the context that Kant helped to develop. The epistemological problem is still uppermost in contemporary philosophy. In our section on the contemporary context, we will deal with the diverse schools of thought that have evolved since Kant.

The work of Descartes, Hume, and Kant truly laid the foundations of the contemporary era. As we deepen our understanding of them, we will better comprehend the intellectual factors that have shaped our lives.

STUDY QUESTIONS & EXERCISES

I. Give an overview of the modern era in your own words.

II. What are the names associated with the Reformation and why are these important?

III. What are the names associated with the Scientific Revolution and why are these important?

IV. What are the names associated with the Continental rationalist and why are these important?

V. What are the names associated with the empiricists and why are these important?

Chapter 12
Continental Rationalist

A. René Descartes (1596-1650)

I think, therefore, I am. ***Descartes***

Chapter 12
Continental Rationalist

Responding to the shocking news that the Catholic Church had condemned Galileo, René Descartes wrote:

> I cannot imagine that an Italian, and especially one well thought of by the Pope from what I have heard, could have been labeled a criminal for nothing other than wanting to establish the movement of the earth. I know that this had been censured formerly by a few cardinals, but I thought that since that time one was allowed to teach it publicly even in Rome. I confess that if this is false, then all the principles of my philosophy are false also.[64]

In the year 1633, it seemed incredible that such a thing could happen. Galileo's *Dialogue on the Two Chief Systems*, which sought to prove that the earth revolved around the sun, was hardly irreligious. Still, the Pope had declared that it was in error, and Galileo was being punished. As Descartes considered the forthcoming publication of his *Le Monde* ("The World"), he wondered what he should do. Living in Protestant

Holland, he was beyond the reach of the Catholic Church. But Descartes wanted his ideas accepted in Paris and Rome as well as in Holland. Should he proceed with the publication of his work, knowing that the church would probably condemn it? Or should he wait until a more judicious occasion? What insights could his newly discovered method bring to this issue?

Early Life

René Descartes was born in Touraine, France, on March 31, 1596. His paternal grandfather was a doctor and his father a member of the nobility. His family was independently wealthy, and young René never had to work. In 1606, at the age of ten, Descartes began a nine-year course of study at the Royal Jesuit College of La Fleche. During his first six years at the college, Descartes studied the humanities and theology. The next three years were spend studying philosophy. Philosophy, which was not distinguished from the special sciences at that time, included morals, logic, mathematics, physics, and metaphysics.

Descartes was a good student and did well at the College. But as his studies ended Descartes came to a very negative conclusion about his education. As he later wrote:

> From my childhood I have been familiar with letters; and as I was given to believe that by their means a clear and assured knowledge can be acquired of all that is useful in life, I was extremely eager for instruction in them. As soon, however, as I had completed the course of study, at the close of which it is customary to be admitted into the order of the learned, I entirely changed my opinion. For I found myself entangled in so many doubts and errors that, as it seemed to me, the endeavor to instruct myself had served only to disclose to me more and more of my ignorance. [I was led] to conclude that there was no body of knowledge in the world of such worth as I had previously been led to expect.[65]

There was, however, one subject that Descartes found to be of value: mathematics. In the rigors of mathematics, Descartes found the certainty that was so lacking in all of the other disciplines. Whereas the humanities and the sciences of the time were based on conflicting, unprovable presuppositions, mathematics was based on the certainty of deductive reasoning. In fact, it seemed odd to Descartes that a foundation “so firm and solid should have nothing loftier erected upon [it].”[66]

Descartes’ interest in mathematics grew after he left the college. Following some study at Poitiers, he joined the army of Maurice of Nassau in 1618 and served as a gentleman volunteer. Having been left a sizable inheritance by his father, Descartes was free to pursue his own interests. While serving as a volunteer, he carried on intense mental struggles over the place of mathematical reasoning in science. Descartes became more and more convinced that the whole approach to understanding of the world was incorrect. In 1619, following a period of especially intense reasoning, he had a series of dreams that convinced him that the “spirit of truth” had been inspiring him and that his mathematical studies had divine approval. Traveling, soldiering, and writing, Descartes spent the next ten years developing and testing his new principles. In 1629, he moved to Holland, where there was a greater degree of intellectual freedom than anywhere else on the continent, and began to prepare his writings for publication.

The Rules

Throughout his studies, Descartes found uncertainty and contradiction. Each thinker he encountered seemed to have a different approach to the quest for truth that conflicted with other thinkers. Many learned men of the past had relied on the authority of the church or sacred writings to guide them. But this dependence on authority also led to contradictory results. As Descartes continued his studies, he became “obsessed by the eager desire to learn to distinguish the true from the false, that [he] might see clearly what [his] actions ought to be, and so as to have assurance as to the path to be followed in this life.”[67] It seemed to Descartes that mathematics was the only discipline that supplied the kind of certainty he was seeking. Therefore, he decided to use the principles of mathematics to construct a system of knowledge. He began by establishing twenty-one Rules for the Direction of the Mind. The most important of these rules were the following:

> *Rule 3.* In treating of objects proposed for investigation what we have to examine is not what others have opined, nor what we ourselves may conjecture, but what we can clearly and evidently intuit, or can deduce with certainty: knowledge is not obtainable in any other way. . . .

> By intuition I understand, not the fluctuating testimony of the sense, nor the misleading judgment of a wrongly combining imagination, but the apprehension which the mind, pure and attentive, gives us so easily and so distinctively that we are thereby freed from all doubt as to what it is that we are apprehending. . .
>
> By way of deduction. . . we understand all that is necessarily concluded from other certainly known data. . .
>
> *Rule 4*. In the search for the truth of things method is indispensable.
>
> *Rule 5*. Method consists entirely in the orderly handling of the things upon which the mind's attention has to be concentrated, if any truth bearing on them is to be discovered. We shall comply with it exactly, if we resolve involved and obscure data step by step into those which are simpler, and starting from the intuition of those which are simplest, endeavor to ascend to the knowledge of all the others, doing so by corresponding steps.[68]

To find certain truth, then, one must begin with what could be "clearly and evidently intuited." Such "clear and evident" intuitions could not be derived from sense-perception. The senses provided only blurred information. Certain knowledge had to come from someplace else. But if "clear and evident" intuitions did not come from the senses, then where did they come from?

Following Plato's theory of Forms, Descartes claimed that they were innate. One could never derive, for example, the concept of a perfect triangle from sense experience. Any attempt to draw a triangle would necessarily fall short of the mark. No matter how carefully drawn, the triangle would always have imperfections. But the "clear and evident" intuition or idea of a "plane figure formed by three lines intersecting by twos in three points" could be known apart from sense experience. It could be known with certainty.

Plato held that sense experience served to remind people of the eternal truths they already knew. Aquinas, following Aristotle, held that sense experience provided the basis for one's knowledge of universals. But for Descartes sense experience played no role whatsoever in the search for truth.

Once one had established "clear and evident" intuitions, Descartes claimed, then one could move deductively to build on them. Just as mathematics began with basic postulates and then used these to form theorems, Descartes began with basic intuitions and then used them to discover other certain knowledge.

Descartes began with himself, with his own ideas, in his search for truth. He put aside the authority of past thinkers, the church, sacred writings, and even his own sense experience and sought to discover ultimate truth by using only his reason.

Methodological Doubts

The key issue for Descartes was to find the "clear and evident" intuition (or intuitions) that would lead him to truth. It seemed to Descartes that the best way to find such intuitions was the process of methodological doubt. This process involved examining every idea that he had been taught or had come to believe to see whether there was a chance it might be incorrect. If there was a chance of being mistaken, however remote, the idea was to be set aside or "doubted." In this manner, Descartes hoped to find one (or more) things that could not be doubted. As he explained it:

> In respect . . . of the opinions which I have hitherto been entertaining, I thought that I could not do better than decided on emptying my mind of them one and all, with a view to the replacing of them by others more tenable, or, it may be, to the re-admitting of them, on their being shown to be in conformity with reason.[69]

Descartes began his methodological doubt by doubting everything he had been taught. Holding that they could possibly be mistaken, he doubted every theory of science that was held in his time. After all, Galileo was attempting to prove that the earth rotated around the sun, not the sun around the earth, as was commonly supposed. If the commonly held opinion was wrong in this instance, could one trust it in other cases? He doubted all of the theology and metaphysics that he had learned from the Jesuits. Next he doubted ideas that seemed more certain: his own bodily existence and the truths of mathematics. Descartes came to the conclusion that even in the matters he might possibly be mistaken. There was always the possibility that he might be insane or even that some evil god was deceiving him. As Descartes explained this process of methodological doubt:

It may be said, although the senses sometimes deceive us regarding minute objects ... There are yet many other things which . . . are too evident to be doubted; as for instance, that I am in this place, seated by the fire, attired in a dressing-gown, having this paper in my hands, and other similar seeming certainties. Can I deny that these hands and this body are mine, save perhaps by comparing myself to those who are insane. . . . None the less I must bear in mind that I am a man, and am therefore in the habit of sleeping, and that what the insane represent to themselves in their waking moments I represent to myself, with other things even less probable in my dreams. How often, indeed, have I dreamt of myself being in this place, . . . lying undressed in bed! . . . On more careful study . . . I see that there are no certain marks distinguishing waking from sleep . . . Let us, then, suppose ourselves to be asleep, and that all these particulars---namely, that we open our eyes, move the head, extend the hands---are false and illusory; and let us reflect that our hands perhaps, and the whole body, are not what we see them as being. . . . This, perhaps, is why we not unreasonably conclude that physics, astronomy, medicine, and all others disciplines treating of composite things are of doubtful character, and that arithmetic, geometry, etc. . . . have a content that is certain and indubitable. For whether I am awake or dreaming, 2 and 3 are 5. . . . Yet even these truths can be questioned. . . . How . . . do I know that [God] has not arranged that there be no earth, no heavens, no extended thing, no shape, no magnitude, no location, while at the same time securing that all these things appear to me to exist precisely as they now do? Others, as I sometimes think, deceive themselves in the things which they believe they know best. How do I know that I am not myself deceived everytime I add 2 and 3? . . . But perhaps God has not been willing that I should be thus deceived, for He is said to be supremely good. . . .[But] I shall now suppose, not that a true God, who as such must be supremely good and the fountain of truth, but that some malignant genius exceedingly powerful and cunning has devoted all his powers in the deceiving of me. . . What is there, then, which can be esteemed true? Perhaps only this, that nothing whatsoever is certain.[70]

Cogito Ergo Sum

While in the process of this universal, all-encompassing doubt, Descartes came across one thing that he simply could not doubt: that he doubted. Even if there was a "malignant genius" who was misleading him at every point, there still had to be a "him" to mislead. There had to be a person who was doubting. This led Descartes to affirm the one proposition that could not be doubted, "*Cogito ergo sum*---I think, therefore, I am." Descartes reflected:

But I immediately became aware that while I was thus disposed to think that all was false, it was absolutely necessary that I who thus thought should be somewhat; and noting that this truth *I think, therefore I am*, was so steadfast and so assured that the suppositions of the skeptics, to whatever extreme they might all be carried, could not avail to shake it, I concluded that I might without scruple accept it as being the first principle of the philosophy I was seeking.[71]

Having established that there was at least an "I" that was doubting, Descartes went on to examine the nature of this "I." It seemed clear to Descartes that this "I" was, by nature, a thinking thing. He wrote:

> What then is it that I am? A thinking thing. What is a thinking thing? It is a thing that doubts, understands, affirms, denies, wills, abstains from willing, that also can be aware of images and sensations.[72]

Proof of God's Existence

Included among the ideas that this "thinking thing" had was the idea of God. Where did such an idea come from? Certainly the idea of God did not come from within the "thinking thing" itself, because the self was finite and could not conceive of something infinite. In fact, the awareness that this "thinking thing"was finite only came through comparison with something infinite. The idea of God, then, had to come from a source outside the "thinking thing." Futhermore, this idea of God had to come from a source adequate to produce such an idea. The only source was God. Descartes explained:

> I resolved to inquire whence I had learned to think of something more perfect than I myself was; and I saw clearly that it must proceed from some nature that was indeed more perfect. . . . Thus [I am] committed to the conclusion that [the idea of something more perfect] has been placed in me by a nature which is veritably more perfect than I am, and which has indeed within itself all the perfections of which I have any idea, that is to say, in a single word, that is God.[73]

Having proved that there was a perfect God, Descartes argued: "it is impossible that He should ever deceive me, since in all fraud and deception there is some element of imperfection."[74] Therefore, he concluded that his God-given judgment, if used properly, could never lead him astray. Even his senses could be trusted---if they were subject to his reason. By using his reason alone, Descartes was able to come to truth.

Body and Mind

The affirmation "I think, therefore, I am" was absolutely certain because it applied only to the conscious self. The "I" that Descartes found at the conclusion of his methodological doubt was not "that assemblage of limbs we call the human body."[75] What then was the relation of this conscious self or mind to the body?

According to Descartes, the body was a part of the material world. As part of the material world, two important things about the body became clear. Like all other objects, the body was subject to the laws of motion. Some antecedent movement determined each bodily motion. So the body, taken by itself, was simply a complex machine. Like all other objects in the material world, the body's essential characteristic was extension. Using a piece of wax as an example, Descartes explained what he meant by extension. One could easily describe the taste, color, shape, and size of the wax. But when the wax melts "What remains of the tastes exhales, the odor evaporates, the color changes, the shape is destroyed, its size increases,"[76] and so on. Yet through all of these changes, the piece of wax remained a piece of wax before and after heating---and common to all material things, including the body---was the "character of being spacially extended. It is the capacity to assume, under certain and different conditions, this or that determinate size and this or that determinate shape."[77]

The mind, on the other hand, had nothing whatsoever to do with the material world. Whereas the body was determined by the laws of motion, the mind was totally free. The

essential characteristic of the mind was thought. The mind was the "self" Descartes found at the end of his process of doubt.

From this distinction between body and mind, Descartes concluded that the world of experience was dual. On the other hand, there were the material objects, which were distinguished by extension: the world of bodies. On the other hand, there were the human-selves, which are distinguished by thought: the world of minds. This is the **Cartesian Dualism**

The problem that remained for Descartes was to explain the interaction of the body and the mind. If they belonged to such totally different world, how could one affect the other? How could the body, for example, cause the mind to direct the body to write down ideas?

Descartes attempted to answer this question by referring to the pineal gland. This small gland, attached to the brain, provided the bridge between "thinking substance" (mind) and "corporeal substance" (body). When some material object acting on the senses stimulated the body, one of two things happened. Either the body responded on its own, or else through the pineal gland the body caused changes in the mind. For example, if one's hand became hot from being too near a flame, the body would independently respond to the heat stimulus by causing the hand to move away. If another person held one's hand over a flame, the body would act on the pineal gland, causing a change of mind. The mind would then understand that the other person was up to something evil and might attempt to do that person harm.

Conversely, the mind could act on the body through the pineal gland. If, for example, the mind should desire intellectual stimulation, it might direct the body to move to the library. Descartes contended, "Solely because it desires something, [the mind] causes the little gland to which it is closely united to move in the way requisite to produce the effect which relates to this desire."[78]

Galileo's Condemnation

In 1604 a new star appeared in the constellation of Cassiopeia. The appearance of this new star was devastating to the intellectual life of Europe. Ptolemy and even Copernicus had held that the starts were fixed. The stars were the furthest things away from the fallen earth and the closest things to God. It was inconceivable that these perfect creations of God could ever change.

Around this time, an Italian by the name of Galileo began experimenting with lenses. In 1609, Galileo built a telescope that could enlarge by thirty diameters. Pointing this telescope at the heavens, Galileo made several starling discoveries. He discovered that the Milky Way was actually an incredible number of stars. He discovered that the planet Jupiter had at least four moons---much like the moons of earth. And, most important, he discovered that the earth's moon had mountains.

Galileo's discoveries and his conclusions, which supported a position similar to that of Copernicus, were unacceptable to the Roman Catholic Church. Whereas Copernicus had written in a period of relative freedom of ideas, Galileo was writing in a period of fear and distrust following the Reformation. Whereas Copernicus had based his theories on mathematical principles and a desire for simplicity, Galileo based his theories on observation. Whereas Copernicus' theories had left medieval theology essentially undisturbed, Galileo's discoveries threatened to undermine it. That mountains, the symbols of sin, could be found in the perfection of the heavens was unthinkable! In 1616 Galileo was "strongly counseled" by the Pope not to publish any findings that he might make. However, in 1632 Galileo finally published his theories in the *Dialogue on the Two Chief Systems*. In 1633, the Roman Catholic Church declared Galileo's work heretical. Galileo was called before the Inquisition and forced to renounce his ideas. He spent the rest of his life under house arrest at his small estate near Florence.

When Descartes heard the news, he was dumbfounded. He had thought that Galileo's work was gaining general acceptance everywhere. The severities of the sentence especially frightened him and force him to rethink his plan to publish his work. Although his method was different from that of Galileo, he came to many of the same conclusions. In his application of mathematics to astronomy, he, too, held that the earth revolved around the sun. But even apart from this specific area, his whole work was radically new and would probably breed controversy. He had begun with the self, the thinking "I." God had been found to be a useful aid in humankind's quest for knowledge. Surely, the Roman Catholic Church would condemn such a philosophy.

As Descartes considered publication, he was uncertain as to his course of action. He could proceed with publication, knowing that his work would probably be censured. But that would mean his ideas would not reach the centers of learning in the church-controlled universities. He could postpone publication and hope for a softening of the church's hard-line position. But was such a change forthcoming? By waiting, he would rob himself of the opportunity to interact with other thinkers about his ideas. In confusion, Descartes pondered his alternatives.

STUDY QUESTIONS & EXERCISES

I. Describe Descartes' process of methodological doubt. Indicate several implications of the conclusion to which he came at the end of his doubting process.

II. Explain how Descartes arrived at each of the following certainties, and show how each of the certainties relate to each other.

a. Certainty 1. I think, therefore I am.
b. Certainty 2. God exists.
c. Certainty 3. Within the bounds of reason, the senses can be trusted.

III. Sketch Descartes' argument for the existence of God. What was it like and how was it different from the ontological argument of Anselm?

IV. What were the characteristics of body and mind for Descartes? How were they related to each other?

V. In what ways are body-mind dualisms with us today? Give examples.

Chapter 13
Continental Rationalist

B. Baruch Spinoza (1632-1677)

… For reason is the light of the mind, and without her all things are dreams and phantoms. ***Spinoza***

Chapter 13
Continental Rationalist

B**aruch** Spinoza was one of the great philosophers of the age of Rationalism and a major influence afterward. Feared and detested across Europe as a precarious atheist, Spinoza led a reclusive existence; most of what little work he was able to publish was written anonymously.

However, Spinoza did obtain affectionate friends and some measure of favorable reputation. He was among the most ethical men ever to have lived. Although Jews, Christians, Catholics and Protetsant alike and also freethinkers, have attacked him; nevertheless, others admired him for his moral character. He made a living for a while by grinding lenses, where the dust had damaged his lungs. The pension that his friends later obtained for him did not prevent him from dying at the young age of 45. His opportunity for an established academic career, with an offer from a German university, was rejected, because of the confessional conformity that would have been required. Spinoza's life, consequently, though not inherently horrible, seems on the whole sad, isolated, and shattered.

His Life

Spinoza was born in Amsterdam in 1632 to Jewish parents who had fled to Holland from the Iberian Peninsula. His first name was Baruch or, as it was often rendered in its Latin equivalent, Benedictus. He received his early education in the Jewish academy of Amsterdam, where he acquired knowledge of Hebrew Scripture and of medieval Hebrew philosophy.

He favored rationalism while he was a student for the rabbinate, and this resulted in his being invited to retract certain views that were considered profane. However, in 1656, when he refused to make the retraction, he was expelled and excommunicated from the Synagogue of Amsterdam, and exiled from the city by the Protestant authority. Spinoza was thoroughly educated in both Jewish and Christian philosophy, but his unorthodox opinions caused him to be excommunicated from Hollnad, at a time when Holland was the most liberal nation in Europe.

Pantheism: God as immanent

Spinoza employed a very simple phrase that showed his ideology in relationship to God: God is *everything*. This implies that God is identical to the universe. He wanted to develop a concept about God that would not leave us with a terrible distance between the Supreme Being and ourselves. Also, he seemed to have wanted to leave room open, for different religions and conceptions about God, without insisting that any of them was the only "true" religion.

This is a principle that this writer believes and agrees with. In today's world, we do find many closed systems of beliefs. These ideologies, usually religions, believe in absolutes, they present the idea that God has signed a contract of exclusivity with a specific group. Therefore, any form of conviction that just happens to be different from their own, must be considered to be false and invalid. Stricly, from a philosophical point of view, this argument is totally unsound and artificial. The **truth**, from a philosophical point of view is not an absolute; it is relative to one's education, social and emotional conditions and experiences. Therefore, it is impossible to claim to have found the "true religion."

According to Spinoza, we are God, not individuals. Humanity as a whole is an integral part of the whole universe. He called this "**One Substance**." Therefore, we are an integral part of God as well. He rejected the idea of a relation *between* God and man.

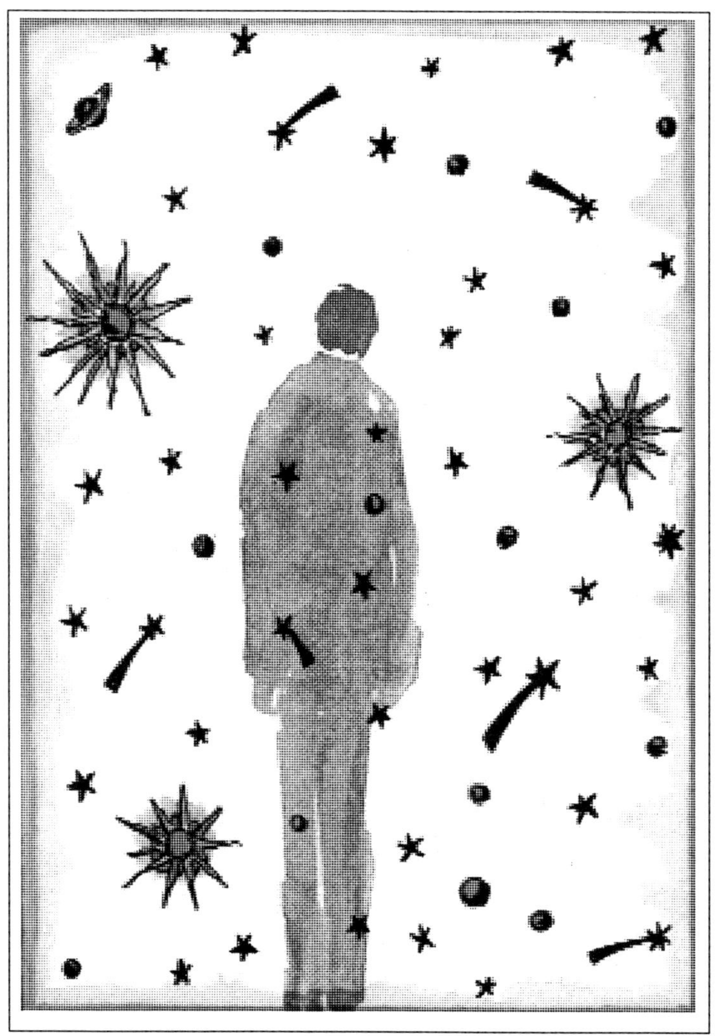

Rather, he believed there is a basic *unity* between these two. He defines God the following way: "God I understand to be a being absolutely infinite, that is, a substance consisting of infinite attributes, each of which expresses eternal and infinite essence." Spinoza regards all individual beings, whatever is popularly supposed to be a real thing, as mere modifications of one infinite substance, which has an infinite number of attributes. However, only two are perceptible by man, namely, thought and extension.

Spinoza uses a methaphor to illustrate his point. Each of us is like a tiny worm in the blood inside the body of some great being. We see only our immediate surroundings and have a tendency to treat that alone as reality, with some vague idea of some greater being "outside of us." Yet, we are *part* of that great being, and once we realize this, we transcend our limited perceptions and our idea of something outside us. When this takes place, we become aware and can see ourselves being a part of the package of that great being.

In his book *Ethics*, Spinoza presents 250 **axioms** or **theorems**, each of which he tried to derive by careful deductive logical thinking. Spinoza was able to prove that there are no multiple substances, as Descartes believed, instead, there is only one infinite substance. Spinoza equated this substance with God. We must be careful to keep in mind that Spinoza is not taking about the personal Judeo-Christian God; rather, it is the sum of everything there is.

In this context Spinoza might be taking about nature as a whole.

STUDY QUESTIONS AND EXCERCISES

I. Go to the *Encyclopedia of Philosophy* and find the name Spinoza. Write a summary on the article.

II. Mention at least five items in relationship with the life of Spinoza.

III. What is the concept of God according to Spinoza?

IV. What is the name and the definition of Spinoza's idea about God?

V. How is Spinoza viewed by different faiths?

VI. Use the concept of God as presented by Spinoza and write a short story that would explain the origin of the world.

Chapter 14
British Empiricism

Chapter 14
British Empiricism

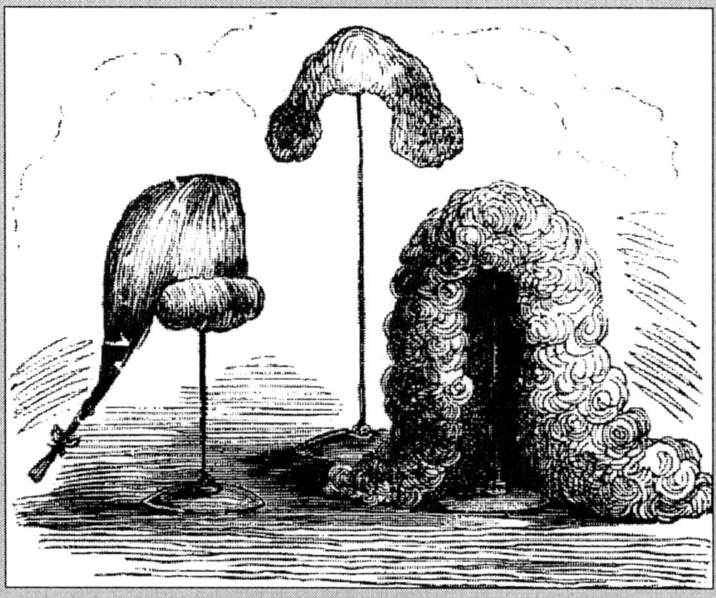

British Empiricism refers to the 18th century philosophical movement in Great Britain that maintained that all knowledge comes from sense experience. **Continental Rationalists** maintained that knowledge comes from foundational concepts known intuitively through reason.

René Descartes was the first of the "continental rationalist." These thinkers, who dominated the philosophy of the continent of Europe until the end of the 1700s, held that truth was derived from reason. All knowledge was deducible from certain "clear and evident" ideas. Reason was independent of sense experience. In fact, reason was prior to and superior to sense experience. Among the philosophers who held to this view of knowledge were **Benedict Spinoza** and **Gottfried Wilhelm Leibniz**.

However, philosophy developed quite differently in the British Isles. The British Empiricists, as they were called, believed that there was no such thing as an innate idea. A person was not born with certain truths already implanted in the mind. Rather, knowledge came from observation, from sense experience. Even the idea of God, was not innate---it was a conclusion drawn from observations.

Chapter 14
British Empiricism

For most **empiricists**, experience includes inner experience-reflection upon the mind and its operations as well as sense perception. This position is opposed to rationalism in that it denies the existence of innate ideas. According to the empiricist, all ideas are derived from sense experience. Therefore, knowledge of the physical world can be nothing more than a generalization from particular instances and can never reach more than a high degree of probability. Most empiricists recognize the existence of at least some a priori truths, e.g., those of mathematics and logic. Empiricism has been the dominant but not the only tradition in British philosophy.

Although Empiricists rejected innate ideas in favor of ideas from experience, it is important to note that they did not eliminate the notion of instinct. They believed that we have inborn predispositions that regulate our bodily functions, poroduce emotions, and even direct our thinking. What Empiricists denied, is that we are born with detailed, picture-like concepts, such as the concept of God, casuality, and even mathemathics.

Chapter 15
British Empiricism

A. John Locke (1632-1704)

It is ambition enough to be employed as an underlabourer in clearing the ground a little, and removing some of the rubbish which lies in the way of knowledge.

John Locke

Chapter 15
British Empiricism

John Locke (1632-1704) was the first philosopher clearly to lay out a form of empiricism. He was an English philosopher and political theorist who attempted to center philosophy on an analysis of the extent and capabilities of the human mind.

His life

John Locke was born on August 29, 1632, in Wrington, in Somerset, where his mother's family resided. She died during his infancy, and Locke was raised by his father, who was an attorney in the small town of Pensford near Bristol. John was tutored at home because of his always-delicate health and the outbreak of civil war in 1642. When he was 14, he entered Westminster School, where he remained for six years. He then went to Christ Church, Oxford. In 1658 he was elected a senior student at his college. In this capacity he taught Greek and moral philosophy. Under conditions at the time he would have had to be ordained to retain his fellowship. Instead he changed to another faculty, medicine, and eventually received a license to practice. During the same period Locke made the acquaintance of Robert Boyle, the distinguished scientist and one of the founders of the Royal Society, and, under Boyle's direction, took up study of natural science. Finally, in 1668, Locke was made a fellow of the Royal Society.

In 1665, Locke traveled to the Continent as secretary to the English ambassador to the Brandenburg court. Upon his return to England he went to medically attend Lord Ashley, First Earl of Shaftsbury, and later Lord Chancellor of England. Their friendship and lifelong association drew Locke into political affairs. He attended Shaftesbury as physician and adviser, and in this latter capacity Locke drafted *The Fundamental Constitutions of Carolina* and served as secretary to the Board of Trade. In 1676 Locke went to France due to his health.

An inheritance from his father made him financially independent, and he remained in Montpellier for three years. Locke rejoined Shaftesbury's service, and when the latter fled to Holland, the philosopher followed. He remained in exile from 1683 to 1689, and during these years he was deprived of his studentship by express order of Charles III. Most of his important writings were composed during this period. After the Glorious Revolution of 1689 Locke returned to England and later served with distinction as a commissioner of trade until 1700. He spent his retirement at Oates in Essex as the guest of the Mashams. Lady Masham was the daughter of Ralph Cudworth, the philosopher. Locke died there on October 28, 1704.

His philosophy

According to Locke, the mind was at birth a tabula rasa, a blank tablet. All ideas that were imprinted on this blank tablet came from experience. Experience could be either external, coming from sensations produced by objects outside the person, or internal, coming from reflection on external experience. In either case, all knowledge had to originate in sense experience.

Sense experience, and reflection on sense experience, gave rise to simple ideas. These simple ideas could be any one of four kinds. There were those simple ideas received through one sense only, such as ideas of taste, color, and smell. Next, there were the simple ideas that were obtained by a combination of two or more senses, such as the ideas of space, extension, and motions. Thirdly, there were the simple ideas that were obtained by reflection alone. These ideas included such things as remembering, judging, and knowing. Finally, there were those simple ideas that arose from both sense and reflection. Such ideas included the idea of pleasure, existence, and unity. These simply ideas were combined by the mind to form an infinite number of complex ideas. The idea of God, for example, was a combination of the simple ideas of existence, unity, knowledge, and so on. This meant, for Locke, that no matter how complex and idea might be it could in principle be reduced to simple ideas that came from sense experience. Therefore, all knowledge was derived from the senses.

Locke also made a distinction between simple and complex ideas and external objects. Ideas, whether simple or complex, were caused by "things outside" the person. These "things outside" the person had certain powers that included the power to cause changes in other objects and the power to produce sensations. So all ideas came from sensations, and all sensations came from external objects.

Locke used this concept of the power of external objects to prove God's existence. His "first-cause argument" was similar to the first of Aquinas' "five ways." The world is known by ideas that are caused by sensations. External objects cause these sensations. It follows, said Locke, that something must have caused these external objects. This "something" that caused external objects must, in turn, have a cause, and so on. Locke posited that there could not be an endless series of causes and effects, so he concluded that there had to be a first cause. Because external objects ultimately gave rise to the orderly perceptions and ideas by which the universe was known, these objects must have been created in an orderly manner. Because thinking was the end product of the power of objects, thinking must have caused the objects in the first place. Therefore, there had to be a supreme thinking source that corresponded to (and ultimately gave rise to) the complex idea of a divine being.

The identification of God as the first cause of the universe led Locke to affirm a religion of Deism. According to the Deists, God created the world to operate in a certain way. God both caused the world to begin and established the law of nature to govern it. Having laid down the laws of nature, God would not violate them. Hence, God did not work miracles, answer prayer, or in any other way interfere with the operation of natural laws. Humankind's job was to discover these natural laws and live in accordance with them.

STUDY QUESTIONS & EXERCISES

I. Write a summary of the life of John Locke.

II. Explain his concept of tabula rasa.

III. What is Locke philosophy dealing with sense experience, reflection on sense experience and simple and complex ideas?

IV. Describe Locke's proof for the existence of God. Compare and contrast it with one of Thomas Aquinas' five ways of knowing God.

Chapter 16
British Empiricism

B. David Hume (1711-1776)

The mind has never anything to it but…perceptions, and cannot possibly reach any experience of their connection with [eternal] objects.

David Hume

Chapter 16
British Empiricism

With all the religious controversy going on in England at the time, **David Hume** wanted to be sure that his ***Treatise of Human Nature*** was not misunderstood. The **Deist** and the orthodox Christians were attacking one another in almost every book that appeared in the 1730s, and Hume wanted to do more than simply defend one side. In fact, he felt that his *Treatise* would show both sides of the controversy to be wrong.

But Hume's desire to avoid religious controversy ran counter to his desire to include in the Treatise a chapter on miracles. Entitled **"Reasonings Concerning Miracles,"** this chapter pointed out the problems associated with miracles. Using the principles established at the beginning of the *Treatise*, Hume argued that one could never provide even a probable argument for the occurrence of miracles.

As Hume completed the *Treatise* and began to look for a publisher, he had second thoughts about including this chapter. Would his views on miracles force him into the middle of the Deist-Christian controversy? Would he appear to be simply another Deist as well as a traditional Christian? If he did not include the chapter, would the *Treatise* be damaged? Would people be able to realize the staggering implications of Hume's reworking of Locke's philosophy without examples such as "Reasoning concerning Miracles?" As Hume considered these questions, he realized he had a difficult decision to make.

His life

David Hume was born in Edinburgh, Scotland, in 1711. His father, Joseph, was a lawyer who died before young David was two years old. As Hume later recalled his childhood, his father's death left him "with an elder Brother and Sister under the care of our Mother, who, though young and handsome, devoted herself entirely to the rearing and educating of her children."[79] David's mother, Katherine, was a deeply religious person who raised her children to be God-fearing members of the Scottish Church. Young David also took his religion seriously. While still a young boy, he made list of his vices so that he might properly seek forgiveness from God.

Even though he grew up under the strict rules of the Scottish Presbyterian Church, David had a pleasant childhood. The family estate, called Ninewells, sat on a bluff overlooking the Whiteadder River in southern Scotland. As a boy, Hume lived part of the year in this charming country estate and part of the year in a small flat in Edinburgh. When he was twelve years old, Hume went to the University of Edinburgh. Like his father before him, he did not study for a degree. As Hume described his university life: "I passed through the ordinary Courses of Education with Success . . . and was seized early with a passion for Literature."[80] While a student, Hume encountered the writings of John Locke. As a result of his readings in Locke and other philosophers, Hume abandoned his religious beliefs.

The Hume family was certainly not poor, but neither were they rich. When Joseph died, he did not leave David enough money to live a leisurely life of studying and writing. As a result, David's family encouraged him to learn a profession. Because his father had been a lawyer, it was decided that he should be a lawyer too. Hume later explained:

> My studious Disposition, my Sobriety, and my Industry gave my Family a Notion that the law was a proper profession for me: But I found an insurmountable Aversion to everything but the pursuits of Philosophy and general learning; and while they fancyed I was pouring over Voet and Vinnius, Cicero and Virgil were the Authors which I was secretly devouring.[81]

In 1729, Hume made what he considered to be some startlingly new discoveries in philosophy. He found what he held to be "A new Science of Thought, which transported [me] beyond measure and made [me], with an ardour natural to a young man, throw up every other pleasure or business to apply entirely to it."[82] He announced to his family that he was going to give up his pretense to law and become a philosopher. For the next several years, Hume worked on developing his new ideas. The pace at which he worked on his studies soon made him quite ill. He moved to France, where the weather was less severe and his limited money would go further.

In 1735, Hume retired to the town of La Fleche. The college in this small town where Descartes had gone to school was one of the centers of continental rationalism. Living quietly in a small cottage, Hume continued his studies and his writing. In 1738, Hume finished the *Treatise of Human Nature*.

The Treatise: Impressions and Ideas

A monumental work, the *Treatise* contained sections dealing with logic, morals, criticism, and politics. Logic, which Hume held to be an explanation of "the principles and operations of our reasoning faculty and the nature of our ideas," took up the whole of Book 1.

Hume agreed with Locke that there is no such thing as an innate idea. He also agreed that all knowledge must come through sense experience. But as he worked out the implications of his empirical (or "sense-experience") theory of knowledge, he came to some very different conclusions from those of Locke.

Hume began his exposition in the *Treatise* by dividing the perceptions of the human mind into impressions and ideas.

> All the perceptions of the human mind resolve themselves into two distinct kinds, which I shall call impressions and ideas. The difference between these consists in the degrees of force and liveliness, with which they strike upon the mind, and make their way into our thought or consciousness. Those perceptions which enter with most force and violence, we may name *impressions*; and under this name I comprehend all our sensations, passions, and emotions, as they make their first appearance in the soul. By *ideas* I mean the faint images of these in thinking and reasoning; such as, for instance, are all the perceptions excited by

> the present discourse, excepting only those which arise from the sight and touch, and excepting the immediate pleasure or uneasiness it may occasion.[83]

In distinguishing between impressions and ideas, Hume used empirical distinction: impressions strike the mind with more "force and liveliness" than ideas. He made no assumptions about where these impressions came from or why they had more "force" than ideas. To deal with such questions would have been to move beyond the world of sense experience. Next, Hume divided impressions and ideas into simple and complex.

> Simple perceptions, or impressions and ideas, are such as admit of no distinction nor separation. The complex are the contrary to these, and may be distinguished into parts. Through a particular colour, and smell, are qualities all united together in this apple, it is easy to perceive they are not the same, but are at least distinguishable from each other.[84]

At this point, Hume did make one nonempirical assumption. Just as Locke had assumed that all complex ideas could be reduced to distinct simple ideas, Hume assumed that every simple impression was a distinct, single unit. He further assumed that every simple idea was a memory copy of a simple impression.

Besides the distinction between simple and complex, impressions could be further divided into impressions of sensations and impression of reflection. Impressions of sensations were the original impressions, the cause of which was unknown. Impressions of reflection were derived from ideas. Hume outline the process:

> An impression first strikes upon the senses, and makes us perceive heat or cold, thirst or hunger, pleasure or pain, of some kind or other. Of this impression there is a copy taken by the mind, which remains after the impression ceases; and this we call an idea. This idea of pleasure or pain, when it returns upon the soul, produces the new impressions of desire and aversion, hope and fear, which may properly be called impressions of reflection, because derived from it.[85]

Because every simple idea was a distinct unit, it should follow that any one idea might precede or follow any other idea. But this was clearly not the case. Ideas in the mind followed one another in an orderly progression. Hume concluded that there must be "some universal principles" that connected ideas. He wrote in the *Treatise*:

> Were ideas entirely loose and unconnected, chance alone would join them; and it is impossible the same ideas should fall regularly into complex ones (as they commonly do) without some bond of union among them, some associating quality, by which one idea naturally introduces another. [86]

Treatise: Cause and Effect

There were, according to Hume, three principles by which the mind moved from one idea to another: resemblance, contiguity in space and time, and cause and effect. These three principles were not ideas because they did not come from impressions. Rather, they reflected the habitual way the mind worked. Hume explained the principles of resemblance and contiguity in space and time in the following way:

> It is plain, that in the course of our thinking . . . our imagination runs easily from one idea to any other that *resembles* it, and that this quality alone is to the fancy a sufficient bond and association. It is likewise evident, that as the senses, in changing their objects, are necessitated to change them regularly, and take them as they lie *contiguous* to each other, the imagination must long custom acquire the same method of thinking.[87]

By means of the principle of resemblance, the mind connected ideas that appeared similar to one another. By means of the principle of contiguity in time and place, the mind connected ideas that appeared to arise from sensory objects that followed one another. Hume gave an example:

> That these principles serve to connect ideas will not, I believe, be much doub ted. A picture naturally leads our thoughts to the original [resemblance]: the mention of one apartment in a building naturally introduces an enquiry or discourse concerning the others [contiguity in space and time]: and if we think of a

> wound, we can scarcely forbear reflecting on the pain which follows it [cause and effect].[88]

The principle of cause and effect was of special interest to Hume. Locke had held that external objects had the power to cause changes in their objects and to give rise to sensations. In fact, all philosophers before Hume, whether rationalist or empiricists, Platonic or Aristotelian, had held that every effect must necessarily have a cause. For every event that occurred, the thinking went, something must have caused it.

Hume denied that there was such a necessary connection between cause and effect. According to Hume, people simply experienced one impression followed by another. After a period of time, people concluded that the second impression was caused by the first. But no one could ever give a reason for believing that any occurrence should follow another. No one could ever have an impression of one thing *causing* another. Hume declared:

> When we look about us towards external objects, and considered the operation of causes, we are never able, in a single instance, to discover any power or necessary connexion; any quality, which binds the effect to the cause, and renders the one an infallible consequence of the other. We only find, that the one does actually, in fact, follow the other . . . we never can observe any tie between them. They seem *conjoined* but never *connected*. And as we can have no idea of any thing which never appeared to our outward sense [impressions of sensation] or inward sentiment [impressions of reflection], the necessary conclusion *seems* to be that we have no idea of connexion or power at all, and that these words are absolutely without any meaning, when employed either in philosophical reasonings or common life.[89]

For example, when a person repeatedly observed the movement of one billiard ball followed by the movement of another, he or she inferred that there was a necessary causal connection. The movement of the first ball seemed to be *causing* the second ball to move. In truth, there was nothing necessary about the second ball's movement. The reason people assumed that there was a necessary connection was that they were accustomed to seeing one ball's movement follow the others. For Hume, the cause and effect relation was simply a matter of habit.

Treatise: Empirical Criterion of Meaning

According to Hume, all complex ideas were combinations of simple ideas and all simple ideas were copies of simple impressions. Because all ideas ultimately came from impressions, any given idea had meaning only if there was an impression (or combination of impressions) that it was copying. For example, the idea *house* arose from a combination of impressions of certain colors, shapes, and sizes.

This criterion of meaning led Hume to question ideas that had been accepted by philosophers for centuries. The idea of *substance*, that which was left when all sensory properties of a thing were removed, had been an important idea in the philosophy of Aristotle and others. But Hume found it to be a meaningless idea. As he put it:

> I would fain ask . . . philosophers . . . whether the idea of *substance* be derived from the impressions of sensations or reflections? If it be conveyed to us by our senses, I ask, which of them, and after what manner? If it be perceived by the eyes, it must be colour; if by the ears, a sound; if by the palate, a taste; and so on of the others senses. But I believe none will assert, that substance is either a colour, a sound, or a taste. The idea of substance must, therefore, be derived from an impression of reflection, if it really exists. But the impressions of reflection resolve themselves into our passions and emotions; none of which can possibly represent a substance. We have therefore no idea of substance, distinct from that of a collection of particular qualities, nor have we any other meaning when we either talk or reason concerning it.[90]

Locke had assumed that all sensations ultimately arose from external objects. These external objects in an external world were beyond-sense experience. They gave rise to sense experience but could not themselves be experienced. According to Hume, the idea of an external world was meaningless. There were no impressions that could give rise to such an idea. The senses, which provided all knowledge, could never get outside of themselves to experience their own relationship to some supposed external world. Hume concluded that there were impressions *of* something was a question that could not be answered.

Finally, Hume held that the idea of *self* was also meaningless. Descartes had founded his philosophy on the "clear and evident" intuition "I think, therefore I am." But for Hume, there was no such thing as an "I": no self. He asserted:

> When I enter most intimately into what I call *myself*, I always stumble on some particular perception or other, of heat or cold, light or shade, love or hatred, pain or pleasure. I never can catch myself at any time without a perception, and never can observe anything but the perception.[91]

Hume concluded, therefore, that the self or "I" was nothing but "a bundle or collection of different perceptions, which succeed each other with an inconceivable rapidity, and are in a perpetual flux and movement."[92]

Miracles

Given that all knowledge began with impressions or the relations of ideas, Hume held that metaphysical systems that talked about God, the nature of what was real, and so on, had no meaning. Because it was not possible to have a simple impression of things that transcended human experience, it was not possible to talk meaningfully about such matters. More specifically, because there was no necessary relation between cause and effect, all proofs for God's existence that depended on God's being the necessary cause of some feature in the world were meaningless. Thus the five ways of Thomas Aquinas and the first-cause argument of Locke were worthless. Further, any proofs for God's existence that sought to build necessary connections between the idea of God and the idea of something separate from the idea of an object, it was ridiculous to conclude that the idea of God (which was meaningless itself) had the unique characteristic of entailing the idea of existence. Thus the ontological proof of Anselm and Descartes' proof of God's existence on the basis of the idea of God were also doomed to failure.

Applying his philosophy to miracles, Hume pointed out that a miracle was, by definition, a violation of a law of nature, But the laws of nature that were known were founded on repeated observation. They were based on extensive and carefully recorded experience. For that reason, known laws of nature had the highest degree of probability. Therefore, Hume concluded that one should believe the testimony for a miracle, a violation of the law of nature, only if it would require more of a miracle for the testimony to be false than for there to have been an actual miracle. For example, someone might claim that they had seen an entire mountain moved. This person's testimony should be believed, according to Hume, only if the possibility of this person's lying or being mistaken was less that the possibility of a mountain moving. It was hard to image someone whose testimony would be that sure. It was, of course, possible that this could happen. The laws of nature were sometimes in need of revision. Perhaps this person had seen an earthquake or a force not previously observed. But it was usually more likely that such testimony to a miracle was either false or at least confused.

Hume took this argument a step further by claiming that there was not really even a probable argument for miracles. In the first place, most miracles were reported among ignorant and barbarous nations. In the second place, the testimony for miracles in the past had been less than unimpeachable. In fact, the history of supposed miracles seemed so tainted to Hume that he concluded it was always more probable that a miracle had been made up than that one had actually occurred. Finally, all religions claimed miracles. But not all religions could be true[93], because they had conflicting truth claims. Therefore, many of these claimed miracles had to be deceptions. Hume concluded that given any miracle claim, there was always a very good chance that it was false. In no way could such suspect miracles be taken as proof of any religion.

Publication

It was obvious that the orthodox Christians would not appreciate this commentary on miracles. However, Hume also opposed the Deists. Holding that there was a God who, as the first cause, established universal and immutable laws, the Deists engaged in metaphysical speculation that was meaningless for Hume. The whole notion of a first cause was absurd.

Still, as he considered the upcoming publication of the *Treatise*, Hume was wary. His attack on miracles was directed much more obviously at traditional Christians than at Deists. Did he want to bring on the wrath of the Christian community with a frontal attack? If he did not included the section on miracles, would the book be taken more seriously as a philosophical work? Would his readers be able to grasp the implications of his philosophy and his reaction to Locke without the specific example of "Reasonings Concerning Miracles"?

STUDY QUESTIONS & EXERCISES

I. Examine and outline the differing premises about how knowledge was acquired and held by the seventeenth century continental rationalist and the eighteenth century British empiricists.

II. Define the terms impressions and ideas in Hume's philosophy. What were their various sources and how were they related to each other?

III. Discuss Hume's treatment of the concept of cause and effect. Explain his treatment, using the illustration of billiard balls striking each other.

IV. What was Hume's attitude toward miracles? Give an example of a miracle reported by someone in your lifetime. Examine it, using Hume's criteria of validity. Reflect on Hume's criteria in light of his discussion of cause and effect.

Chapter 17
Late Modern Philosophy

C. Immanuel Kant (1724-1804)

Two things fill the mind with ever new and increasing admiration and awe…the starry heavens above me and the moral law within me.

Kant

Immanuel Kant felt that he was near the end of what had been a quiet life. He read the edict once more before making his reply. For over seventy years, he had lived in Königsberg, Prussia, developing his philosophy under the approving eye of Frederick the Great. Now in 1794, eight years after Frederick's religiously orthodox nephew had succeeded to the throne, the aging Kant was being censored for his religious beliefs. Did his philosophy provide a new and adequate basis for thinking and talking about God? How could he defend his innovative theory of knowledge without attacking the religious powers? What kind of response could he make that would bring out his philosophy without further offending the authorities? Slowly he began to pen his painful reply.

Kant's Early Life

Kant was born in 1724 of poor parents in the university town of Königsberg. His parents belonged to the pietism movement, which stressed both the personal aspects of religion and high moral standards. It was through his mother's favorite preacher that the young Immanuel was able to begin his studies. This man was both a professor at the university and the director of a local high school, to which Kant was admitted at the age of eight. There he received a pietistic education with solid training in the classics. Kant studied there until at the age of sixteen he was admitted to the university.

At the university, Kant entered the department of philosophy. He was influenced greatly by a professor, Martin Knutzen, who introduced Kant to mathematics and Newtonian physics. Under the influence of Knutzen, Kant developed a great interest in the philosophy of Christian Wolff, an extreme rationalist who followed Descartes and Leibniz.

Kant heard lectures for some years at the university. Following this, he spent a few years tutoring in the Königsberg area.

In 1755, Kant returned to the university as an instructor. He continued in this position for fifteen years becoming very popular not only with students, but also with men of high ranks. During his early years as a lecturer, Kant's interest was primarily in the external world. Along with his lectures on logic, metaphysics, and mathematics, he dealt specially with physics. He initiated the first lectures on physical geography at the university. In 1755, he published a work called *Universal History of Nature and Theory of the Heavens*, in which he attempted to explain the structure of the universe exclusively on the basis of Newtonian physics. In this system, there was absolutely no need for the intervention of God. Kant felt that true religion had no interest in limiting mechanical explanations of the universe.

During the 1760s, Kant's interests began to shift toward the inner world of human beings and their moral nature, as was the general movement of the time. He began to move away from the mathematical orientation of such thinkers as Descartes and became acquainted with the writings of Hume. Hume's writings presented a challenge to the whole rationalist approach. This challenge forced Kant to rethink much of his philosophy. He later declared that Hume's writings had awakened him from his dogmatic slumbers. The writings of Rousseau also had a profound influence on Kant. While Hume provided a challenge to Kant, Rousseau gave him a new direction. From this French thinker, Kant developed a new valuation of knowledge: the primacy of the moral over the intellectual. Moral reflection came to replace metaphysical speculation as primary in Kant's thinking.

In 1770, Kant received the professorship in logic and metaphysics at Königsberg he had so long desired. One major factor in his appointment was the high esteem in which many prominent officials held him. Another important consideration was that many of the current professors were being replaced because they would not cooperate with the government. In his inaugural address, entitled *Dissertation on the Form and Principles of Sensible and Intelligible Worlds*, Kant revealed his intention to reconstruct philosophy. This intention was fulfilled in 1781 with the publication of his *Critique of Pure Reason*.

Kant's Critique of Pure Reason

In the Critique of Pure Reason, Kant elaborated his basic theory of knowledge. He presented the mind as active in knowing, as asking specific questions of accumulated data and demanding specific answers. The mind was not merely a blank tablet on which data was deposited. Knowledge involved both the mind of the knower and the object known. Using this model, Kant argued that the mind has fixed laws according to which it organized data just as science had theories according to which it organized its data.

Kant concurred with the British empiricists, Locke and Hume, that sensation was the source of these data. However, Hume had taken the argument to the extreme by holding that it was unnecessary to assume sensation to be anything but a state of mind, a tingle in the brain. This led Hume to deny the necessity of a world external to the mind. Kant rejected this conclusion, holding that it was absurd to think there could be an appearance without there being something that appeared. Kant held that there was a world outside experience that was made up of "things-in-themselves." These "things-in-themselves" were the "noumenal" world and gave rise to the things that were in the world of experience, called the "phenomenal world." For example, the color, texture, and shape of a chair could be experienced, but the "essence" of a chair could not. The experienced characteristics of the chair belonged to the phenomenal world, while the essence (or being) belonged to the noumenal world. Still, although there was a noumenal world, it was beyond the world of experience and so could not be known by the reason. People were limited by their reason to the phenomenal world, that is, to experience.

With the rationalists (Descartes, Spinoza, Leibniz), Kant agreed that concepts were formed by the mind. Sensations, taken by themselves, could not lead to concepts. The mind had to play an active role in developing concepts. But, whereas the rationalists had held that knowledge could be found apart from sensations, Kant held that knowledge resulted from a combination of mind and sensations. Sensations, apart from the concept-forming mind, were meaningless and chaotic. The mind, apart from data-proving sensations, was ignorant and blind. Using Aristotle's terminology, the "matter" of knowledge came from the senses, as the empiricists claimed. The "form" of knowledge came from the understanding---which was similar to the positions of the rationalists.

Kant felt that he had performed a Copernican revolution in philosophy. Copernicus had rejected the notion that heavenly bodies around earthly observes of them, and instead "made the spectator to revolve and the stars to remain at rest."[94] Kant's revolution reversed the relationship between human knowledge and its objects. Kant declared:

> Hitherto it has been assumed that all our knowledge must conform to objects... We must therefore make trial whether we may not have more success in task of metaphysics, if we suppose that objects conform to our knowledge. [95]

Certain factors, structures, or elements within the human mind imposed ordered relationships on the world of sense experience, according to Kant. Nature was, by definition, a system of objects manifesting an order on which predictions could be based. For Kant, then, there was the possibility of human understanding "prescribing laws of nature, and even of making nature possible."[96] The factors within the mind that imposed meaningful order on the world external to the human knower, for Kant, were three: the forms of intuition, the categories of the understanding, and the ideas of reason.

The Forms of Intuition

In all knowledge that one could have about the phenomenal world, there were three factors that had to be considered. In the first place, everything that occurred in the phenomenal world occurred in space and time. All people apprehended (or experience) whatever occurred to them as being ordered in space and time. All people thought and spoke in these categories" "This house is to the left of that tree;" "Karl went to the store after Fritz came home."

All people experience what they considered to be objects outside themselves. Kant said: "By means of outer sense, a property of our mind, we represent to ourselves objects as outside us, and all without exception in space."[97] This space was not some real thing. It "does not represent any property of things in themselves."[98] Neither was space an empirical concept derived from experience. Instead, it was the precondition for experiencing anything as outer. In short, it was simply a form of intuition: one of the ways the mind worked.

Similarly, all people experienced what they considered to be the succession of one idea following another or one event following another. All experience, whether of external objects or of inner states seemed to take place in time. Kant stated:

> Time is the formal *a priori* (or necessary) condition of all appearances whatsoever. Space, as the pure form of all *outer* intuition, is so far limited; it serves as the *a priori* condition only of outer appearances. But since all representations, whether they have for their objects outer things or not, belong, in themselves, as determinations of the mind, to our inner state.[99]

Like space, time was neither some real thing nor some empirical concept derived from experience. It was simply another form of intuition. Space and time were the preconditions for a person ever experiencing anything.

The Categories of Understanding

A second factor in gaining knowledge was the unifying activity of the mind. Everything that was perceived by the mind was organized according to certain categories into concepts. Through the senses, the mind received intuitions that were spontaneously acted upon by the categories. This yielded understanding of the intuitions as concepts. Kant claimed that by carefully analyzing the basic level of knowledge he discovered that there were twelve categories. Two of these categories were those of substance and cause.

Kant believed that one never had an experience of substance or cause. Rather, those were structures of the mind that brought together sensations. Kant did not believe that the categories were God-given nor innate ideas of something enduring beyond sense experience with an empirical relation: endurance through time. A substance was a collection of sensations that were experienced as permanent and unified.

Hume had denied that there could ever be a necessary cause-and-effect relationship between two things. People talked about such a relationship because they observed one thing following another often enough to expect a connection. When people saw one billiard ball's movement followed by another ball's movement often enough, they assumed that there was a necessary causual relation. Kant agreed that the cause-and effect relation did not arise from experience. Agreeing with Hume that no one ever had a sensation of a cause-and-effect relation, he concluded that the relation was supplied by the understanding.

According to Kant, there were two ways in which one sensation (or impression, using Hume's terminology) followed another. In the first case, there were those times when Sensation B followed Sensation A because the mind's attention had been turned from A to B. In this case, the mind could have done otherwise. Using Kant's example, this was similar to a person looking at a house from top to bottom. He or she received a series of sensations that followed one another, bottom to top or from side to side. On the other hand, there were times when in the example of the house, one had to begin at the bottom in building a house. In this kind of case, there was a necessary connection between one sensation and another. This connection was supplied by the category of cause.

The Ideas of Reason

The third group of factors within the mind that imposed meaningful order on the world external to the human knower Kant called the *ideas of reason*. Kant held that these were the three unifying, guiding ideals of complete knowledge. These three were (1) "The absolute unity of the thinking subject" (the soul or the mind), (2) "The absolute unity of the series of conditions of appearance" (the world), and (3) "The absolute unity of the condition of all objects of thought in general" (God).[100]

For Kant, as for Hume, none of these three ideas were really part of experience. No one ever had an experience of his or her own soul, the world (that is, the noumenal world), or God. Hence, no one could ever have knowledge of these things. But these ideas were important as guides to knowledge. These ideas, did not give information, only the senses gave information. But they directed the investigation of objects. Knowledge was always of appearances, the phenomenal world---not of things-in-themselves. But without the ideas of a soul, a world, and a God, there would be no way to organize knowledge. These three ideas were useful tools rather than actual things existing beyond the world of experience.

So all one could know for sure was his or her own mental states. Although there had to be something beyond these mental states, one could never know what it was. Hence, knowledge about the soul, the world, and God was impossible. Neither from sense experience nor from reason could one gain knowledge of what really is. The ideas of reason were important as a regulative force. They gave direction to the search for knowledge and limited the reason itself to the phenomenal or empirical world. Kant asserted:

> It is thus evident that reason has here no other purpose than to prescribe its own formal rule for the extension of its empirical employment, and not any extension *beyond all limits of empirical employment*.[101]

For Kant, these great ideals (self, world, and God) gave meaningful unity to human experience and stimulated the pursuit of knowledge. Metaphysics, the search for knowledge of reality as a whole, could never be a science but remained a disposition of the human mind. The ideas of reason did not describe realities in the phenomenal world but pointed beyond themselves to possibilities in the noumenal world where science could not reach. Reason thus gave certain knowledge---but only of appearances in the phenomenal world of sensation. To gain knowledge of realities in the noumenal world of ideas and things-in-themselves, Kant sought another avenue, not the pure reason, but the practical reason.

Kant's Critique of Practical Reason

Kant wrote a second extensive critique called the *Critique of Practical Reason*. It was designed to ensure objectivity in the area of moral judgments and moral behavior despite the limited and relative character of science. Kant contended that moral action was demanded by the very nature of rational human beings. Morality, for Kant, was a categorical imperative. An act was good only if one behaved according to a built-in moral law rather than because such an act would benefit the doer. Kant stated the command of this inner moral law in two formulations:

> Act only on that maxim whereby thou canst at the same time will that it should become a universal law. [And,] so act as to treat humanity, whether in thine own person, or in that of any other, in every case as an end withal, never as means only.[102]

Because, according to Kant, this moral law was present within all rational beings he felt justified in drawing certain conclusions about human beings and reality in the noumenal world. First of all, humans were free. Kant reasoned that of people felt obligated to obey the moral law within them then they had to be able to do so. Thus, people had free will. Human beings were citizens of two worlds, in Kant's view. As a part of the phenomenal (appearance) world, a human was subject to causal laws. But as a member of the noumenal (thing-in-itself) world a human enjoyed freedom. In the phenomenal world persons were objects. In the noumenal world, humans were subjects, imposing laws on themselves.

Kant drew a second conclusion from his awareness of the moral law within people. Humans were immortal. The moral law demanded perfection. So perfection had to be within human power. Yet people were not perfect in this world. Thus humans had to live on beyond this life in order to have further opportunity to advance toward the goal of perfection.

Finally, Kant postulated that God must exist. Humans desired that obedience to the inner moral law be accompanied by happiness. But happiness belonged to the (phenomenal) realm of what was while duty operated only in the (noumenal) realm of what ought to be. Kant held that it was a rational faith to believe that God existed who brought the two realms together and united obedience to the moral law with happiness.

Kant's Moral Religion

Kant had remained a pious person throughout his life. For him, this piety was not inconsistent with his attack on the traditional empirical or rational arguments for the existence of God. Kant pointed to flaws in the evidence or logic of each of the arguments for God's existence. But he ultimately rejected empirical or rational proofs for God because they were applicable only to objects in the phenomenal world of time and space. Arguments therefore could neither prove nor disprove God's existence. God transcended the phenomenal realm to which empirical and rational demonstrations applied.

Kant felt that he had not threatened religion. He had only placed it on a more firm foundation, that of morality.

> Morality thus leads ineluctably to religion, through which it extends itself to the idea of a powerful moral lawgiver, outside of mankind, for Whose will that is the final end of creation which at the same time can and ought to be man's final end.[103]

Far from being an enemy of religion, as some apparently thought him, Kant felt that he had done the cause of religion a service. He had shown that one could not make vital affirmations such as the reality of God, freedom, and immortality on the basis of scientific (pure) reason. Only in the realm of duty, that of the practical reason, could these values be found. Kant expressed his intellectual and religious choice unambiguously: "I have therefore found it necessary to deny *knowledge*, in order to make room for faith."[104]

The Edict

Kant had feared that the edict would come. The authorities had opposed publication of *Religion Within the Limits of Reason Alone*, but it contained the results of his life's work. Did it offer a different but viable way of thinking and speaking about God? How could he deny the logical conclusions of his own theory of knowledge? Was it possible still to hold to the orthodox theology of his day without denying his theories? What effect would all of this have on his quiet way of life? It was time to make a response.

Chapter 17
Late Modern Philosophy

STUDY QUESTIONS & EXERCISES

I. Discuss the influences on Kant from seventeenth century rationalist and the eighteen century empiricists. How did he respond to these influences?

II. Illustrate and explain the factors present in the mind, according to Kant, that give meaningful shape to our sense data.

a. The forms of intuition
b. The categories of the understanding
c. The ideas of reason

III. Argue from Kant's perspective, against Anselm's ontological proof and Aquinas' cosmological proof for the existence of God. On what rational grounds did Kant find belief in God justified?

IV. Define Kant's "categorical imperative." What are its implications for morality?

V. Describe the phenomenal and the noumenal worlds as Kant did. How was the human person related to each?

VI. Debate the following proposition: "In our society today, Kant would be considered a conservative."

Chapter 18
19th Century Philosophy

A. Søren Kierkegaard (1813-1855)

The biggest danger, that of losing oneself, can pass off in the world as quietly as if were nothing; every other loss, an arm, a leg, five dollars, a wife, etc. is bound to be noticed.

Kierkegaard

Chapter 18
19th Century Philosophy

As **Emil Boesen** sat in the deserted restaurant, he reflected on the events of that evening in 1841. **Søren Kierkegaard** had met him at a theater in Copenhagen to inform him of his broken engagement with his fiancée. Was Kierkegaard really acting on the rationale he had worked out for breaking with Regine? Was he acting as a "**knight of faith**"? Or was he simply shackled to the past, the melancholy his father had inflicted on him? Could it be that, by giving up Regine, Kierkegaard thought that God would return her to him?

Nineteenth-Century Denmark

The first half of the nineteenth century in Denmark was a time of turmoil, reform, and nationalism. Denmark began the century with an absolute monarchy and a kingdom nearly large enough to rival major European powers. But by 1815, because of it collaboration with Napoleon, the country had been stripped of Norway as a possession. Denmark was thrown into a severe economic depression that lasted over a decade. Just as Denmark began to regain its economic strength, the nation's political life was threatened by the revolutions that took place in Germany in the 1830s. Aware of new forces that demanded a share in the government, King Frederick VI of Denmark and his successors responded with a series of practical reforms.

Denmark's catastrophic economic conditions and its altered political status following the Napoleonic Wars compelled the nation to discover a new source of spiritual strength. Neither orthodox Christianity nor the new rationalistic Deism seemed capable of providing a spiritual vision. Orthodox Christianity's historical reliability, apologetic value, and moral authority had been eroded by the Enlightenment. Deism, on the other hand, had been dealt a blow by the contentions of Hume and Kant that rationalistic proofs of God's existence were impossible. The deistic idea of a "watchmaker God" was collapsing.

Kierkegaard and the philosophy of G.H.F. Hegel

Denmark's intellectuals began to examine the new works of the German idealist, **Georg Wilhelm Friedrich Hegel**. Hegel was the foremost thinker in Germany at the time. His **idealism** proclaimed the existence of an objective truth (the Idea) that **transcended** and controlled the course of history. Hegel described the Idea as a dynamic force that moved history toward it conclusion through what he called a " **dialectical development**."

By "dialectical development," Hegel meant that there was a progressive manifestation of the Idea in history. This manifestation was progressive because the Idea was only partially manifested in any one historical period. Each partial manifestation of the Idea produced its own antithesis, or countermovement. This antithesis was a corrective thrust, which sought to overcome the deficiencies of the thesis, the original manifestation of the Idea. But this antithesis was also partial. Therefore, it too, had to be overcome. This movement, overcoming the inadequacies of the thesis and the antithesis, led to synthesis, or the combination of what was strongest in the thesis and the antithesis. However, this new synthesis was also inadequate. Therefore, it too had to be superseded. The synthesis became the new thesis, and a new antithesis and a new synthesis arose. This process Hegel called "dialectical development." Put into schematic form, "dialectical development" looked like this:

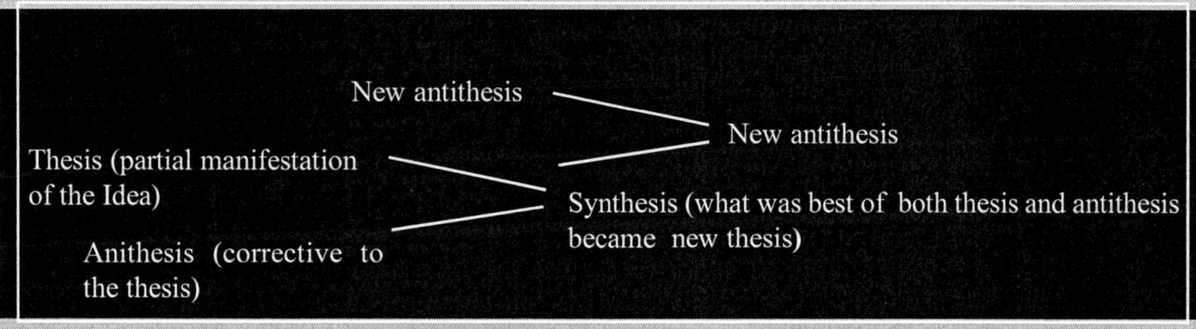

Thus Hegel saw an ongoing dialectical development in history in which each successive historical period was generated out of the tensions and shortcomings of the previous period. This movement would reach fulfillment only at the end of history.

According to Hegel, Christianity exemplified this process. Apostolic Christianity represented one stage in the expression of truth, while the heresies of the early church were the antithesis to that expression. The inadequacies of these two movements in turn gave rise to early medieval Catholicism, which was a synthesis of the partial truth contained in apostolic faith and the heresies of people like Marcion and Arius. Medieval Catholicism, in turn, became the new thesis. The Reformation became the new antithesis, and the Danish Lutheran Church was believed by many to be the new, and perhaps final, synthesis. Put schematically:

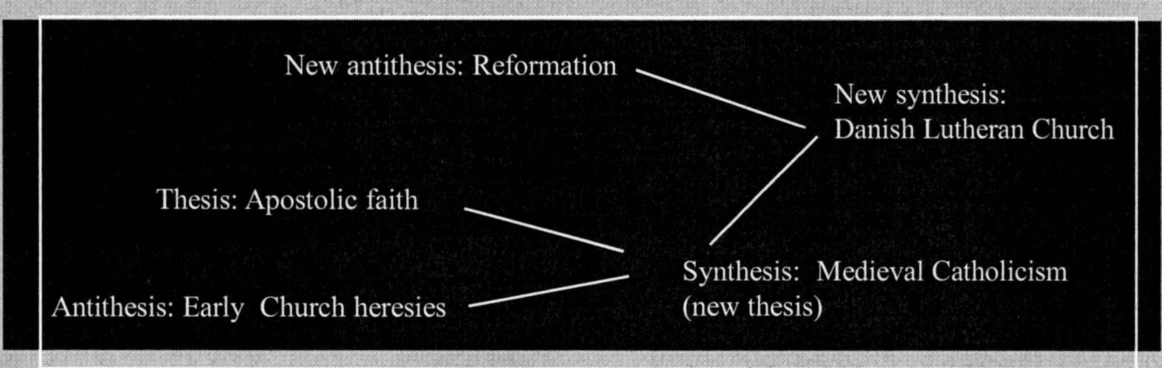

Hegel's theories had a special appeal for the church of Denmark. Hegelianism provided a sophisticated way of reconciling faith and reason. Hegel saw human reason as the self-manifestation of God actualizing his own essence throughout history. The bearers of this absolute Idea were nations and cultures, each of which constituted a necessary element in the Idea's progressive self-actualization. Because the Idea of God was thought to be actualized in the culture of nineteenth-century Denmark, the state church was believed to be the guardian and repository of true religion. To be faithful to the state and to the state church was to be faithful to God.

Kierkegaard's Early Life

Kierkegaard's father, Michael Pedersen Kierkegaard, was born in 1768. While still a young boy herding sheep as a serf in the bleak northern area of Jutland, Michael cursed God because of his wretched life. At age twenty-one, Michael was released from serfdom. With the help of an uncle, he became a cloth merchant in Copenhagen and soon became quite wealthy. At age twenty-six, he married the sister of a business associate, but she died after two years of marriage. Within the year, he married his wife's maid, Anne Lund, and five months later they had their first child. Five more children followed before Søren who was born in 1813, the child of middle-aged parents. By the time Søren was twenty-two, everyone in his family, save his father and one brother, had died.

Young Søren was raised in an atmosphere of deep personal faith and strong imagination coupled with anguish and melancholy. Michael Kierkegaard was committed to Moravian piety. The Moravians were a sectarian group that rejected the established religion and demanded a commitment beyond that of the state church. Michael was given to using his imagination to take young Søren on "trips of fantasy" while conversing with him in the family library. But coupled with this faith and imagination was a deep sense of anguish and personal guilt. Having cursed God as a boy and having slept with his deceased wife's maid before marrying her, he was convinced that God had damned him. As Søren's older brother, Peter, wrote of their father:

> The memory of this curse in his childhood never left the boy, the man, the patriarch—and seeing that God's grace from that very moment showered temporal blessings upon him, so that instead of tasting the divine wrath he was over whelmed with riches, marvelously gifted children, universal esteem—then

> solemn anxiousness and dread gripped his soul most deeply. God *did* exist, and *he* had cursed this God—was not this the sin against the Holy Ghost which never can be forgiven? It was for this reason the old man's soul continued in anxious dread, for this reason he beheld his children condemned to "the silent despair," for this reason he laid upon their shoulders in tender years the sternest requirements of Christianity—for this reason he was a prey to temptation and in constant conflict of soul.[105]

Søren Kierkegaard as a Young Man

Following the wishes of his father, Søren entered the university in 1831 and studied for a career in theology. But he soon lost all interest in a church vocation. As he wrote in his journal:

> In Christianity itself the contradictions are so great that, to say the least, they prevent a clear view. As you know, I grew up, so to speak, in orthodoxy, but as soon as I began to think for myself the tremendous colossus began to totter...I am supposed to read for a theological degree, an occupation which does not interest me at all and so does not advance particularly quickly.[106]

His father and his older brother, Peter who by this time was a respected Danish churchman, were disappointed and angered when they learned of Søren's change of interests. To make matters worse, Søren had begun to adopt the profligate life-style of a rich man's son. He frequented the fashionable theaters and cafes in Copenhagen and spent large amounts of money on clothes, liquor, and tobacco. Much of his time was spent in the company of a few friends who were part of Copenhagen's literary circles. He affected the life-style of a dilettante.

One night in 1836 Kierkegaard went out with some friends for a night on the town. He was in the habit of drinking quite a bit that year, and on this evening he became completely drunk. Seeing that he was in a drunken stupor, his friends drove him to a brothel in Copenhagen, where he awoke in bed the next morning. Precisely what happened late that night was a jealously guarded secret that Kierkegaard refused to divulge even to his journal. However, there were frequent references to guilt among the journal entries following this date, and they suggested the depth of his feelings.

The thought began to take shape in Søren Kierkegaard's mind that not only his father but his entire family lay under a divine curse. Because of his father's cursing of God, because of his own doubts about the Christian faith, because of his drunken night out, he concluded that perhaps he too was cursed by God. Despite his externally frivolous life-style, he became internally more and more serious. The thought of suicide was never far from his mind. A wry description entered in his journal in 1836 characterized this period of his life:

> I have just returned from a party of which I was the life and soul; wit poured from my lips, everyone laughed and admired me—but I went away—and the dash should be as long as the earth's
> Orbit-------------------------------------and I wanted to shoot myself.[107]

Conversion

Against his background, Kierkegaard made an entry in his journal on May 19, 1838, that presented a startling contrast:

> *May 19.* Half- past ten in the morning. There is an indescribable joy which enkindles us as inexplicably as the apostle's outburst comes gratuitously: "Rejoice I say unto you, and again I say unto you rejoice"—Not a joy over this or that but the soul's mighty song "with tongue and mouth, from the bottom of the heart": "I rejoice through my joy, in, at, with, over, by, and with my joy"—a heavenly refrain, as it were, suddenly breaks off our other song: a joy which cools and refreshes us like a breath of wind, a wave of air, from the trade wind which blows from the plains of Mamre to the everlasting habitations.[108]

This entry marked the return of the prodigal. It was the most direct reference in all his writing to a conversion, but it was so cryptic that one could only guess at the nature of his experience. That this experience marked a turning point in his life, however, could not be doubted. Kierkegaard was reconciled to his father, who died shortly afterward. He then resumed his theological studies and completed them in 1839.

The Penitent

Kierkegaard's return to Christianity was marked by several important commitments. Certain ideas that he conceived during his "prodigal period" began to appear in his writing, and these ideas became the central points in his own psychological and intellectual development. The first point was Kierkegaard's conception of himself as a penitent. Certainly the doom that he believed lay over his family and the guilt feelings that he retained from his prodigal period contributed to this self-conception.

When Kierkegaard spoke of himself as a penitent, he was thinking primarily of one who could not live like people who went to church on Sunday and pursued the normal occupations of life the rest of the week. For him, to be a penitent was to renounce all claims on the world, to forget the possibility of living a normal life, and to be consumed by the task that God has set before him: to make people aware of true Christianity.

The Critic of Hegel

Kierkegaard also became committed to criticizing Hegel's philosophy and Hegel's influence on current Lutheran theology. Kierkegaard was very disconcerted by Hegel's system. In the first place, it failed to affirm the freedom of the individual. If each society, each period of history, was the only step in the progressive manifestation of the absolute Idea, then what was left for the individual? The individual was simply an insignificant part of a culture in which the Idea was partially manifested. Kierkegaard's contemporaries believed that to deviate from the latest historical expression of the Idea was not an act of freedom but an act of insanity, a flight from reason and truth.

Second, Kierkegaard objected that Hegel's system did not describe the world in which Kierkegaard lived. Although Hegel could look forward to the end of history when all the contradictions of history would be explained, Kierkegaard observed that the supposed end of history had little influence on the choices he had to make each day. It was one thing to affirm that all contradictions would be reconciled, all theses and antitheses joined into syntheses. It was another thing to live in a world that was full of contradictions and to have to make choices before the contradictions were resolved. Hegel's system, Kierkegaard maintained, was not very instructive for the business of living. Kierkegaard argued that the more one tried to become more objective the more one lost touch with real life.

Then Kierkegaard conceived a thoroughly frightening idea. If it was true that at any one point in history one could not really know the truth—which was only to be revealed fully at the end of history—why should it be assumed that truth would be knowable or even desirable at the end? Suppose at the end of history the ultimate truth turned out to be ugly, cold, and merciless? There was nothing about the absolute Idea as Hegel conceived it that warranted people's affection and adoration.

Kierkegaard's fourth objection to Hegel was that his system was in fact antithetical to faith. When faith became natural and reasonable, it was in serious danger of ceasing to be faith. Kierkegaard expressed himself in a paragraph in his *Concluding Unscientific Postscript*:

> How strange is the way of the world! Once it was at the risk of his life that a man dared to profess himself a Christian; now it is to make oneself suspect to venture to doubt that one is a Christian. Especially when this doubt does not mean that the individual launches a violent attack against Christianity with a view to abolishing it; for in that case it would perhaps be admitted that there was some thing in it. But if a man were to say quite simply and unassumingly, that he was concerned for himself, lest perhaps he had no right to call himself a Christian, he would indeed not suffer persecution or be put to death, but he would be smothered in angry glances, and people would say: "How tiresome to make such a fuss about nothing at all; why can't he behave like the rest of us, who are all Christians? It is just as it is with F.F., who refuses to wear a hat on his head like others, but insists on dressing differently."[109]

The Opponent of a State Church

This last objection focused the third important theme that characterized Kierkegaard's newly discovered faith commitments. Kierkegaard objected to the entire concept of a state religion. Faith could become a completely external matter, completely lacking commitment, once Christianity became the official religion of the state. In an entry in his journal, Kierkegaard mused,

> Let us try a thought-experiment. If one could establish the fact that Christ had never existed, nor the Apostles either, that the whole thing was a poetical invention—in case nothing was done on the part of the State or the congregations, no hint that they would suppress [the pastors] livings, I should like to see how many parsons would resign their posts.[110]

As Kierkegaard saw it, even the cows in Denmark deserved to be called Christian, because they had been born in a Christian country. So, Kierkegaard published a number of articles criticizing the Danish Lutheran Church for conspiring to produce faith without commitment.

Kierkegaard's Concept of Faith

In contrast to what he considered the sterile stance of the state church, Kierkegaard stressed the need for personal faith, First, faith had to be passionate. Kierkegaard deplored the idea that faith could be defined as the affirmation of an orthodox confession. Systematic theology held no interest for him. In his opinion the dominant Hegelian theological system actually undermined faith. The specific nature of Christian faith, as Kierkegaard understood it, was not determined by what it asked one to believe but by the act of faith it required of the believer.

Second, for Kierkegaard, this passion, of faith was a totally consuming one. It was not like the desire for pleasure, which could be turned off at will. It was like love, which seized a person, commanded his or her entire attention, and grew more consuming each day. Was this rational? Kierkegaard responded with an emphatic "No!" At the center of Christian faith was something that reason could not grasp—the incarnation. According to the Christian faith, the eternal God had become limited, a temporal creature. Being a Christian did not remove the paradox inherent in the incarnation. For Kierkegaard, faith was thus a passion rather than a process of thought because faith defied mere reason.

The Knight of Faith versus the Knight of Infinite Resignation

Kierkegaard illustrated this concept of faith in his work *Fear and Trembling*. In this work, the "knight of faith" was contrasted with the "knight of infinite resignation." The knight of infinite resignation was similar to the ancient Stoics or the more modern romantic heroes. He renounced everything in the world without any hope of getting it back. He completely gave up on the finite world and lived in the infinite. "The knights of infinite resignation are easily recognized; their gait is gliding and assured."[111] These were persons who could rise above the mundane world and seize life in its purest forms.

According to Kierkegaard, however, these knights of infinite resignation were not able to live in the finite world. In transcending the banal things of this world, they became strangers to the world. As he described them:

> Whenever they fall down they are not able at once to assume the posture, they vacillate an instant, and this vacillation shows that after all they are strangers in the world. This is more or less strikingly evident in proportion to the art they possess, but even the most artistic knights cannot conceal this vacillation.[112]

In contrast to the knight of infinite resignation was the knight of faith. He, too,

> Has made and every instant is making the movements of infinity. With infinite resignation he has drained the cup of life's profound sadness, he knows the bliss of the infinite, he senses the pain of renouncing everything, the dearest things he possesses in the world, and yet finiteness tastes to him just as good as to one who never knew anything higher…. And yet, and yet the whole earthly form he exhibits is a new creation by virtue of the absurd. He resigned everything infinitely, and then he grasped everything again by virtue of the absurd. He constantly makes the movements of infinity, but he does this with such correctness and assurance that he constantly gets the finite out of it, and there is not a second when one has a notion of anything else.[113]

The knight of faith, then, give up everything just as the knight of infinite resignation did. But "by virtue of the absurd" he believed that he would gain all that he had given up[114]. Believing this to be true, he continued to live in the finite. While the knight of infinite resignation was always "incommensurable" with everyday life, the knight of faith looked and acted "like a tax collector."[115] That is, the knight of faith looked and acted like anyone else.

In order better to explain the difference between the knight of infinite resignation and the knight of faith, Kierkegaard used two examples: Agamemnon and Abraham.

Agamemnon, the Knight of Infinite Resignation

Agamemnon, the Greek commander in the Trojan War, was becalmed at Aulis on the way to the battle at Troy. With the ship's provisions running low, a prophet informed Agamemnon that he had offended the gods, who were withholding the winds as punishment. With the lives of his entire company at stake, he was told that the only way to appease the gods would be to sacrifice his daughter Iphigenia. Kierkegaard described Agamemnon's situation:

> When an undertaking in which a whole nation is concerned is hindered, when such an enterprise is brought to a standstill by the disfavor of heaven, when the angry deity sends a calm which mocks all efforts, when the seer performs his heavy task and proclaims that the deity demands a young maiden as a sacrifice—then will the father heroically make the sacrifice. He will magnanimously conceal his pain....yet soon the whole nation will be cognizant of his pain, but also cognizant of his exploit, that for the welfare of the whole he was willing to sacrifice her, his daughter, the lovely young maiden.[116]

Agamemnon was a tragic hero because he was caught between two conflicting ethical demands. He was Iphigenia's father, and he was the king of Mycenae. In this situation, he had to deny either his obligation to his daughter or his obligation to the state. He resolved the dilemma by offering to sacrifice the individual for the greater good of the state. He resigned himself to the dictates of ethical reason.

Abraham, the Knight of Faith

Without his faith, his hope against hope, Abraham would simply have been, like Agamemnon, a figure or resigned obedience. Kierkegaard described the paradoxical nature of that faith:

> By faith Abraham received the promise that in his seed all the races of the world would be blessed....Time passed, it became unreasonable, Abraham belie ved.....Then came the fullness of time....Then there was a joy in Abraham's house, when Sarah became a bride on the day of their golden wedding. But it

> was not to remain thus......"And God tempted Abraham and said unto him, "Take Isaac, thine only son, whom thou lovest, and get thee into the land of Moriah, and offer him there for a burnt offering upon the mountain which I will show thee." So all was lost—more dreadfully than if it had never come to pass![117]

It looked as if God were only playing with Abraham. Having made the impossible take place, God would snatch Isaac away again. But in spite of the appearance,

> Abraham believed and did not doubt, he believed the preposterous...And Abraham rose early in the morning...He said nothing to Sarah, nothing to Eleazar. Indeed who could understand him? Had not the temptation by its very nature exacted of him an oath of silence? He cleft the wood, he bound Isaac, he lit the pyre, he drew the knife.[118]

Abraham's devotion to God had led him beyond the rational, beyond the limits of ethical reason:

> The ethical expression for what Abraham did is, that he would murder Isaac; the religious expression is, that he would sacrifice Isaac; but precisely in this contradiction consists the dread which can well make a man sleepless, and yet Abraham is not what he is without that dread.[119]

Abraham's faith clung to the promise and to the impossible possibility that, having given up his loved one, he would nevertheless receive him back. Abraham believed that by "virtue of the absurd" he would get Isaac back.

Abraham differed from Agamemnon because he had faith, rather than Agamemnon's resignation. But there was another difference. Like Abraham, Agamemnon was called to sacrifice his child. But unlike Abraham, Agamemnon's act remained within the boundaries of morality. His action was tragic but not immoral in his culture. But what higher principle was served by the sacrifice of Isaac? There was none. God was only testing Abraham's faith. In Abraham's case, the act of faith required a breach, or at least a suspension, of ethics.

The Engagement

In May 1837, Kierkegaard met a young girl of fourteen while attending a garden party in Fredricksberg. The young girl, Regine Olsen, later remembered that he "talked incessantly…his conversation welled up and was in the highest degree captivating." Ironically, the subject of their first conversation concerned under what circumstances an engagement ought to be broken. Regine was not the only one captivated, Kierkegaard, recognizing his attraction to Regine, pursued a secretive and fantasized relationship with her by observing Regine from a coffee shop as she went to her music lessons.

Kierkegaard maintained this imaginary love affair until after he passed his theological examination in 1840. From that July until August, he vacationed in Jutland. On his return to Copenhagen, he decided to take positive action. On the eighth of September, he met Regine outside her house. After inviting himself inside the vacant house, he requested her, as she had so often in the past, to play the piano.

> She did so, and that wouldn't satisfy me. Then suddenly I took the music book, closed it not without a certain vehemence, threw it down on the piano and said, "O what do I care about music! It is you that I want. I have wanted you for two years." [120]

Regine was speechless at the moment, but after a few days, in September tenth, she formally accepted his proposal of marriage.

The Break

Now, eleven months later, Emil Boesen sat pondering the events that had transpired since their engagement. Regine had given her being completely to Kierkegaard, who was truly in love with her. But from the beginning Kierkegaard had been apprehensive of his action. He had communicated to Emil a series of convincing rationalizations, all of which precluded the successful outcome of a marriage between himself and Regine.

Even before he asked her to marry him, Kierkegaard confided, he had gone about pregnant filled with ideas and had fallen in love with the ideal image of her. Reality could not answer his burning desires. Emil remembered Kierkegaard wondering with the poets if "all love like knowledge is remembrance."

Further, Kierkegaard confided, his penitence, his melancholy alienated him from Regine. His ghostly existence in a fundamentally spiritual world served as a barrier to the relationship. He could never initiate her into such terrible things as his melancholy, the dreadful night that brooded in the inmost depths, his wildness, lusts, and excesses. Kierkegaard's overwhelming concern with lust stemmed from his self-diagnosis as an uncommonly erotic individual. He suffered terribly from the guilt of visiting the brothel five years before. Kierkegaard's chosen role of the penitent was inconsistent with that of a husband.

Then there was the age difference. He was ten years her senior temporally, but existentially he saw himself as an eternity too old for her. Besides, his religious task would be endangered if he were to bind himself to anything on earth. His destiny to find truth made him a sacrifice for others, and if he were to pursue his task she must be sacrificed for others.

These ruminations in his shortcomings culminated in Kierkegaard's conception that a divine veto had been cast against his marriage to Regine. This concept of the divine veto was not a recent development, for as early as 1839 he had stated that his commitment to the role of a penitent would affect his personal relationships. Now he was sure that marriage conflicted with his definition of a penitent. He wrote in his journal,

> I saw that I had made a false step. A penitent such as I was, my *vita ante acta*, my melancholy, that was enough. I suffered unspeakably at that time.
> She see med to notice nothing. On the contrary her spirits were so high that once she said she had accepted me out of pity…She gave herself to me, almost worshipping me, asking me to love her, which moved me to such an extent that I was willing to risk all for her. How much I loved her is shown by the fact that I always tried to hide from myself how much she had moved me….Had I not been a penitent, had I not had my *vita ante acta,* had I not been melancholy, my union with her would have made me happier than I had ever dreamed of being. But in so far as I was what, alas, I was, I had to say that I could be happier in my unhappiness without her….There was a divine protest, that is how I understood it.[121]

The Decision

Boesen had watched as his friend wrestled with his predicament. Kierkegaard had left a short while before, crying remorsefully. Regine had left him a note begging him in the name of Christ and the memory of her deceased father not to leave her. He had been deeply disturbed by it and was in a quandary about what to do. Sitting in the deserted restaurant, Boesen reflected on Kierkegaard's predicament. Kierkegaard could still seek a rapprochement with Regine, but that would fly in the face of a divine veto. He could remain resolute in his decision despite Regine's pleadings, but Regine had sworn that if he abandoned her she would die of despair. Emil knew that Kierkegaard feared having Regine's death on his conscience.

Would Kierkegaard be able to break the shackles of his past and live in the existential fulfillment that he himself attributed to marriage, or would he remain eternally imprisoned within his father's melancholy? Was Kierkegaard truly a "knight of faith," or was his act one of infinite resignation? Or could it be that, like Abraham, Kierkegaard thought he would gain Regine by renouncing her? Did Kierkegaard's love of Regine and his duty as a penitent have to conflict?

STUDY QUESTIONS & EXERCISES

I. Outline Hegel's dialectical understanding of history and indicate Kierkegaard's reaction to it.

II. Both psychology and religion deal with guilt. How are these concepts and methods of dealing with guilt similar and different? Apply your findings to the case of Søren Kierkegaard and his father.

III. Describe the two differing models of faith that Kierkegaard offered in the persons of Abraham and Agamemnon.

IV. To which of the preceding models of faith (or what combination of them) did Kierkegaard conform in his relationship to Regine Olsen?

V. Suggest an example from recent history of someone acting against the conventions of society in the name of religious convictions. Evaluate that event from the perspective of Kierkegaard's attitudes.

Chapter 19
19th Century Philosophy

B. Karl Marx (1818-1883)

Religion is the opium of the people.

Marx

Chapter 19
19th Century Philosophy

The Balmy spring air of Paris gave no hint of the intense political drama-taking place in 1871. After two short months of existence, the Paris Commune faced annihilation. Wild rumors of the Commune's revolutionary excesses were rampant. Condemnation was everywhere. Why had the International Working Man's Association not risen to their defense? Did the Commune embody what the workers' had been striving for since the revolutions of 1848? Was this the next stage in the historical progression of the class struggle? Or was it simply a naïve outburst, a spasm out of step with history and doomed to set back the workers' cause? In London, Karl Marx pondered these questions as his friend Friedrich Engels strode into the room. The International' general council was growing exasperated-Engels could stall them no longer. Marx had, to produce the council's communique on the Commune immediately.

Marx's Early Life

The Marx family lived in the ancient Rhineland town of Trier. In fact, Karl Marx's forefathers had been rabbis there for 200 years. Karl's father, Heschel, was an official in the Prussian government. Unlike his brother who followed family tradition and became a rabbi, Heschel was not particularly interested in his Jewish heritage. When, in 1817, a wave of anti-Semitism was forcing Jewish bureaucrats to resign their posts, Heschel preserved his livelihood by changing his name to Heinrich and becoming a baptized Lutheran. A year later, on May 5, 1818, his son, Karl was born.

Karl grew up in comfortable surroundings in Trier. The third of nine children, Karl became the eldest son when his brother Moritz died in 1818. Karl was a solid but undistinguished student in high school. Late in his career there, the mathematics and Hebrew instructors were both dismissed-the former as a materialist and atheist, and the latter as a revolutionary.

In October 1835, Karl embarked on the study of law at the University of Bonn. While there, he engaged fully in the rowdiness of student life. He was wounded in a duel; he once spent a night in jail for drunkenness. In addition to his general rowdiness, Karl had a problem that was to plague him all his life: his inability to manage money. His father complained, " As though we were made of gold my gentleman-son disposes of almost 700 thalers in a single year, in contravention of every agreement and every usage, whereas the richest spend no more than 500."[122] Hoping to curb his son's excesses, Heinrich decided that Karl should transfer to the University of Berlin in 1836.

Conversion to Hegel

On his arrival there, Marx found Berlin in the heyday of Hegelianism. Hegel had developed a philosophy based on the dialectical development of history. Now Hegelian philosophy was being used to explain virtually every field of study. There was Hegelian economics, Hegelian biology, and Hegelian history. Hegel's ideas were being applied everywhere.

At first, the rampant Hegelianism put off Marx. He was more into German romantic tradition than he was in rationalism. As a romantic, Marx was not interested in history or historical development. But because Hegel had died only five years before Marx went to Berlin and because Hegel's thought was so widely accepted, Marx had no choice but to "struggle with philosophy".

Marx soon became impressed with the Hegelian approach. He came to value the historical perspective Hegel brought to his ideas. He came to appreciate the way Hegel looked at situations holistically. Hegel's concept of an evolving history was especially appealing to Marx. The idea that the world was evolving, moving toward a greater realization of the Absolute Idea, was exciting. Hegel had a way with making people want to participate in life, of making one want to be a part of the process. Within a short period of time, Marx became a "convert" to Hegelianism. Marx formalized this "conversion" by joining the Young Hegelian Doctors' Club.

By the late 1830's a split had developed among Hegel's followers. Hegel had seen history as the progressive actualization of the Absolute Idea, but he was somewhat ambiguous about the future. To some extent, he suggested that the Absolute Idea was fully realized: Christianity was the Absolute State. The "Old Hegelians" endorsed this reactionary view-everything was to be kept just as it was. On the other hand, there was some reason to believe that Hegel saw the dialectic movement of history continuing: the current state of affairs would be superseded by even more adequate realizations of the Idea. The "Young Hegelians" endorsed this revolutionary aspect of the master's thought.

Initially, the key topic of discussion for the Young Hegelians was religion, primarily because politics was too dangerous. The first salvo of their attack on the orthodoxies of the day was thus **David Strauss' *Life of Jesus*** in 1835. But the intimate connection between religious and political orthodoxy at that time meant that the Young Hegelians could avoid political criticism. The state church and the state government were too closely linked to permit attacking one without attacking the other. Bruno Bauer's The Christian State in Our Time took up the task of political criticism in 1840. Many suspected that this was based largely on the ideas of Bauer's friend Karl Marx.

Marx's growing involvement with philosophy led him to consider an academic career. He thus began constructing a doctoral thesis on Democritus and Epicurus, whose post-Aristotelian situation Marx saw as a parallel to his own post-Hegelian context. On the advice of Bauer, he sent his manuscript to the University of Jena and was awarded his doctorate in absentia in 1841. Just as Marx became ready to embark on a teaching career, however, the Prussian minister of education decided to purge the unruly Young Hegelians. Marx's friend Bauer was removed from his post, and Marx's own prospects were likewise eliminated.

Feuerbach and the Criticism of Hegel

After casting about for some time, Marx decided to pursue a career in journalism. During this same period, Marx began to deal with some problems he saw in Hegel's thought. Despite his appreciation of Hegelian process of dialectical development, Marx had some real problems with Hegel's notion of the Absolute Idea. It seemed to Marx that Hegel was too idealistic and not realistic enough. Marx came to believe that ideas reflected reality rather than shaped reality. There was not some Absolute Idea that caused the reality one saw around oneself; rather, all ideas arose from a previous reality. Consciousness did not shape existence; rather, existence shaped consciousness.

As Marx continued to deal with these inadequacies of Hegel's system, he came across the works of Ludwig Feuerbach. In 1841, Feuerbach had written the *Essence of Christianity*, a work that directly attacked the supernaturalist idealism of Hegel.

Feuerbach claimed that Hegel's idealism led to a devaluation of humanity, the senses, and the material world. Underneath Hegel's rationalism, Feuerbach saw a religious, other-worldly longing. Feuerbach's critique involved purging Hegelianism of this other-worldly impulse. Feuerbach held that the world of ideas was generated by humanity and the material world, not vice versa. Feuerbach saw his own philosophy as

> Essentially distinguished from the systems hitherto prevalent, in that it corresponds to the real, complete nature of man; but for that reason it is antagonistic to minds perverted and crippled by a superhuman, i.e., anti-human, anti-natural religion and speculation. It does not…regard the pen as the only fit organ for the revelation of truth, but the eye and ear, the hand and foot…it recognizes as the true thing, not the thing as it is an object of the abstract reason, but as it is an object of the real, complete man.[123]

In place of Hegel's ideal, Feuerbach placed the human being. Often referring to his thought as "sensualism," Feuerbach stressed the reality of this world and the primacy of sense knowledge.

Marx saw Feuerbach as developing a kind of materialism, a focus on humanity and this world, that would overcome the problems of Hegelianism. Whereas history was for Hegel the history of Absolute Spirit, now it could be seen in the development of humanity and nature.

As Marx moved further and further away from Hegel's thought, he also moved further and further away from the Young Hegelians. It seemed to Marx that the Young Hegelians were too interested in ideas, speculating about revolution and not nearly enough in practical political action.

In April 1842, he produced his first article for the *Rheinische Zeitung*, a liberal newspaper in Cologne. In this setting, Marx began to focus on politics and, to some extent, economics. This practical engagement further distanced Marx from the speculative ideas of the Young Hegelians. Turning from their flashy but abstract slogans, Marx began his lifelong focus on practical political change.

Eventually, Marx became editor of the paper. His leadership was such that its circulation quickly doubled. In addition, political developments in the Rhineland led Marx increasingly to criticize the government. His January 1843 article on the poverty of the Mosel wine makers finally brought the censors down on his head, and the *Rheinische Zeitung* was suppressed in March.

Economics: Alienated Labor, Class Struggle, and Private Property

With the closing of the paper, Marx became free to accept the offer of his friend Arnold Ruge to become co-editor of a new journal. It was to be a review devoted to political action incorporating both theoretical and practical issues. Publishing in Germany was out of the question, so the decision was made to locate in Paris. With Marx's future given a new base of security, he finally felt free to marry his fiancée, Jenny von Westphalen.

Jenny von Westphalen was four years his senior, and a talented woman. A one-time Queen of the Ball in Trier, she had a quick mind and radical sympathies. Their marriage in June 1843 thus provided Marx with an intellectual partner of tremendous value. Jenny assisted Karl with most of his later publications.

After their honeymoon in Switzerland and an extended stay with Jenny's mother, the two of them headed for Paris. During this time, Marx continued his study of Feuerbach, his criticism of Hegel, and his preparation for the new journal. The first issue of *Deutsch Französische Jahrbücher* came out in February 1844, but because of its poor reception and the growing estrangement between Ruge and Marx, Ruge discontinued publication.

With the demise of *Jahrbücher* and with the receipt of a large sum from the former shareholders of the *Rheinische Zeitung*, Marx was again free to throw himself wholly into economic and political studies. Particularly during the summer, while his wife and newborn daughter were away in Trier, Marx laid the foundations for his later economic and political theories.

In his study of "alienated labor," Marx saw that in a capitalist system

> The worker becomes a cheaper commodity the more commodities he produces…All these consequences follow from the fact that the worker is related to the *product of his labor* as to an *alien* object…The more the worker exerts him self, the more powerful becomes the alien objective world which he fashions against himself…It is the same in religion. The more man attributes to God, the less he retains in himself.[124]

The workers' labor was alien to them because it was not theirs. It belonged to another. The workers' labor belonged to the capitalist, whose ownership of the means of production was also ownership of the workers' labor. In return for the workers' labor, the capitalist paid them a wage, a wage that Marx saw as always barely enough for subsistence. In this arrangement, the worker became thoroughly alienated, for it "makes his life activity, his essence, only a means for his existence."[125]

Over the years, human potential had been so minimized that no one was able to produce the kind of life that was possible. Through alienation from their labor, people became alienated from human existence. Those who were not members of the working class were also alienated. They too were alienated from fulfilling their potential. Although this individual alienation was important, it was not nearly as important as the alienation people had as an economic class. Workers, as a class, were alienated from those who owned the means of production. Those who owned the means of production were, in turn, alienated from the workers.

This alienation gave rise to **class struggle**. The interests of one economic class were always in opposition to the interests of other economic classes. These differing interests led to conflict and struggle, class struggle. This was true of all classes, not just the working classes.

According to Marx, the reason for this class conflict, as well as the reason for the alienation that gave rise to it, was private property. It was because of private property that some people were capitalists and others were workers. In order to get rid of all the oppressive institutions that capitalism had developed (which included religion, the state, the family structure, and so on), one must first get rid of private property. As Marx explained it,

> Religion, family, state, law, morality, science, art, etc., are only particular forms of production and fall under its general law. The positive overcoming of private property as the appropriation of human life is thus the positive overcoming of all alienation and the return of man from his religion, family, state, etc., to his human, that is, social existence.[126]

The overcoming of capitalism's alienation of labor by means of private property was the key to attaining truly human existence.

To overcome alienation, to overcome private property, was, for Marx, the meaning of communism. He criticized the "crude communists" of his time for demanding "the reversion to the unnatural simplicity of the poor and the wantless man who has not gone beyond private property, has not yet even achieved it."[127] At the same time, these "crude communists" advocated the community of women-which Marx saw simply as "communal lust"-and in fact the universalization of alienation, in the form of state capitalism. Against crude communism, Marx envisioned a true communism, a true overcoming of alienation. This would be "the riddle of history solved," the "true resolution of conflict between existence and essence." Marx did not spell out his vision, but he affirmed it would have to be both postcapitalist (using the technology developed by capitalism) and non-alienating. In particular, because it would not rest on alienated labor, communism would not alienate people from each other. Rather, it would affirm the "species-being" or social integration of humanity. Marx felt that further detail on communism was unnecessary, because he saw that "communism is the necessary form and dynamic principle of the immediate future but not as such the goal of human development."[128]

Friendship with Engels

While Marx was intensely engaged in these economic and political studies, he formed what was to become the most important friendship of his life. Friedrich Engels had written an article on economics for the Jahrbücher which impressed Marx greatly. He was thus delighted to make Engel's acquaintance in August, 1844.

During their time together, Marx learned that Engels came from a large family of wealthy, textile industrialists. Since his birth in 1820, Engels had been immersed in the fundamentalist Lutheranism of Barmen in Prussia. Strauss' s *Life of Jesus* had come to Engels as a breath of fresh air while working in his father's factory. Following its lead, he went to Berlin and joined the Young Hegelians. When his father sent him to work at the English branch of the family firm, in Manchester, he became a sharp and critical observer of working class life. It was in Manchester that Engels composed his *Outlines of a Critique of Political Economy*, which Marx had found very helpful. The two men immediately decided to spend ten days together discussing political economy, and planning a joint volume criticizing Bruno Bauer and the other Young Hegelians.

At the same time that Marx was pursuing his study of economics and his project with Engels, he was politically active among the expatriate German workers. He became a frequent contributor to their biweekly paper, *Vorwärts*. Late in the year, the Prussian government became so annoyed with the radical Parisian paper that it began to put diplomatic pressure on the French government. Consequently, in January 1845 *Vorwärts* was suppressed and Marx was expelled from Paris.

Historical Materialism, the Stages of Development, and Revolution

From Paris, Marx went to Brussels, then a haven for political refugees from all over Europe. Without a job, Marx was nonetheless financially secure. He had sold the family's belongings in Paris and had received an advance for the book he was writing on political economy. In addition, his Parisian associates sent him a gift in order to share "communistically" his expenses, and Engels gave him the royalties from his own *The Condition of the Working Classes in England*. This gift from Engels was the first in what would become an extended and life-saving service.

When Engels arrived in Brussels in April, he found that Marx had already made substantial progress intellectually. According to Engels, by seeing that history had to be explained in terms of economics (rather than vice versa), Marx "had already advanced…to the main aspects of his materialist theory of history."[129]

The position toward which Marx was moving combined aspects of Hegel's idealism and Feuerbach's materialism. With Hegel, Marx agreed that history must be understood as a process. History was made up of various stages: each incomplete, each a necessary part of the process, each leading to the next stage. But Marx did not agree with Hegel's characterization of the Absolute Idea as that which guided and directed this process. For Marx, the various stages of history were not to be explained by some "other-worldly" idea. Furthermore, Marx held that the movement from one stage to another was not a gradual, slow, orderly process. Rather it was a sudden and often violently revolutionary change.

With Feuerbach, Marx agreed that the world must be understood in "this-worldly" terms. He agreed with Feuerbach that material forces shaped the world. But Marx felt that Feuerbach did not go far enough. While Feuerbach did criticize Hegel's emphasis on the Absolute Idea, an abstract and non-material notion, he did not tie his criticism to historical development. Marx commented, "As far as Feuerbach is a materialist he does not deal with history, and as far as he considers history he is not a materialist."[130]

Combining what he thought best in Hegel and Feuerbach, Marx developed a view of history called "historical materialism". Most people in nineteenth-century Europe thought of history in political or personal terms. When strong leaders such as Napoleon came along, they altered history by changing the political structure. But Marx held that this view of history was mistaken. Such political changes were not the result of individual people. Rather, they were the result of economic, material conditions in which people found themselves. In fact, most political changes were simply by-products of the "material conditions of life."

According to Marx, there were five stages in the development of history, five "modes of production" that "determine the social, political, and intellectual life processes." Each (except the last) of these five stages was incomplete. Each was a necessary part of the process, and each led inevitably (and sometimes violently) to the next stage.

The first stage was **primitive communism**. This was a society characterized by the absence of private property. With the advent of private property, the next three stages of development were introduced. After primitive communism came **slavery**, **feudalism**, and **capitalism**. Each of these stages was higher, more productive, more developed, and more efficient than the previous one. Each of these stages replaced what was becoming an inefficient and ineffective economic system. Each of these economic stages determined the way people thought and acted in that stage.

The final stage of the economic development of history was **communism**. There was no sixth stage, because private property ceased to exist at the level of communism. There was no longer any division in society between the haves and have-nots. No longer were those who owned the means of production exploiting those who had no control over the means of production. So, after a transitionary period a society would be developed in which all people would be able to achieve the kind of skill, talent, and creativity that they were capable of achieving. People would no longer be restricted by the economic consequences of their actions. They would achieve such a high level of productiveness that all needs of the system could be met.

In response to the criticism that human nature would not allow this to happen, Marx argued that selfishness and greed were parts of any economic system based on private property. People were determined to be selfish and greedy by the "social production of their material lives." Change the mode of production (that is, eliminate private property), and the way people think and act would change too.

The stage Marx was particularly interested in was capitalism. Marx held that capitalism had served an important historical purpose. But it was now time for capitalism to give way to the next and final stage of development: communism. Furthermore, Marx felt that it was not enough simply to theorize about the overthrow of capitalism-one must commit oneself to bringing it about.

Marx gave an example of the practical resulting from his theory when he criticized Feuerbach's communism. Abstracting himself from historical realities, Feuerbach thought communism was simply a particular way of looking at human life. Marx charged that Feuerbach wanted "merely to produce a correct consciousness about an existing fact; whereas for the real communist it is a question of overthrowing the existing state of things." [131]

Marx could not stop with ideas as Feuerbach had. Marx declared, " The philosophers have only *interpreted* the world in various ways; the point is, to *change* it."[132]

Marx's passage beyond the Young Hegelians and Feuerbach consisted of transferring the location of truth from the realm of abstract ideas and attitudes to the arena of historical action. For Marx, truth was not so much known as done. For this reason, Marx could not be romantic about the communist revolution. An ideal revolution needed only to capture the imagination, but a true revolution would have to be founded on the proper economic circumstances.

In the real world, Marx said, to be a communist was not simply to possess a certain attitude, but to be "the follower of a definite revolutionary party."[133] Marx made good on this statement in 1847 when the Communist League was formed. Although he was not an organizer of the League, Marx quickly joined it and was asked-together with Engels-to draft its platform or manifesto.

The ***Communist Manifesto*** in its finished form was almost entirely Marx's own work. His aims were to set out the party's foundation and program. Their foundation was Marx's historical materialism. The program was class struggle and the abolition of private property.

Before the *Manifesto* was even off the presses, revolution had begun to sweep across Europe. When news of the revolution in Paris reached Brussels in late February 1848, the Belgian government expelled all suspect foreigners. After moving first to Paris, Marx continued on to Germany when revolution broke out in Berlin. Together with Engels, Marx quickly resurrected his old newspaper as the *Neue Rheinische Zeitung*. Marx hoped the paper would become a focal point for radical politics throughout Germany. At first it took a relatively moderate line, seeking simply to deepen and consolidate what was in fact a very shallow revolutionary impulse. By the spring of 1849, however, it had sufficiently antagonized the recovered Prussian authorities so that they once again expelled Marx from the country.

Capital and the International

In mid-1849, Karl and his pregnant wife, Jenny, virtually destitute, arrived in London. Their condition was an accurate omen of their future, for the Marxes lived in a substandard existence in London for the next thirty years. At times their condition was so severe that survival was in doubt. Three of their children died due to lack of funds for doctors and medicines. Marx was able to acquire some funds through journalism, as correspondent for the *New York Tribune*. But their primary source of income was always Engels. Engels returned to work in his father's Manchester factory and devoted a large part of his income throughout the 1850s and 1860s to Marx's support.

Beyond his work for the Tribune, Marx's primary occupation for the rest of his life was the study of economics. His earlier work had developed the main outlines of his theory, but now this was sharpened and documented with an enormous wealth of data. Marx became a fixture in the reading room of the British Museum, where he pored over government records, histories, and the writings of other economists. He projected a work of enormous scope that would deal in detail with each of the first four economic stages. However he only completed the portion dealing with capitalism, called *Das Kapital*, or *Capital*.

In *Capital*, Marx set out the rules of capitalism. He explained how capitalism emerged from feudalism and how it must eventually give way to the final stage of development, communism.

The most stirring passages of *Capital* were Marx's documentation of the deprivations of the early Industrial Revolution. Although most of this material was simply objective, Marx did not avoid drama. He wrote,

> The historical movement which changes the producers into wage workers, appears, on the one hand, as their emancipation from serfdom and from the fetters of the guilds...But, on the other hand, these new freedmen became sellers of them selves only after they had been robbed of all their own means of production, and of all the guarantees of existence afforded by the old feudal arrangements.[134]

Marx's historical materialism provided the key for understanding not only capitalism's past, but also its future.

> Along with the constantly diminishing number of the magnates of capital, who usurp and monopolize all advantages of this process of transformation, grows he mass of misery, oppression, slavery, degradation, exploitation; but with this too grows the revolt of the working class, a class always increasing in members, and disciplined, united, and organized by the very mechanism of the process of capitalist production itself. The monopoly of capital becomes a fetter upon the mode of production, which has sprung up and flourished along with, and under it. Centralization of the means of production and socialization of labour at last reach a point where they become incompatible with...capitalism. The death bell of capitalist private property sounds.[135]

Marx predicted that capitalist society would generate its own destruction. By bringing together a large labor force to work in the factories, the capitalists were organizing the workers. It would be only a matter of time before the workers would revolt against the capitalists and abolish private property. He asserted, as he had twenty years before, that with the abolition of private property a non-alienating (communist) society would be born.

At the same time that Marx was putting the finishing touches on Capital, he was again involved in working class politics. In 1864, a number of different workers' groups came together in London to form the International Working Men's Association. Marx was not one of the International's organizers but quickly ascended to its leadership, framing its inaugural address.

From the beginning, the International was a hodge-podge of people with various interests, bound together solely by their commitment to workers and their dissatisfaction with the status quo. It acted as the vanguard of working class aspiration at the time. But Marx came to feel that while its prominence attracted many to the International, its effectiveness could only be maintained by reducing the internal conflict within the International. Consequently, an increasing amount of Marx's time after 1865 was devoted to conflict with rival factions in the International. In all of this, Marx's concern was with historical and therefore political effectiveness in the working class struggle.

The Commune

Not all the agitation in Europe during the late 1860s arose from the working classes. Bismarck, the "Iron Chancellor" of Prussia, had imperial plans for Germany. Consequently, France was provoked to war in July of 1870. First proclaimed by the Germans as a "war of defense," the Franco-Prussian war quickly took on the contours of territorial expansion. When the French emperor, Louis Bonaparte, was captured by the Prussians on September 4, the French government immediately reconstituted itself as a republic. It called itself the "Government of National Defense," but its aims quickly appeared to be otherwise. Working in the interests of the aristocracy and wealthy industrialists, the Republic sought a quick and favorable end to the Prussian disturbance.

Meanwhile, the Prussian advanced on Paris, laying siege to the city on September 18. The main body of Parisians had no relish for the Government of National Defense, because this group appeared more devoted to its own interests than to those of Paris. By January 28, 1871, the Republic had arranged an armistice with Prussia, but still did not have the Parisians' confidence. The final bone of contention was the disarming of the city. The Republic called for it but the citizens refused.

On March 18, troops from the Republic sought to take away the city's cannons by stealth. They were soon discovered and, largely because of the women of Paris, their plan was foiled. In the momentum of the hour, the city's militia took the offensive and drove the forces of the Republic from the city. Almost by accident, the city was free. On March 28, the Paris Commune was proclaimed.

The Commune was a democratically organized coalition of forces administered by a ninety-two member council. It had little coherent policy but drifted toward socialist lines. It acted against the city's oppressive rents, and at the request of the bakers it prevented employers from requiring night work. The Commune aided in the establishment of over forty-three workers' cooperatives, but launched no attacks on private property. The Paris branch of the International played a small role in the Commune, with seventeen of the ninety-two Council seats.

The Commune was quite disorganized. But to the rest of Europe it appeared as a threatening symbol. The Commune had few friends, for the ruling powers saw it as proof of the destructive chaos of worker militancy. On the other hand, many workers' groups saw it as a combination of fringe elements and typical Parisian chauvinism. The International had remained conspicuously silent. Now, as the troops of the Republic began advancing into the city and fighting grew more intense, the workers of Europe wanted to know: should they support the Commune?

The Decision

Marx agonized. If he threw the International onto the side of the Commune and it was crushed, the major political force of the European workers would be crushed along with it. But if he refused to stand with the workers of Paris, would not the International lose credibility with all workers?

> Back in the fall, Marx had told the French workers,
> Any attempt at upsetting the new government in the present crisis...would be a desperate folly. The French workers...must not allow themselves to be swayed by the national souvenirs of 1792...Let them calmly and resolutely improve the opportunities of republican liberty, for the work of their own class organization. It will gift them with fresh herculean powers for the regeneration of France, and our common task-the emancipation of labor.[136]

Sensing that this advice would not be heeded by the Parisians, Engels predicted that a proletarian revolution in 1870 would be crushed, and would "set back another 20 years" the cause of the working class.

In March, two days after the Commune was proclaimed, Marx had written that it had no chance of success. It was not grounded in reality but in abstract ideas of justice and equality. Its foundation was not the historical development of the means of production but a historical accident. Marx exclaimed, "The decisive, unfavourable 'accident' this time is by no means to be found in the general condition of French society, but in the presence of the Prussians in France."[137] And yet the courage of the communards was striking. Marx cried out, "What elasticity, what historical initiative, what a capacity for sacrifice in these Parisians!"[138]

As he watched the struggle develop, Marx had second thoughts. Were the Communards out of touch with historical reality? Or were they moving forward in the development of history? Could the mixed forces of the Commune represent a new breakthrough by the working class? Or did they only represent themselves, another piece of Parisian delirium? Engels rose to leave. Marx had to make up his mind. Europe was waiting.

STUDY QUESTIONS & EXERCISES

I. Describe the political, economic, and religious environment in which Marx grew to maturity. Suggest factors in this environment that appear to have a lasting influence on Marx.

II. How did Marx develop his philosophy by reacting against and incorporating elements of Hegelianism?

III. Outline Marx theory of historical materialism. To what extent was he indebted to Feuerbach, and how did Marx go beyond Feuerbach?

IV. Give reasons why Marx would not want to spurt the Paris Commune and reasons why he would not. Which set of reasons do you think more closely coincides with his theory of historical materialism?

V. Evaluate the impact of Marx's thinking on present day liberation movements in Africa, Latin America, Asia, and the United States.

Chapter 20
19th Century Philosophy

C. Friedreich Nietzsche (1844-1900)

Error has transformed animals into men; is truth perhaps capable of changing man back into an animal?

Nietzsche

Chapter 20
19th Century Philosophy

Friedreich Nietzsche (1844-1900) was the son and grandson of Lutheran ministers. Neverless, he was the herald of judment that "God is dead" and undertook a campain against morality. He was nurtured in an enviroment dominated by females. However, he advocated the most masculine philosophy of the "superman." He called for the fullest expression of human vitality in the name of the "will to power." Yet, he believed that sublimation and control are truly human characteristics. His writings rank among the most lucid ever. At the same time, he ended his days in hopeless insanity.

His life

Nietzsche was born in the province of Saxony on October 15th, 1844. His father, who was a Lutheran minister, died when he was only five years of age. He spent his childhood surrounded by his mother, his sister, and two maiden aunts. After attending a first rate boarding school, he went on to study classical philology at the universities of Bonn and Leipzig. He was unimpressed with the caliber of his fellow students. At 24 years of age, he earned a professorship at Basel, which is where his brilliance came to be more widely recognized.

Nietzsche's first great work, *The Birth of Tragedy*, came in 1872, and was followed by other works, most notably *Human, All too Human* in 1878. His brief military service came during the Franco-Prussian war when Nietzsche left Basel and volunteered as a medical orderly on active duty. His time in the military was short and he returned to Basel in a state of shattered health. In 1879 he resigned from Basel, but instead of waiting to heal, he pushed headlong into a more fervent schedule of writing than ever before.

While Nietzsche continuously kept in contact with his former colleagues, His most productive years were after he left Basel, with the culmination of his work (not to mention notoriety) coming with the writing of *Thus Spoke Zarathustra*. For many years, Nietzsche had been closely associated with the German composer, Richard Wagner. The extent of their relationship is speculation at best, but at some point around 1887-1888, there was a deep rift wedged between the two men. In 1889, less than two weeks after the completion of *Nietzsche contra Wagner*, he broke down, insane. Accounts tell of a frail Nietzsche draping himself around the neck of an old horse, which was being brutally beaten in the street. There are numerous possible explanations for his madness, perhaps the most logical of which is that it was a condition brought on by an advancing case of syphilis. Others have postulated that the sheer weight of his thought and the gravity by which he saw reality ultimately uncoiled even his most tightly wrapped intellect.

Most of his final years were spent in his sister Elisabeth's care. During this time, Elisabeth grew more and more involved in the burgeoning anti-Semitic movements in Germany. While he wasted away, she collected and edited many of his scattered notes and tailored them to suit her own political agenda. The fruition of this was Nietzsche's altered works and philosophy being used as a cornerstone in the Nazi party and Adolf Hitler's personal mantra. In 1900, he died, in 1901; Elisabeth published *The Will to Power*.

His philosophy

Nietzsche believed that people have become enslaved by what he called "**slave morality**." This kind of morality rejects life, celebrates mediocrity and renders people cowardly, reactionary and lacking in purpose. Therefore, Nietzsche rejected the notion that there is a universal absolute system of morality.

People are definitely different; to conceive of morality in universal terms is to disregard basic differences between individuals. It is unrealistic to assume there is only one kind of human nature. Since its direction cannot be prescribed by one set of rules. There is however, one thing that characterizes all human beings, the drive to dominate the environment. This drive is what he called: **the will to power**.

This will to power is more than a simple desire to survive. Nietzsche wrote: "…the strongest and highest will to life does not find expression in a miserable struggle for existence, but in a will to war." This means a will to power, a will to overpower. If someone proposes a universal moral rule, he is denying the fullest expression of people's elemntal vital energies.

He used the Judeo-Christian ethics as a representative of the worst offender. He believed that these kind of ethical rules are contrary to people's basic nature, that it is anti-natural morality and it produces weak lives.

Nietzsche believed in a twofold early history of good and evil. This shows the development of two primary types of morality:

1. **The aristocratic morality**
2. **The slave morality**

The word master means for Nietzsche, high caliber, and noble. Noble people pass judgment on themselves. He identifies these words with the aristocratic morality. Their morality is one of self-glorification. These noble individuals act out of a felling of power, which seeks to overflow. They may help the unfortunate, but not out of pity. Rather, from an impulse generated by abundance of power. They honor power in all its forms. They take pleasure in subjecting themselves to rigor and toughness and have reverence for all that is severe, difficult and hard.

In contrast to aristocratic morality, we find slave morality. The word slave is identified with evil, which means common, plebeian, the abused, the oppressed, the salves and those who are uncertain of themselves. For the slave "good" is the symbol for all those qualities that serve to alleviate the existence of sufferers. Good means sympathy, a helping hand, a warm heart, patience, diligence, humility and friendliness.

This according to Nietzsche is the morality of utility. Whereas goodness refers to whatever is beneficial to those who are weak and powerless. Whereas for the slave morality the person who arouses "fear" is "evil."

He uses two Greek gods to illustrate his point, Dionysus, who is the symbol of the power of dynamic passions. His devotees drank the fruit of the vine in sensuous and frenzied dance. And Apollo and His chariot: they symbolized restraint, order, and rational control of the powerful passions.

Nietzsche hypothesized moral systems developed from within a society. Nietzsche discussed the Master Morality of aristocratic cultures, such as the Roman Empire, and the Slave Morality of Jewish communities. Nietzsche recognized that the two cultures were actually components of one greater society / culture, but the moral systems were markedly different.

The aristocratic class, or ruling class, became leaders through their naturally superior abilities and stronger aggressive instincts. This has improperly led to a belief that Nietzsche thought a race could be naturally superior; his only claim was the individuals could be born superior. As proof, slaves could become citizens and even senators in Rome. These natural leaders, according to Nietzsche, would highly value sexuality based upon Darwin's theories that the strong wish to procreate and continue their power.

Another mark of the ruling class would be an acceptance of aggression and the use of force. As these rulers express power openly, they view the pursuit of power and the defense of self as honorable. For this reason, Nietzsche speculated that these leaders would not hold a grudge against enemies. In fact, they would not view competitors for power as enemies, but rather as opponents in a great game of human ability. These rulers welcome competition, believing that it builds character and teaches valuable lessons. After a battle, they study their failures and openly admit the strengths of others. Nietzsche wrote that such leaders do not see a right and wrong, only a superior and inferior combatant.

In stark contrast to the ruling class, the subservient populations embrace a moral code based upon a mythical equality of individuals. Knowing this, the aristocrats claim to acknowledge this equality in various empty manners -- such as equality under the law, which applies seldom in reality. The subservient, slave class eventually realizes that life cannot be equal, so a religion is developed promising that they are actually superior to those in power on earth.

Nietzsche hypothesized the slave class embraced democracy and the principle of equality in order to bring the naturally superior class down to their own level. Sin and evil are artificial constructs, created by the slaves and adopted by the leaders of this class, who often become leaders in the aristocratic class -- proving they do not believe in this religious myth. The slaves demean sex, human desire, and teach humility instead of respect for power and authority. Nietzsche believed this was a repression of resentments. A minority of religious leaders are either true believers or individuals seeking power, but unable to admit this due to their own repressed natures.

God is dead.

At this point it should be clear how Nietzsche combines his critique of morality with a critique of religion. In his book *The Joyful Wisdom*, he makes a critique of religion explicit in a famous parable. Nietzsche was not a casual atheist who thought that giving up belief in God would make no difference. But he thinks that people are giving up belief without fully realizing the consequences.

The best way to understand Nietzsche's position is to read the famous parable quoted in the next section.

THE JOYFUL WISDOM

The Death of God
Nietzsche

The Madman. – Have you ever heard of the madman who on a bright morning lighted a lantern and ran to the market place calling out unceasingly: "I seek God! I seek God!"—As there were many people standing about who did not believe in God, he caused a great deal of amusement. Why? Is he lost? Said one. Has he strayed away like a child? Said another. Or does he keep himself hidden? Is he afraid of us? Has he taken a sea voyage? Has he emigrated? – the people cried out laughingly, all in a hubbub. The insane man jumped into their midst and transfixed them with his glances. "Where is God gone?" he called out. "I mean to tell you. We have killed him—you and I. We are all his murderers. But how have we done it? How were we able to drink up the sea? Who gave us the sponge to wipe away the whole horizon? What did we do when we loosened this earth from its sun? Whither does it now move? Whither do we move? Away from all suns? Do we not dash on unceasingly? Backwards, sideways, forward, in all directions? Is there still and above and below? Do we not stray as through infinite nothingness? Does not empty space breath upon us."

"Has it not become colder? Does not night come on continually, darker and darker? Shall we not have to light lanterns in the morning? Do we not hear the noise of the gravediggers who are burying God? Do we not smell the divine putrefaction? For even Gods putrefy. God is dead. God remains dead. And we have killed him. For even Gods putrefy. God is dead. God remains dead. And we have killed him. How shall we console ourselves, the most murderous of all murderers? The holiest and the mightiest that the world has hitherto possessed has bled to death under our knife—who will wipe the blood from us? With what water could we cleanse ourselves? What lustrums, what sacred games shall we have to devise? Is not the magnitude of this deed to great for us? Shall we not ourselves have to become Gods, merely to seem worthy of it? There never was a greater event, and on account of it, all who are born after us belong to a higher history than any history hitherto"—Here the madman was silent and looked again at his hearers; they also were silent and looked at him in surprise. At last he threw his lantern

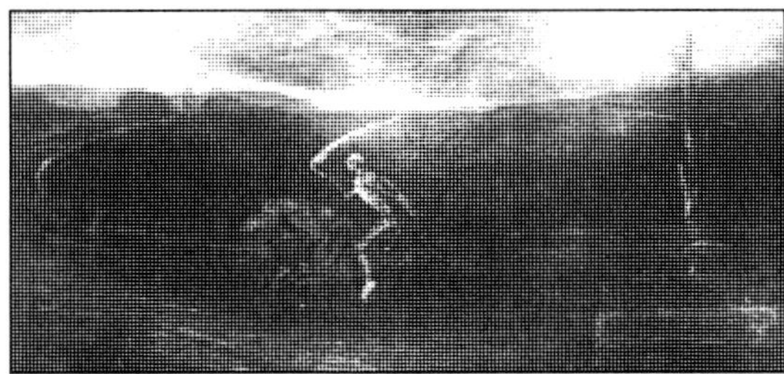

on the ground, so that it broke in pieces and was extinguished. "I come too early," he then said, "I am not yet at the right time. This prodigious event is still on its way, and is traveling—it has not yet reached men's ears. Lightning and thunder need time, the light of the stars need time, deeds need time, even after they are done, to be seen and heard. This deed is as yet further from them than the furthest star and ye they have done it!"—It is further stated that the madman mad his way into different churches on the same day, and there intoned his Requiem aetername deo. When led out and called to account, he always gave the reply: "What are these churches now, if they are not the tombs and monument of God?"

...It is always a metaphysical belief on which our belief in science rests—and that even we knowing one of today, the godless and anti-metaphysical, still take our fire from the conflagration kindled by a belief a millennium old, the Christian belief, which was also the belief of Plato, that God is truth, that the truth is divine.... But what if this itself always become more untrustworthy, what if nothing any longer proves itself divine, except it to be error, blindness, and falsehood; what if God himself turns out to be our most persistent lie?

The most important of the more recent events—that "God is dead," that the belief in the Christian God has become unworthy of belief—already begins to cast its first shadows over Europe. To the few at least whose eye, whose suspecting glance is strong enough and subtle enough for this drama, some sun seems to have set some old, profound confidence seems to have changed into doubt: our old world must seem to them daily more darksome, distrustful, strange, and "old." In the main, however, one may say that the event itself is far too great, too remote, too much beyond most people's power of apprehension for one to suppose that so much as the report of it could have reached them; not to speak of many who already know what had already taken place, and what must all collapse now that this belief had been undermined—because so much was built upon it, so much rested on it, and had become one with it: for example, our entire European morality. This lengthy, vast, and uninterrupted process of crumbling, destruction, ruin, and overthrow which is now imminent: who has realized it sufficiently today to have to stand up as the teacher and herald of such a tremendous logic of terror, as the prophet of a period of gloom and eclipse, the like of which has probably never taken place on earth before?...Even we, the born riddle-readers, who wait as it were on the mountains posted 'twixt today and tomorrow, and engirt by their contradiction, we, the firstlings and premature children of the coming century, into whose sight especially the shadows which must forthwith envelope Europe should already have come—how is it that even we, without genuine sympathy for this period of gloom, contemplate its advent without any personal solicitude or fear?

Believers and their Need of Belief. How much faith a person required in order to flourish, how much "fixed opinion" he requires which he does not wish to have shaken, because he holds himself thereby—is a measure of his power (or more plainly speaking, of his weakness). Most people in old Europe, as it seems to me, still need Christianity at present, and on that account it still find belief. For such is man: a theological dogma might be refuted to him a thousand time—provided however, that the had need of it, he would again and again accept it as "true" according to the famous "proof of power" of which the Bible Speaks. Some have still need of metaphysics; but also the impatient longing for certainty which at present discharges itself in scientific, positivist fashion among large numbers of the people, the longing by all means to get at something stable (while on account of the warmth of the longing the establishing of the certainty is more leisurely and negligently undertaken): even this is still the longing for a hold, a support; in short, the instinct of weakness, which, while not actually creating religions, metaphysics, and conviction of all kinds, nevertheless, preserves them. In fact, around these positivist systems there fume the vapors of a certain pessimistic gloom, something of weariness, fatalism, disillusionment, and fear of new disillusionment—or else manifest animosity, ill-humored, anarchic exasperation, and whatever there is of symptom of masquerade of the feeling of weakness. Even the readiness with which our cleverest contemporaries get lost in wretched corners and alleys, for example, in Vaterliinderei (so I designate Jingoism, called chavinisme in France, and deutsch in German) [i.e., extreme patriotism], or in petty aesthetic creeds in the manner of Parisian nature (which only bring into prominence and uncovers that aspect of nature which excites simultaneously disgust and astonishment, they like at present to call this aspect la verite vraie), or in

Nihilism and the St. Petersburg style (that is to say, in the belief in unbelief, even to martyrdom for it): this shows always and above all the need of belief, support, backbone, and buttress…

Belief is always most desired, most pressingly needed where there is lack of will for the will, as emotion of command, is the distinguishing characteristic of sovereignty and power. That is to say, the less a person knows how to command, the more urgent is his desire for one who commands, who command sternly—a God, a prince, a caste, a physician, a confessor, a dogma, a party conscience. From whence perhaps it could be inferred that the two world religions, Buddhism and Christianity, might well have had the cause of their rise, and especially of their rapid extension, in an extraordinary malady of the will. And in truth it has been so: both religions lighted upon a longing, monstrously exaggerated by malady of the will, for an imperative, a "Thou shalt," a longing going the length of despair; both religions were teachers of fanaticism in times of slackness of will power, and thereby offered to innumerable persons a support, a new possibility of exercising will, and enjoyment in willing. For in fact fanaticism is the sole "volitional strength" to which the weak and irresolute can be excited as a sort of hypnotizing of the entire sensory-intellectual system, in favor of the overabundant nutrition (hypertrophy) of particular point of view and a particular sentiment, which then dominates—the Christian calls it his faith. When a man arrives at the fundamental conviction that he requires to be commanded, he becomes "a believer." Reversely, one could imagine a delight and a power of self determining, and a freedom of will whereby a spirit could bid farewell to every belief, to every wish for certainty, accustomed as it would be support itself on slender cords and possibilities, and to dance even on the verge of abysses. Such a spirit would be the free spirit par excellence.

Our Note of Interrogation. But you don't understand it? As a matter of fact, an effort will be necessary in order to understand us. We seek for words; we seek perhaps also for ears. Who are we after all? If we wanted simply to call ourselves in older phraseology, atheists, unbelievers, or even immoralists, we should still be far from thinking ourselves designated thereby: we are all three in too late a phase for people generally to conceive, for you, my inquisitive friends, to be able to conceive, what is our state of mind under the circumstances. No, we have no longer the bitterness and passion of him who as broken loose, who has to make for himself a belief, a goal, and even a martyrdom out of his unbelief! We have become saturated with the conviction (and have grown cold and hard in it) that things are not at all divinely ordered in this world, nor even according to human standards do they go on rationally, mercifully, or justly: we know the fact that the world in which we live is ungodly, immoral and "inhuman"; we have far too long interpreted it to ourselves falsely and mendaciously, according to the wish and will of our veneration, that is to say, according to our need.

For man is a venerating animal. But he is also a distrustful animal: and that the world is not worth what we have believed it to be worth is about the surest thing our distrust has at last managed to grasp. So much distrust, so much philosophy! We take good care not to say that the world is of less value; it seems to us at present absolutely ridiculous when man claims to devise values to surpass the values of the actual world; it is precisely from that point that we have retraced our steps; as from an extravagant error of human conceit and irrationality, which for a long period had not been recognized as such. This error had its last expression in modern Pessimism; and older and stronger manifestation in the teaching of Buddha; but Christianity also contains it, more dubiously, to be sure, and more ambiguously, but nonetheless seductive on that account. The whole attitude of "man as the standard of the value of things, as judge of the world, who in the end puts existence itself on his scales and finds it too light—the monstrous impertinence of this attitude has dawned upon us as such, and has disgusted us—we now laugh when we find, "Man and World" placed beside one another, separated by the sub-lime presumption of the little word "and." But how is it? Have we not in our very laughing just made a further step in despising mankind? And consequently also in Pessimism, in despising the existence of cognizable by us? Have we not just thereby become liable to a suspicion of an opposition between the world in which we have hitherto been at home with our veneration—for the sake of which we perhaps endure life—and another world which we ourselves are: an inexorable, radical, most profound suspicion concerning ourselves, which is continually getting us Europeans more annoying into its power, and could easily face the coming generation with the terrible alternative: Either do away with your venerations, or with yourselves! The later would be Nihilism: but would not the former also be Nihilism? This is our note of interrogation.

STUDY QUESTIONS & EXERCISES

I. Give a small summary of the life of Nietzsche.

II. Explain his concept of the will to power.

III. How does Nietzsche divide society?

IV. Nietzsche's concept of God is dead presents several challenges to the believer. What are these and how can they be answer.

Chapter 21
The Contemporary Context

Chapter 21
The Contemporary Context

THE NINETEENTH century has been called the **Age of Progress**.[139] Although there were social upheavals: by 1848 there had been political uprisings in France, Germany, Austria, Italy, and Hungary-in general, people were optimistic. In England, especially, all was placid. Queen Victoria was on the throne. At mid-point in the century, in 1851, England held a Great Exhibition to display "the Works of Industry of All Nations." Its theme was "Progress." Inspired by the Queen's consort, Prince Albert, the exhibition was housed in a "Crystal Palace" of glass that enclosed nineteen acres of Hyde Park. The building itself illustrated the theme as one of the first examples of prefabrication and mass production. More than 6 million viewers passed through the exhibit hall to gaze at displays of raw materials, manufactured goods, and especially the great machines-locomotives, hydraulic presses, power looms.

At the beginning of the century, nearly two-thirds of all Europeans lived on farms. Sustenance came from the land. Tools were made by hand. Power came from wind and water and human effort. Travel was done by horse or sail. By mid-century, machines were providing transport and power and manufacture. Population was shifting from the country to the city. The revolution that England celebrated in 1851 was the **Industrial Revolution**. Change, which had occurred so slowly for centuries, now suddenly accelerated. And it seemed all to the good.

Karl Mark sat in the British Museum Library researching and writing his critique on capitalism. And in Denmark Søren Kierkegaard deplored the conformity of most people to the dictates of the state and church. But to most Victorians, the future promised a continuity of progress.

Scientific Developments

Technological developments from 1851 until the outbreak of World War I in 1914 continued to change everyone's lifestyle. The telephone, the streetlight, the fountain pen, the box camera, and the wireless telegraph were all invented. **Louis Pasteur**, **Joseph Lister**, and the Curies were making discoveries that made surgery safer and more effective. Industrialists were perfecting ways to make steel, aluminum, and combustion engines as well as dynamite and machine guns. In 1903, **Henry Ford** established his first factory, and the **Wright brothers** made the first powered flight in an airplane.

Breakthroughs in scientific theory opened a new era in thought and application. In physics, Einstein introduced the special theory of relativity, and Max Planck formulated quantum mechanics. In mathematics, non-Euclidean approaches to geometry were being investigated, and attempts were made to found a universal algebra. Between 1910 and 1913, a three-volume work appeared, entitled *Principia Mathematica*, co-authored by Bertrand Russell and Alfred North Whitehead. It attempted to demonstrate that all mathematics could be deduced from a few principles of formal logic. It caused ferment in an area that had been fixed since Aristotle.

A scientific approach to the human and social sciences was blossoming in the second half of the nineteenth century. **Sigmund Freud** was born in 1856 and **Emile Durkheim** in 1858. Their names became synonymous with psychology and sociology. Anthropology as a systematic study of primitive human societies began. And archaeologists unearthed evidence in Egypt, Crete, and Troy of the gradual emergence of civilization.

A positive attitude toward change was the new intellectual element in the nineteenth century. In 1867, British Prime Minister **Benjamin Disraeli**, declared, "Change is inevitable, in a progressive country change is constant".[140] No idea was more responsible for that attitude than the theory of evolution. **Charles Darwin** published his ***On the Origin of Species*** in 1859. By the end of the century, nearly all scientists accepted some sort of evolutionary hypothesis. To some lay people, the idea of evolution undermined the authority of the Bible and traditional morality. Others were more optimistic. They saw evolution as the guarantee of inevitable human progress. Developments in science, medicine, and technology gave powerful support to their conviction.

Philosophers of Progress

John Stuart Mill (1806-1873) was an influential philosopher in the English-speaking world during the nineteenth century. His social and political philosophy stressed the importance of individual freedom and the development of strong individual character. Mill was one of the first Englishmen to advocate the equality of women. Religiously, Mill concluded that skepticism was the proper religious attitude toward supernatural religion. But he maintained that it was appropriate to encourage religious hopes. He entertained the theory of a limited deity with whom humans could cooperate to bring about improvement in the world.

Other philosophers developed ideas of process and becoming. **Herbert Spencer** (1820-1903) popularized Darwin's views and applied them to society. **Henri Bergson** (1859-1941) wrote of a vital force that guided unceasing evolution and could be known by intuition and instinct. The poet **William Wordsworth** inspired people with a sense of humankind's continuity with nature. These elements of empiricism and pragmatism were linked by the American philosopher William James (1842-1910). John Dewey (1859-1952) continued James's work and applied it especially to American education.

Twentieth Century Disillusionment

The optimistic nineteenth century ended in 1914. During the next four years, 30 nations, representing 1.4 billion people on six continents, were engaged in the most devastating conflict that humankind had ever seen. Science and technology, which had symbolized the promise of inevitable progress, were used to devise instruments of mass destruction. By the time of armistice in 1918, 10 million were dead and another 20 million wounded. Another 10 million innocent lives were lost to disease and famine.

After a brief decade of economic recovery, humankind's faith in progress was again stunned. The United States fell into an economic depression with the collapse of the stock market in 1929. In the next several years, the depression spread to other industrialized nations of Europe. Factories shut down, banks closed, and million lost their jobs. Anxiety, hopelessness, and despair scarred an entire generation.

In the bitter aftermath of war and depression, totalitarian movements arose that regimented people and suppressed their individuality for the sake of achieving nationalistic dreams of conquest and expansion. Before the 1930's were over, World War II had begun. This time, literally the whole world was involved. Seventy million people fought in the war, and 30 million died, civilians as well as soldiers. During the conflict, the Nazi's attempted systematically to exterminate Europe's Jewish population. Jews were herded in to concentration camps, where 6 million were murdered.

The conclusion of World War II marked the beginning of a new and more ominous era-the Atomic Age. On August 6, 1945, an atomic bomb, secretly prepared by European and American scientists, was dropped on Hiroshima, Japan. The single explosion was 2,000 times more powerful than any previous bomb. It destroyed most of the city, killed 68,000 people, and left a radioactive atmosphere that injured thousands more.

Existentialist Reaction

In the immediate aftermath of World War II, the dominant philosophy was existentialism. It paralleled the earlier work of Kierkegaard, but it was decisively focused by the despair of a world in which all traditional cultural values seemed to have collapsed. **Jean-Paul Sartre** (1905-1980) had worked in the French underground movement resist-

ing Nazism. He and his companion **Simone de Beauvoir** (1908-1986) spoke for a generation that believed that it had to order its own world and create its own values. A human being just existed and had to create its own essence. Sartre pessimistically proclaimed that a human being was "condemned to be free." He rejected God and anything that seemed to limit human freedom. For Sartre, "Hell is other people," and death was the final absurdity of existence.

Divisions After Kant

The major philosophical thinkers of the nineteenth and twentieth centuries responded to and exemplified the motifs of the cultures in which they lived. Philosophical trends, like cultural ones, exhibited the tension between (1) the rise of science and its attendant hope for human progress and (2) the perverse uses of science for destruction and the attendant human despair. The case studies of nineteenth-and twentieth century philosophers that follow illustrate this dialectic tension.

Early in the nineteenth century the Kantian synthesis collapsed. Kant had combined elements of seventeenth-century rationalism and eighteenth-century empiricism. He had attempted to synthesize the felt reality of the free human spirit and the sensory evidence of the cause and effect controlled material world. Philosophers following Kant seized on one dimension of his synthesis and separated it from the other. We still struggle with the dichotomies between human values and scientific facts that were implicit in Kant and became explicit in the nineteenth and twentieth centuries. The problem of knowledge, epistemology, overshadowed all other concerns. Most philosophers felt that a comprehensive view of reality was impossible and contented themselves with a specialized focus on one problem or dimension of reality. Many rejected the possibility of metaphysics. Even Whitehead, who attempted philosophy on the grand scale, did so primarily from the premises of modern mathematics and physics.

The Nineteenth Century

Johann Gottlieb Fichte (1792-1814) rejected Kant's belief that things-in-themselves existed even though they were beyond the reach of human knowledge. For Fichte, only ideas were real. Human ideas and judgments were considered to be true if they formed a coherent system.

Hegel sought to remove the restrictions that Kant had placed on reason. Hegel acknowledged that human understanding encountered apparent paradoxes. He boldly asserted, however, that reason could find a synthesis that would resolve the apparent contradictions between these and their antithesis. His dialectical method enabled him to posit a continual progress of thought from a thesis to its antithesis to a new synthesis.

For Hegel, finally, only the whole was true. Ultimate reality was an "absolute spirit," or "mind," which came to expression through historical events. Extensions of the approach Hegel developed were classified as idealism.

Near the end of Hegel's career, and in the immediately ensuing years, his views became widely accepted. For right-wing Hegelians, the "absolute spirit" was realized in the state and church of their time and, of course, in Hegelian philosophy.

In Denmark, Kierkegaard reacted violently to what he considered an idolatrous conformity to merely human institutions and ideologies. Kierkegaard contended that the Christian story of God becoming a human being in Jesus Christ posed a paradox that human reason could never resolve. The infinite qualitative difference between God and humanity could never be absorbed into a higher synthesis.

For Kierkegaard, a person's own personal, subjective commitment alone was truth. Young Søren had been raised as the last child of an older-than-usual father. Søren had been initiated into intense introspection. He believed that his family suffered under a "curse." Kierkegaard could not live like others in conformity to society. He wished to be known only as "that individual." Kierkegaard sketched three differing attitudes toward life: the esthetic, which viewed life objectively, at a distance; the ethical, which lived life in conformity to rigid rules; and the existential approach to life lived in the risk of personal faith was authentically human. Thus, Kierkegaard laid the groundwork for subsequent philosophies of existentialism.

Another different reaction to idealism was developed as dialectical materialism. Marx (1818-1883) studied philosophy in Berlin five years after the death of Hegel. Marx fell in with a group of younger, left wing Hegelians. They rejected the right-wing assumption that Hegel's thought represented the culmination of all thought and that the German state was the perfect form of institutional life. Rather, the left-wing Hegelians emphasized their master's concept of continuing dialectical development. This led these youthful radicals, including Marx, to espouse revolution in the church and state and rigorous transformation of traditional patterns of thought.

Because of his commitment to radical ideas and causes, Marx was a political refugee all of his life. He attempted to make a living as a journalist, but the government soon suppressed each newspaper and journal for which he worked. He was exiled from Germany, France, and Belgium and lived the last thirty years of his life in England. His wife, Jenny, who shared his radical views, aided Marx. They lived in extreme poverty, which led to the early death of three of their children. Their financial support came primarily from gifts from Friedrich Engels, the son of a wealthy textile manufacturer. Together, Marx and Engels produced *The Communist Manifesto* in 1848.

Marx spent most of the last three decades of his life poring over economic data in the British Museum Library. His statistical and historical studies formed the basis for a massive analysis of capitalism, one volume of which was published in his lifetime. Marx did not view himself as a philosopher. He categorized his work as "scientific" research, free of philosophical, religious, or ethical speculations.

Karl Marx identified with the cause of the common laborer. He joined British workingmen's association and served as a theoretician and propagandist for them. Marx's fundamental concept was a revolutionary one in philosophy. He declared: "The philosophers have only interpreted the world in various ways; the point is to change it."[141] This approach put praxis, active involvement in the struggle for justice, above theoretical thought. The fundamental reality was "labor," which common working people produced. Because of this, some people question whether Marx can be classed as a philosopher. Marx is usually identified as a dialectical materialist.

If the nineteenth century actually ended with the beginning of World War I in 1914, then **William James** (1842-1910) was a nineteenth-century person. His philosophy of pragmatism brought into singular focus another aspect of Kant's earlier synthesis; namely, the importance of the practical reason. James emphasized the freedom of human will and declared that truth was judged by its practical consequences. An idea was true if it made a difference in the world.

James graduated from Harvard Medical School in 1870. He soon returned to teach anatomy and physiology in 1873. By 1875, he was teaching psychology, and by 1879 he was lecturing in philosophy. For James, the progression was quite natural. He had always probed scientific questions for the more general, philosophical considerations that lay behind them.

In both psychology and philosophy, James was essentially self-taught. His wealthy father had reacted against his own earlier rigid indoctrination in religion and education by raising his children in a succession of schools so that they would continually question and think for themselves. William James's *Principles of Psychology* in 1890 established his reputation as an original mind. His later studies in religious phenomena and philosophy remain as an original, distinctively American, contribution. His pragmatic philosophy captured the optimistic, nineteenth-century spirit of a young nation in which all things seemed possible by the exertion of one's will.

The Twentieth Century

The two eminent twentieth-century philosophers whose cases we will study were both formed in a milieu that continued the nineteenth-century emphasis on scientific progress.

Alfred North Whitehead lived until nearly the middle of the twentieth-century. He experienced two world wars, a great economic depression, and the development and destructive use of the atomic bomb. But throughout it all he never lost faith in progress. Victor Lowe, one of Whitehead's students, and his biographer concluded:

> The nineteenth century was a peaceful century, and sheltered the pursuit of thought. Whitehead was fifty-three years old at the beginning of the World War I. As a youth, he went to Cambridge during one of her great ages. Fortunate occasions arose, at various times for the exercise of his powers.... If it be also true that mathematics and metaphysics are naturally akin, then it is impossible to imagine a set of conditions more favorable for the creation of a philosophy. The man fitted the conditions perfectly. The philosophy of organism is the ultimate intellectual achievement of the nineteenth century.[142]

Whitehead's early training was in the British preparatory school tradition of Latin and Greek classics. After studying at Cambridge, he stayed on to teach mathematics. At nearly fifty years of age, Whitehead suddenly moved to London where he studied and taught philosophy of science until near to retirement. At age sixty-two, Whitehead unexpectedly received an offer to teach philosophy at Harvard. Although Whitehead had never formally studied or taught philosophy, he became a professor in that field and during the next thirteen years did his most creative writing.

Whitehead's thought offers a dynamic and sometimes confusing blend of two dominant influences in his background: classical philosophy and contemporary science. Like the classical realists of Greece's Golden Age, Whitehead believed that there was a real world in which everything was interrelated and that the human task was to understand it. But the answers the Greeks had given in metaphysics and epistemology were no longer adequate. Modern science had changed the focus of philosophy. Reality was now understood not in terms of substances and essences. Reality in science was described in terms of relationships and processes. Physicists do not have to define what an atom is; they only need to understand how it acts. Psychologists no longer ask the question "What is a human?" The issues now are "How do humans behave?" and "How can they adjust to their environment?" Whitehead's philosophy took these changes of focus into account.

But in the end Whitehead was not a scientist, but a philosopher. The task of science is specialization and analysis. The task of philosophy is generalization and synthesis. "It follows that Philosophy is not a science," Whitehead declared.[143] Whitehead was a modern man, at home with the thought of Planck and Einstein. But Whitehead was also a classical metaphysician, equally comfortable with Plato and Aristotle.

Whitehead's process philosophy endeavored to unify all of human knowledge and experience. He attempted new ways to blend into organic relations traditional opposites: thought and feeling, spirit and matter, fact and value. His method was to understand these elements, not as essences but as relationships. In doing so, he took modern physics and philosophy since Kant with utter seriousness. A person perceiving was viewed as a natural organism both reacting to and a part of the environment being perceived. Whitehead repudiated the traditional dichotomies that had dominated from Aristotle to Hume: subject and predicate, substance and quality, particular and universal. For people trained to think in those terms, Whitehead is terribly difficult to understand. It remains to be seen whether future generations trained in new math, relativity physics, and ecological biology will find Whitehead's way of thinking more conformable to common sense.

Ludwig Wittgenstein was born into a wealthy family of brilliant, talented and strong-willed parents and siblings. Two of Ludwig's elder brothers committed suicide when their father insisted that they follow him into the family steel industry rather than pursue artistic careers. Ludwig Wittgenstein thus was well acquainted with tragedy. Karl Wittgenstein, the father, died of cancer in 1913 when Ludwig was twenty-four years old. Another older brother committed suicide rather than be captured during World War I.

In his formal training, Wittgenstein pursued engineering. Informally, he read widely and was impressed with Kierkegaard and Tolstoy. Throughout his life, Wittgenstein felt the need for the personal purity and simplicity that Tolstoy advocated and lived with an intense individualism reminiscent of Kierkegaard.

Wittgenstein went to England to study aerodynamics. In 1911, he moved to Cambridge to study mathematics under Bertrand Russell. From math he moved to philosophy and was soon being treated as a peer by the Cambridge faculty.

Ludwig Wittgenstein became the father of two, quite distinct schools of contemporary philosophy: logical positivism and linguistic analysis. Both schools shared an anti-metaphysical stance: philosophy is viewed as an activity, not a set of theories, the object of which is to remove confusions in our language.

After two years at Cambridge, Wittgenstein withdrew for a year to a remote cabin in Norway. In 1914, he enlisted in the Austrian army. The notebooks he kept while serving on the eastern front and in an Italian prison camp became his first book, *Tractatus Logico-Philosophicus*. The Tractatus declared that words are like pictures of things. When the referrents of these pictures are known and proper grammatical form is used, all problems are solved.

A group of philosophers of science called the Vienna Circle took up Wittgenstein's idea and developed them into the philosophy of logical positivism. They held that the only statements that could meaningfully be made were those which could be verified either by empirical science or by logic. All other statements, including metaphysical, religious, and ethical statements were treated as nonsense.

After finishing the *Tractatus*, Wittgenstein felt that all of the essential philosophical questions had been answered. He gave away his inheritance and took a job teaching at a boy's school in an Austrian village. Listening to his students convinced Wittgenstein that ordinary human language was more complex than he previously realized. In 1929, he returned to Cambridge where he was accepted as a faculty member on the basis of his *Tractatus*.

During the rest of his life, Wittgenstein lectured yearly at Cambridge, except for a period as a hospital orderly during World War II. He continually revised his former views but published only one article. His posthumously published volume *Philosophical Investigations* provided the basis for a new school of philosophy, linguistic analysis or "*ordinary language philosophy*."

The later Wittgenstein characterized language not as pictures, but as games. Wittgenstein felt that every statement had it own logic, which was established by listening to its use in ordinary language in a particular context, form of life, or language game. Metaphysical, religious, and ethical utterances were not nonsense. They were meaningful in the context of various forms of life that were not scientific or logical language games.

As he came to the end of his life, Wittgenstein was not satisfied that he had been successful in eliminating philosophical problems. He had, however, unintentionally fostered two vital and influential schools of contemporary philosophy.

Contemporary Philosophy and You

Three decades have passed since the deaths of Whitehead and Wittgenstein. Not only their thought, but also that of Kierkegaard, Marx, and James still has articulate and active adherents in the philosophical community. No other figures of their stature have yet risen to establish other alternate forms of doing philosophy in our time. Nor does any one school dominate philosophical reflection in North America at the moment. Part of the reality of our pluralistic era is that a variety of philosophical perspectives inform and energize theory and action in religion, politics, science and the arts at present. Part of the benefit of studying the cases in our contemporary context will be a better understanding the presuppositions that motivate contemporary movements. A further and even more valuable effect of interacting with these contemporary philosophers will be the stimulus to think for yourself, to propose alternate solutions to theirs, and to conceive of new questions that need to be asked.

STUDY QUESTIONS & EXERSISES

I. Write in your own words a summary of the Contemporary Context. Include in your answer all the philosophical movements, tendencies and names of important philosophers of this time.

II. What philosophical aspects of the 20th century, do you see at the beginning of the 21st century?

III. Taking into consideration every single philosopher we have studied so far. Try to create your own personal philosophy, basing yourself in all the different ideas presented in this text.

Chapter 22
20th Century Philosophy

A. William James (1842-1910)

Ideas (which themselves are but parts of our experience) become true just in so far as they help us to get into satisfactory relation with other parts of our experience.

James

Chapter 22
20th Century Philosophy

William James sat in his study at Harvard University. It was spring, 1910, and he was tired. After a year of intense effort, his manuscript was almost ready. James knew that The Meaning of Truth was the sum of his career as a philosopher, and yet a nagging doubt remained. His theory of truth and his concept of free will ran counter to traditional scientific and religious ideas. He knew that. The book would be controversial, but that did not frighten him. The real issue, the fundamental one, James thought , was "Can I trust my own judgement? How can I know that I am right? Does my free choice, of an answer, or an action, really matter?"

His mind wandered restlessly back to another spring forty years before, to an entry scrawled in his journal.

> I think that yesterday was a crisis in my life. I finished Renouvier's second Essay and see no reason why his definition of free will-the sustaining of a thought because I choose to when I might have other thoughts-need be illusory. At any rate, I will assume for the present that it is no illusion. My first act of free will shall be to believe in free will.[144]

For James, the first conscious statement of free will had not been effortless. During the preceding two years at Harvard Medical School, he had been haunted by a sense of moral impotence, faced with the apparently inescapable dilemma of trying to maintain free will in the light of religious determinism on one side and scientific determinism on the other. He had rejected both the notion that all things were rigidly fixed by God's will and the concept that all reality was governed by fixed natural laws of cause and effect.

Now in 1910 as he wrote in his journal, James felt more and more certain that human effort had to count for something, that it must make a difference. He pondered the alternatives. Could God be all-powerful and humans therefore powerless? Were humans, mere outgrowths of evolutionary process and all their efforts of no significance? Most crucial of all, had his own decision to act out of free will been rooted in reality or illusion? Was there really freedom to choose? Or was his need to believe in free will just a fabrication, a mental ploy to escape the crushing control of total determinism?

The James Dynasty

William James was born on January 11, 1842. The James family typified the energy, enterprise, and restlessness of a young and growing America.

William James's grandfather, William, came to Albany, New York, from Ireland in 1789 at the age of eighteen. Poor, but hardworking and thrifty, he parlayed his earnings through careful investments into a fortune of $3 million. He died in 1832, an eminent banker, trustee of Union College, staunch Calvinist, and father of eleven children.

His son, Henry, Sr. (William James's father), became a respected theological writer and thinker in New York and New England. A restless man with a lively intellect, he was surprisingly active in spite of a leg amputated as a youth-the result of trying to stamp out a barn fire.

With his strict Calvinist background, religion was a family tradition. After graduating from Union College in 1830, Henry Sr., began studying for the Presbyterian ministry. He attended Prineton Theological Seminary from 1835 to 1837 but became disenchanted with the absence of spirituality in what he called "professional religion." He left the seminary but continued to spend much of his spare time studying the Bible. At age thirty-three, he was preparing a paper on the book of Genesis. Then, one quiet afternoon following a cheerful meal, a dreadful apparition struck him:

> Fear came upon me, and trembling, which made all my bones shake. It was a perfectly insane and abject terror…some damned shape squatting, invisible to me within the room and raying out from his fetid personality influences fatal to life. The thing had not lasted ten seconds before I felt myself a wreck, reduced from a state of firm, vigorous manhood to almost helpless infancy. [145]

After a prolonged rest cure on the seacoast, he decided he no longer wanted to study the Bible. He put his notes and commentaries away and never looked at them again. At this point, his landlady introduced him to the mysticism of Emanuel Swedenborg, and particularly the concept of purgation, regeneration, and illumination that Swedenborg called *vastation*. Henry, Sr. was convinced that his breakdown had been an instance of just such a vastationary change. He therefore renounced the God of strict Calvinism and became totally immersed in Swedenborgianism.

The Family Context

Henry, Sr., and his Scotch-Irish wife, Mary, encouraged cheerful anarchy as the norm in their family life. The James homes-and there were many, for the family constantly uprooted itself-were not noted for their peace or quiet. Their five children-William, Henry, Jr., Garth, Robertson, and Alice-"fought like cats and dogs." Meals were dominated by lively, often heated, debate in which the children were expected to expound and defend their own views, even when they ran counter to parental opinion. Guests at the Jameses' table included illustrious literary and political figures of the day: Ralph Waldo Emerson, Charles Dana, Felix Darley, William Thackeray, Washington Irving, Oliver Wendell Holmes, and James Russell Lowell.

Amid the chaos, Mary James, described by her son Henry as "soundless, sleepless, and selfless," presided as the calm eye of the hurricane, the "keystone of the family arch." She worshipped her husband, and he relied on her completely. He said that while she had not had intellectually speaking a liberal education, "she really did arouse my heart."[146]

Formal schooling for the James children was, as Henry, Jr., later said, "administered in small vague spasms." The family moved frequently, often several times a year, and often to Europe. Henry, Sr., cited the children's educations as the reason. Remembering his joyless Calvinist childhood, he was determined that his children not be subjected to dogma, pedantry, or rigidity in any form. His idea of intellectual freedom was to throw William and Henry, Jr., into as many schools as possible and let them formulate their own ideas.

London, Paris, New York, Geneva, Newport, Bonn, Albany-while most of the eastern United States pushed toward new lands and gold, the Jameses restlessly wandered to Europe and back, staying only for brief periods in one place. William and Henry called themselves "hotel children." Both they and their brothers and sister experiences chronic ill health during these years of wandering.

William James's Development

In 1850 while living in Bonn, William decided to pursue the study of art. His father reacted violently, thinking William suited for science and engineering. Yet just a few months later Henry, Sr., wrote a friend announcing his decision to return to America so "William could study art." Apparently Henry, Sr., became amenable to this when he decided that none of the children seemed to be "cut out for intellectual labors."

The family moved to Newport, Rhode Island, where eighteen-year-old William studied painting with well-known artist William Hunt. A year's effort convinced him he would never be more than mediocre. Accordingly, he abandoned his brushes to enroll in Lawrence Scientific School.

By 1864, his interest in natural sciences led William to Harvard, where he studied undert he eminent naturalist Louis Agassiz, accompanying him on an expedition to Brazil. It was in Brazil that William contracted a serious case of smallpox that undermined his health for the next fifteen years.

James traveled to Germany to study experimental physiology in 1867. There he became interested in medicine and returned to Harvard Medical School, from which he received his degree in 1869. By 1873, he was a professor of physiology and anatomy, by 1878 of psychology, and in 1879 professor of philosophy. He later remarked,

> I originally studied medicine in order to be a physiologist, but I drifted into psychology and philosophy from a sort of fatality. I never had any philosophic instruction, and the first lecture on psychology I ever heard was the first one I ever gave.[147]

William and his brother, Henry, born only sixteen months apart, had a relationship characterized by deep empathy and intense rivalry. Henry wrote short stories and novels using European and American sites of their boyhood as settings. Both highly successful in their respective fields, they always felt a sense of their, "inexhaustible brotherhood," as Henry put it. Henry felt outclassed and ignored by William, while William felt intimidated by Henry's impressive earnings as a young writer. Both experienced serious back problems that seemed to activate at the other's successes, as well as digestive disorders, nervousness, and eye problems.

Only when William married Alice Howe Gibbens in 1878 did his health improve. The chronic depressions and backaches ceased as he seemed to gain a new sense of purpose in life.

In 1890, William James published his first major work, *The Principles of Psychology.* It was an outgrowth of James's interest in the natural sciences, a descriptive work assembling facts and theories with the view that the world could only be known through pure experience. A two-volume work, Principles was one of the first attempts to treat psychology, not as a superstition or philosophy, but as a legitimate, experimental science. *The Principles of Psychology* was soon viewed as the standard work in its field.

The Nature of Consciousness

Like Descartes, James was an interactionist who posited a psychic and mental chain of ideas interacting with a physical and material causal chain. Yet James was not a confirmed dualist. He had examined the mind-body solutions of other philosophers and rejected them all. For him, there was no separate "mind," but an organ called the brain capable of processing sensory data (thinking). As the brain acted, a thought occurred. What humans called consciousness was a series of isolated ideas associated by mental bonds, a continuum or stream of consciousness that flowed ceaselessly and changed constantly.

Each individual formed his or her own identity by selecting out of this stream of consciousness the parts that seemed biologically, esthetically, or morally useful. The mind worked on sensory data as a sculptor worked on stone. Each person's world was composed of the segments that ancestors and he or she selected or carved out from the mass of possible sensations.

According to James, consciousness was personal, or individualistic. It was always changing, a process rather than a static identity. It was sensibly continuous: in spite of gaps, individual identity was always maintained. And it was selective, using the criteria of relevance and continuity.

In addition, consciousness was purposeful. Its function was to allow humans to make choices that would help them to adapt and survive.

Finally, consciousness could not be considered apart from the body. James felt that sensory processes expressed themselves as motor processes unless inhibited. Similarly, ideas, unless inhibited by other ideas, would lead to action. When asked for an example of this, James theorized that if one had problems arising in the morning all that was necessary was to picture the "getting up process" in the mind and at the same time to clear away all conflicting ideas. The result: that person would soon be standing up.[148]

Pragmatism

By the year 1896, James's intellectual priorities had shifted. Prior to this time, he had considered himself a psychologist with some interest in philosophical and theological problems. Now he began to consider philosophy his primary interest.

The seeds of James's philosophy had been planted in his approach to psychology. At the center was his theory of pragmatism, which stated that the validity of any knowledge had to be seen in terms of its consequences, value, or usefulness.

Mathematician and philosopher Charles S. Pierce, who had in turn borrowed it from Kant, introduced the term pragmatism in America in 1878. James adopted it to describe his "method of settling metaphysical disputes" that otherwise might have been "interminable…and of interpreting each notion by tracing its respective consequences."[149]

For James, any statement that claimed to be true had to have practical consequences. It had to allow for the possibility of some future action and the formation of a willingness to act accordingly in all circumstances of the given kind. So, for any object to which a person would be prepared to apply an idea-such as "banana"-there were certain expected practical outcomes. One had to expect specific sense experiences from the object. And one had to be prepared to perform certain actions in response to it. This active element, this prospective, rather than retrospective, orientation was what set William James's empiricism apart from traditional British empiricism. James's view was characterized as functionalism. James said,

> The truth of a thing or idea is its meaning, or its destiny, that which grows out of it. This would be a doctrine reversing the opinion of the empiricists that the meaning of an idea is that which it has grown from.[150]

In addition to reorienting thought from past to future, James's radical empiricism implied a mind that actively participated. It actively operated on ideas in order to project them into the future; it selected ideas; it ordered and organized them. It acted on present ideas to create a guide to the future that would "seek to assure experiences which it desires and repress those it wishes to avoid."[151]

According to James, the mind was far from being the passive recipient of sensory impressions that it was in Locke's t*abula rasa*. For James, the mind was active, and ideas were "plans for action." The "meaning" of an idea lay in its implications for the future. "Truth" was a property exhibited by any idea that successfully dealt with life experience. Truth was what one could do with statements or ideas.

The Pragmatic Idea of Truth

Prior to James, philosophical idealists such as Berkeley had assumed that truth was a fixed relation. Once one discovered the truth about something, there was no further discussion. Nothing else had to follow that rational climax. Epistemologically, truth was a state of stable equilibrium.

James pragmatism, on the other hand, took a different tack. He asked,

> Grant an idea or belief to be true, and what concrete difference will its being true make in experience? What would be different than the results if that belief were false? What, experientially speaking, is the truth's "cash value?" [152]

James answered his own question, saying that true ideas could be validated and verified. False ideas could not. The truth of an idea was established in its verification process, its test of functionalism. The idea literally became true in the process of verification as it exhibited satisfactory consequences. It was like a scientist who made a statement about a chemical. The importance of the statement would be magnified as the properties of the chemical were tested and verified.

James refused to go beyond his pragmatic definition of truth to a more idealistic definition that "unconditionally demanded to be recognized." To do so, James felt, would be to subvert truth to arbitrariness and thereby deny its meaning.

The Deterministic Dilemma and the Will to Believe

By the mid-nineteenth century, the Calvinistic determinism that had pervaded much of American thought was beginning to retreat in the face of a widespread recognition that science taught that present reality was the result of complex development. The world was no longer seen as fixed forever but as in process of evolutionary change.

The unyielding predestinarian beliefs that had governed the life of William James's grandfather and terrified his father, burning the conviction of God' supernatural being into him "as with a red-hot iron,"[1153] were giving way to a new spirit of exploration and investigation of geographical and intellectual frontiers. The pioneering spirit that swept the country reaffirmed people's roles in shaping their own destinies.

For James, the philosophical implications were inescapable. He intentionally placed himself in the center of the conflict.

Prior to Darwin, the reach of science had not been thought of as extending to human beings. All living organisms, and especially humans, were exempt from science's absolute laws of cause and effect. One of the most dramatic effects of Darwin's evolutionary theory was its overt challenge to the notion that humans were not subject to the laws of science. The work of Darwin, Pavlov, and Freud (who had just visited America) all supported the idea that scientific methodology could apply to life processes. Every organic event was controlled by its causes.

The question for James was one of freedom of will. Was human behavior completely determined by environmental forces and inherited structures? Or were humans free to act in ways not controlled by those forces?

James could not accept the human being as an impotent creature squirming under the thumb of an omnipotent God. Nor could he believe people to be helpless cogs in the evolutionary process, with no intrinsic significance beyond their biological function. If either were the case life would be a farce; there would be no reason to live, no will to believe. There had to be some freedom of will, some human power capable of determining the future. But how could it be proved?

The Subjective Mode

James admitted that freedom of will could not be proved objectively true, but he felt that it could subjectively be assumed. For example, people developed theories about the world and discussed them as a way of better understanding things. If there were two theories about the world and one seemed more rational, then a person would be entitled to feel that the more rational theory was the more true of the two.

> If a certain formula for expressing the nature of the world violates my own moral demand, I shall feel as free to throw it overboard-or at least-to doubt it-as if it disappointed my scientific demand for uniformity of sequence; the one demand being, so far as I can see, quite as subjective and emotional as the other is.[154]

Freewill could not be proved true or false by some external criterion. The alternative was to let one's subjective nature choose! One could pick the view one would like to have true, the view that would make the most sense, seem the most fitting and the most relevant. The test of a theory's success was always the degree to which it defined a universe consonant with one's active powers and provided a sense of familiarity in the world. In James's view, a world in which there were no tasks for the will to perform would not be rational. A world in which anything could happen would not be rational either. This "sentiment of rationality" worked with subjective feeling to enable one to make balanced choices. Whether one chose determinism or freewill, the undeniable implication was that where choice was possible there must be freedom to choose, hence freewill.

An unspoken corollary to the implication of freewill was the fact that there was never any final truth. Whether in physics or in philosophy, truth was always in process. James wrote, "There can be no final truth until the last man has had his experience and said his say."[155] Each person experienced, interpreted, and chose individually: each sculptor carved a different statue.

Metaphysics

By the turn of the century, James's interests had become increasingly metaphysical. In 1902 he published The Varieties of Religious Experience, in 1907 Pragmatism, and in 1909 A Pluralistic Universe.

Throughout his career, he sought a midpoint between the dichotomous extremes he typified as "tough-minded" and "tender-minded." Was the universe supernatural-was there a being beyond the natural world of time and space? Or, was it natural, consisting of empirical reality only? William James had been born into a pre-Darwinian, supernaturalist, Calvinistic world. His father, although not a Calvinist, was an adherent of supernatural Swedenborgian mysticism. Yet all of James's professional training was rational and scientific. He could deny the validity of neither the supernatural nor the natural. In attempting to resolve his dilemma, he focused on the problem of evil.

William James defined "good" as that which allowed a satisfactory life and "evil" as that which destroyed life or frustrated satisfaction. James believed that the world was not completely evil or completely good but was capable of being improved by human effort.

Because there were real possibilities for evil as well as for good James held that no good, all-powerful God could have created the world as we know it. If people were to be allowed any determinative powers at all, then God would have to be invested with correspondingly less power. The degree of human freedom of will dictated the degree of God's limits. Evil, in James's view, was something that God did not approve, but, nevertheless, could not prevent. God existed, but this God was not omnipotent. God was limited in power, or in knowledge, or perhaps both.

The Experiment

James put down his pen, pondering the implications of an indeterministic universe. Freedom of will meant that the human mind did not come on a world complete in itself. Was the character of the world given, or capable of being predetermined? Was the mind a passive spectator in existence or an active participant? Was reality changeless, or full of ever-changing possibilities that people could shape?

The human responsibility implied by such questions was immense. James realized that his views put him on the frontier of an uncertain future. But where else could he be? He could retreat back to the settled security of predestination or evolutionary rationalism, but that would be to deny human worth and significance. Would the alternative-publication of his ideas about truth and freewill-be of any use? If the theory were wrong and freewill did not exist, would life be worth living at all?

Chapter 22
20th Century Philosophy

James looked at the manuscript. Even now in the bright spring of 1910, the memory of his decision to believe forty years before cast a shadow across his mind. Was the freedom to choose real or illusory? How could he know that he was right? Could he trust his own judgment?

STUDY QUESTIONS & EXERCISES

I. How did the experiences of William James's early life influence his concept of human freedom?

II. Describe the major changes that took place in American intellectual life in the last half of the nineteenth century. Asses their significance for the development of James's thought.

III. Explain the nature of consciousness according to James.

IV. Trace the origin and define the meaning of the term pragmatism as used by James.

V. Discuss the subjective character of truth in science, as James saw it and as you understand it now.

VI. Do you believe that you have genuine freedom to determine the course of your own life? How do you account for the influence of other potentially determining factors, such as heredity, environment, chance, and God?

Chapter 23
20th Century Philosophy

B. Alfred North Whitehead (1861-1947)

The safest general characterization of the European philosophical tradition is that it consists of a series of footnotes to Plato.

Whitehead

Chapter 23
20th Century Philosophy

Lucien Price, editorial writer for the Boston Globe, sat at his typewriter. It was November 12, 1947. On the previous day, he had taken advantage of the Armistice Day holiday to visit his friend, the retired Harvard philosopher **Alfred North Whitehead.** Now he was recording the conversation from memory, as he had done following their regular visits over the past fifteen years. Price felt that it was perhaps their last visit. Whitehead was eighty-six years old and failing in health. Yet Whitehead's mind and conversation had been lucid as always.

Price thought of publishing the conversations after Whitehead was gone. Whitehead had given permission. But what would be the reaction of the public? In the aftermath of a world war, people were suspicious of science and sure of the sinfulness of humanity. In philosophy, the existentialists with their pessimistic individualism were popular. And in theology the crisis theologians were dominant with their doctrine of a God totally other than and above humankind. How would people respond to this gentle philosopher with his liberal views, and his sense of adventure, and his hope for the future? Could they be interested in a philosophy in harmony with modern science that saw all of reality in a state of continually changing process? And how would they react to

Whitehead's vision of God as involved with humankind and interacting with the world? Price looked at Whitehead's words as he had just typed them and wondered.

Whitehead's Early Life

Alfred North Whitehead was born on February 15, 1861, in the English village of Ramsgate, Kent. His grandfather and father had been successively headmaster of the same private school in the village. A year before Alfred was born, his father was ordained a clergyman in the Church of England and later gave up his school post to serve a rural parish in the area. Whitehead later commented,

> I watched the history of England by my vision of grandfather, Archbishop Tait of Canterbury…and others. When the Baptist minister in the parish was dying, it was my father who read the Bible to him. Such was England in those days, guided by local men with strong mutual antagonisms and intimate community of feeling. This vision was one source of my interest in history, and in education.[156]

The surrounding land also influenced Whitehead's personality. "Geography," he said, "is half of character".[157] Roman forts and Norman churches marked the area. Near Whitehead's home had stood the oak under which the Saxon King Ethelbert had been converted to Christianity by St. Augustine in the sixth century. Young Alfred enjoyed regular trips to Canterbury Cathedral sixteen miles away. He knew the spot where Becket fell in A.D. 1170 and gazed at the tomb of Edward, the Black Prince, who died in A.D. 1376. Whitehead later reflected on the influence of his environment and said, "It shows how historical tradition is handed down by the direct experience of physical surroundings."[158]

Alfred was a frail child, he was taught at home by his father and encouraged to spend much time outdoors in the company of an old gardener. Each year in the late spring he visited his grandmother in London. From her windows overlooking Green Park he often saw Queen Victoria ride by in her carriage, a little figure in black, belonging, for him, to the unquestioned order of the universe.

At the age of fourteen, Alfred went away to Sherborne in Dorsetshire, one of England's oldest schools. There, too, he was surrounded by history. He later remarked,

> We had plenty of evidence that things had been going on for a long time. It never entered into anybody's mind to regard six thousand years seriously as the age of mankind--not because we took up with revolutionary ideas, but because our continuity with nature was a patent, visible fact…There were incredible quantities of fossils about…the stones were built out of fossils, welded together.[159]

His education was classical. The boys at the school read Greek and Roman history and imbibed classical ideals. The prayer, which each boy successively had to read daily in chapel, stated that they were being trained to serve God in Church and State. Roman and especially Greek political philosophies were sufficient for that purpose for boys who were comparatively ignorant of the problems of modern industrial society. Their religion as well came in Greek. Whitehead remembered,

> Thus we read the New Testament in Greek. At school--except in chapel, which did not count--I never heard of anyone reading it in English. It would suggest an uncultivated religious state of mind. We were very religious, but with that moderation natural to people who take their religion in Greek.[160]

In addition to the classics, young Whitehead enjoyed reading poetry and studying mathematics, which was the best taught of the subjects. Sports also played a large part in the school's program. Having overcome his earlier frailty, Whitehead captained the football and cricket teams. These experiences made a deep impression:

> Being tackled at Rugby, there is the Real. Nobody who hasn't been knocked down has the slightest notion of what the Real is…They used to hack at your shins to make you surrender the ball…but the question was how you took it--your own self-creation. Freedom lies in summoning up a mentality which transforms the situations, as against letting organic reactions take their course.[161]

After five years at Sherborne, Whitehead was offered a scholarship to Trinity College, Cambridge, in either classics or mathematics. He chose mathematics, and during his whole undergraduate period he studied only mathematics, pure and applied, and never went inside another lecture room. This intensely narrow concentration in class was complemented by continual conversation with friends, faculty, and alumni every evening after dinner. This discussion covered politics, religion, philosophy, and literature. Although he never formally studied philosophy, Whitehead later noted that by the end of his five years as an undergraduate he nearly knew by heart parts of Kant's *Critique of Pure Reason.*

Whitehead's Career, Phase 1: Cambridge

In 1885, Alfred North Whitehead was given a fellowship at Trinity and a teaching post. He remained there for twenty-five years. It was a period of great personal stability and equally great intellectual stimulation. Darwin's published work was only two decades old. Non-Euclidean approaches to geometry were beginning to be discussed, along with new approaches to logic and attempts at a universal mathematics. And most challenging of all, were new discoveries in physics. Whitehead's reaction was

> We supposed that nearly everything of importance about physics was known…But…the whole science blew up, and the Newtonian physics, which had been supposed to be fixed as the Everlasting Seat, were gone. Oh, they were and still are useful as a way of looking at things, but regarded as a final description of reality, no longer valid. Certitude was gone.[162]

In 1890, Whitehead married Evelyn Willoughby Wade, an Irish girl who had been educated in France and only come to live in England at the age of seventeen. They were devoted to each other, and Whitehead freely acknowledged his wife's influence on his thought.

> The effect of my wife upon my outlook on the world has been so fundamental, that it must be mentioned as an essential factor in my philosophic output. Her vivid life has taught me that beauty, moral and aesthetic, is the aim of existence; and that kindness, and love, and artistic satisfaction are among its modes of attainment.[163]

The years of 1891 to 1898 were formative in many ways for the Whiteheads. Four children were born to them. One died at birth. Later, all three children exemplified the family sense of duty, serving during World War I. The youngest son, Eric, was killed when his plane was shot down over France in March 1918.

Also during this period, the Whiteheads were both somewhat disaffected with Anglicanism. They made a serious and intensive study of the literature of Roman Catholicism, but at the end of seven years of study, no conversion occurred. Whitehead took all his theology books to a local bookstore and sold them.

In 1898, Whitehead's first book was published. A *Treatise on Universal Algebra*. In the next few years, he was deeply involved in community affairs. He argued for the equality of women in a losing debate at the university. And he spoke for the Liberal party at local meetings in the country villages of his district.

Whitehead's Career, Phase 2: London

In 1910, a second period of Whitehead's life abruptly began. At nearly fifty years of age, and with three children, Whitehead and his wife left Cambridge and moved to London. Having no teaching position there Whitehead took a bottle-washing job at London University. In 1911, he began teaching a University College. After four years, he was made a professor at the Imperial College of Science and Technology. During the next dozen years, he became first dean of the faculty of science and then president of the senate of the University of London.

During this period, Whitehead was deeply involved in the technical problems of mathematics and philosophy of science, as well as in the general questions of university education and administration. Regarding mathematics, he pondered two kinds of questions: "Which formal theory best fits the facts of nature?" and "How can mathematics be made understandable to the general public?" He published an extremely technical and innovative three-volume work, *Principia Mathematica*, co-authored with his former student Bertrand Russell, during 1910-1913. In 1911, he issued his elementary and very readable *Introduction to Mathematics*. He produced several books in the philosophy of science including *The Concept of Nature* (1920). In 1922, he published *The Principle of Relativity with Applications to Physical Science* to introduce an alternative mathematical formulation to that of Einstein's theory of relativity.

Whitehead's Career, Phase 3: Harvard

In 1924, Whitehead was sixty-three years old. He faced mandatory retirement as a civil servant in two years. As a complete surprise to him, he received an invitation to join the faculty of Harvard University in the philosophy department. His wife handed him the letter on a dismal London afternoon. After they had both read it, she asked him, "What do you think of it?" To her great surprise he replied, "I would rather do that than anything in the world"[164]

The original offer from Harvard was for a five-year appointment. After two years, Whitehead was asked to stay as long as he was able. During his thirteen-year tenure at Harvard, Whitehead wrote eight books and numerous articles. He also lectured three times a week and gave himself generously to students in conference. He declined to teach students the thoughts of others but used the classroom to develop his own ideas.

Whitehead continually and eagerly learned from others. He offered a joint seminar with the philosopher W. E. Hocking, one of the first examples of "team teaching" in the United States. And he felt that he learned from his students. He said, "It is all nonsense to suppose that the old cannot learn from the young."[165] During all his years at Harvard, the Whiteheads held open house to students one night a week. The fare was hot chocolate, cake, and conversation with both the Whiteheads. Alfred once remarked, "By myself I am only one more professor, but with Evelyn I am first-rate."[166]

While at Harvard, Whitehead's interest in nature led him further to the question of human nature and that, in turn, led him to investigate the nature of all reality. He began to create a new metaphysic, a comprehensive theory of reality. For Whitehead, that meant dealing wit the nature of God. In *Science and the Modern World*, Whitehead challenged "scientific materialism" as being an inadequate description of the richness of reality as we experience it. He wrote, "The only way of mitigating mechanism is by the discovery that it is not mechanism."[167] At the same time, Whitehead confronted static notions of religion. He said, "Religion will not regain its old power until it can face change in the same spirit as does science."[168] The book was immediately hailed by many American thinkers, among them John Dewey, as providing a more adequate framework for relating both scientific facts and personal values.

The next year Whitehead gave four lectures at King's Chapel in Boston, published as Religion in the Making (1926). He argued that religion is seeking a metaphysic. He asserted, “The Buddha gave his doctrine to enlighten the world: Christ gave his life. It is for Christians to discern the doctrine.”[169] Whitehead devoted himself to developing that metaphysic.

Process Thought: Metaphysics

The metaphysic that Whitehead developed was one of process. He sometimes called it a “philosophy of organism.” According to Whitehead, there were three notions that made up the “category of the ultimate.” The first of these notions was *creativity*. The other two notions were the *many* and the *one*. Creativity was central to his understanding of process. It was the ongoing process by which a novel one came into being from the many and then perished back into the many again.

At any moment, the universe consists of a diversity--the many. But, according to Whitehead, "it lies in the nature of things that the many enter into complex unity."[170] The unique *one* that resulted from this moment of unification (which Whitehead called a *concrescence*) was an *actual entity*. This unity differed from a traditional substance, however, in that it was temporary and was interrelated with all other actual entities. These

actual entities were drops of experience, complex and interdependent. They were microcosmic entities like atoms, groups of which, called societies, formed the macrocosmic things of everyday experience--rocks, plants, and people. To call these realities of which the world was made up "drops of experience" was not to imply that they all had consciousness. Consciousness only emerged in very sophisticated societies of entities like the society we call the human brain.

Nor did these actual entities have an enduring or continuous existence. Whitehead defined an actual entity as the unity to be attributed to a particular instance of concrescence. A concrescence was a growing together of remnants of the perishing past into a unique, immediate unity. The process by which entities related to other entities was called *prehending* (grasping) or *feeling* (sympathizing). This was the process by which actual entities incorporated the data of other objects into themselves. That growing together of the separate feelings of diverse entities from the past into one unity of feeling Whitehead termed the satisfaction of the actual entity. In the moment of attaining its satisfaction, an actual entity perished. It now had an objective immortality in that it could become a datum for new instances of concrescence.

Actual entities were not things that had enduring substances, but activities that occurred in a moment and then became a part of the past. Yet, for Whitehead, this was a meaningful description of life:

> Now as a first approximation the notion of life implies a certain absoluteness of self-enjoyment. This must mean a certain immediate individuality, which is a

> complex process of appropriating into a unity of existence the many data presented as relevant by the physical processes of nature. Life implies the absolute, individual self-enjoyment arising out of this process of appropriation. I have, in my recent writings, used the word "prehension" to express this process of appropriation. Also, I have termed each individual act of immediate self-enjoy ment an "occasion of experience" I hold that these unities of existence, these occasions of experience, are the really real things which in their collective unity compose the evolving universe, even plunging into the creative advance.[171]

Process Thought: God

How did God fit into this process? God was not a person, but for Whitehead, God was a conscious, personal reality. Whitehead had written,

> God is an actual entity, and so is the most trivial puff of existence, in far-off empty space. But, though there are gradations of importance, and diversities of function, yet in the principles which actuality exemplifies all are on the same level.[172]

Whitehead was a thoroughgoing empiricist. He accepted only what could be grounded in experience. He said, "God is not to be treated as an exception to all metaphysical principles, invoked to save their collapse. He is their chief exemplification."[173] God, for Whitehead, was the entity in which all others existed, and God was the persuasive power that related entities to each other and guided the whole process toward fulfillment. Whitehead declared, "Everything must be somewhere; and here 'somewhere' is the non-temporal actual entity…the primordial mind of God."[174]

God had not one nature but two: a bipolar nature. God's primordial nature was a non-temporal actual entity conceptually valuing the timeless realm of eternal objects. But God's consequent nature physically prehended, or incorporated into itself, and preserved the actual entities of the temporal world. God related entities to each other on a grand order as God integrated the physical feelings of God's consequent nature with the conceptual feelings of God's primordial nature. Whitehead wrote of God,

> He saves the world as it passes into the immediacy of his own life. It is the judgment of a tenderness which loses nothing that can be saved. It is also the judgment of a wisdom which uses what in the temporal world is mere wreckage.[175]

God was not before all creation, rather, but was with all creation. According to Whitehead, God was "that factor in the universe whereby there is importance, value, and ideal beyond the actual."[176] God set before each actual entity an initial subjective aim, a vision of what it might become. This initial subjective aim offered an ideal growth on the part of the entity that would result in the kind of world filled with novelty and yet order that would provide a maximum intensity of satisfaction for God. For Whitehead, "all order is therefore aesthetic order, and the aesthetic order is derived from the immanence of God."[177]

Process Thought: Evil

What of instability, disorder, and evil? How could he reconcile his understanding of God with the evil in the world? Whitehead recognized that evil was a fact in the world. He wrote, "Now evil is exhibited in physical suffering, mental suffering, and loss of the higher experience in favour of the lower experience." [178] Things that we may call evil might be good in themselves but had the character of destructive agents among things greater than themselves. Whitehead responded to the problem of evil by claiming that God could not prevent the occurrence of evil because God was not all-powerful. God was good and persuasive and sought to bring order from instability and constructive outcomes from evil. But God did not exercise coercive control over reality. According to Whitehead, "God has in his nature the knowledge of evil, of pain, and of degradation, but it is there as overcome with what is good."[179] This overcoming of evil by good within God's nature was what Whitehead called the "kingdom of heaven." However, God's concepts of goodness and morality were necessarily different from those of human beings. According to Whitehead, God as creative and persuasive love was a "little oblivious" as to morals. What was good from God's perspective did not always seem good to persons. According to Whitehead's vision of God: "He does not create the world, he saves it; or, more accurately, he is the poet of the world, with tender patience leading it by his vision of truth, beauty and goodness."[180] For Whitehead, therefore, "The power of God is the worship He inspires."[181] We perceive God in the world not in the image of a ruling Caesar, or a moral absolutist, nor an unmoved mover, but in that "brief Galilean vision of humility" that "dwells upon the tender elements in the world, which slowly and in quietness operate by love." [182]

Reflection

Lucien Price looked up from his typewriter and paused. Whitehead's health was failing and he probably would not live much longer. The time for publishing their conversations might be coming soon. Price mused over the meaning of possibly his last conversation with Whitehead.

> It was a mistake, as the Hebrews tried, to conceive of God as creating the world from the outside, at one go. An all-foreseeing Creator, who could have made the world as we find it now-what could we think of such a being? Foreseeing every thing and yet putting it into all sorts of imperfections to redeem which it was necessary to send his only son to suffer torture and hideous death; outrageous ideas. The Hellenic religion was a better approach; the Greeks conceived of creation as going on everywhere all the time within the universe…
>
> God is in the world, or nowhere, creating continually in us and around us. This creative principle is everywhere, in animate and so-called inanimate matter, in the ether, water, earth, human hearts. But this creation is a continuing process, and "the process is itself the actuality," since no sooner do you arrive than you start on a fresh journey. In so far as man partakes of this creative process does he partake of the divine, of God, and that participation is his immortality, reducing the question of whether his individuality survives death of the body to an estate of irrelevancy. His true destiny as co-creator in the universe is his dignity and his grandeur.[183]

How would people in a post-war world respond to Whitehead's adventurous vision? Would they affirm Whitehead's philosophy of science, which held that all of reality was in a constant process of becoming and perishing? Could they accept the idea of a patient and persuasive God in process of intimate interaction with people and the world? Price wondered as he pulled the paper from his typewriter.

STUDY QUESTIONS & EXERCISES

I. How did Whitehead deal with the problem of change? Compare his views with those of the following early Greek philosophers:

a. The Pre-Socratics
b. Plato
c. Aristotle

II. To what extent was Whitehead's thought rooted in his life experience?

a. Select central elements of his philosophy and show evidence from his life experience that helps to explain them
b. Pick significant experiences in his life and seek embodiments of those expe riences in his philosophy

III. Outline Whitehead's metaphysical system. Be sure to define terms such as

a. Actual entity
b. Creativity
c. Prehending
d. Satisfaction
e. Objective immortality

IV. Describe Whitehead's concept of a dipolar God and God's relationship to the world.

V. What role did esthetics play in Whitehead's philosophy?

VI. Discuss Whitehead's response to the problem of evil. Consider the following issues:

a. In what ways does Whitehead's response solve traditional problems?
b. What rational needs does Whitehead's view leave unmet?
c. What is your own solution to the problem of evil? Argue for its adequacy.

Chapter 24
20th Century Philosophy

C. Ludwing Wittgenstein

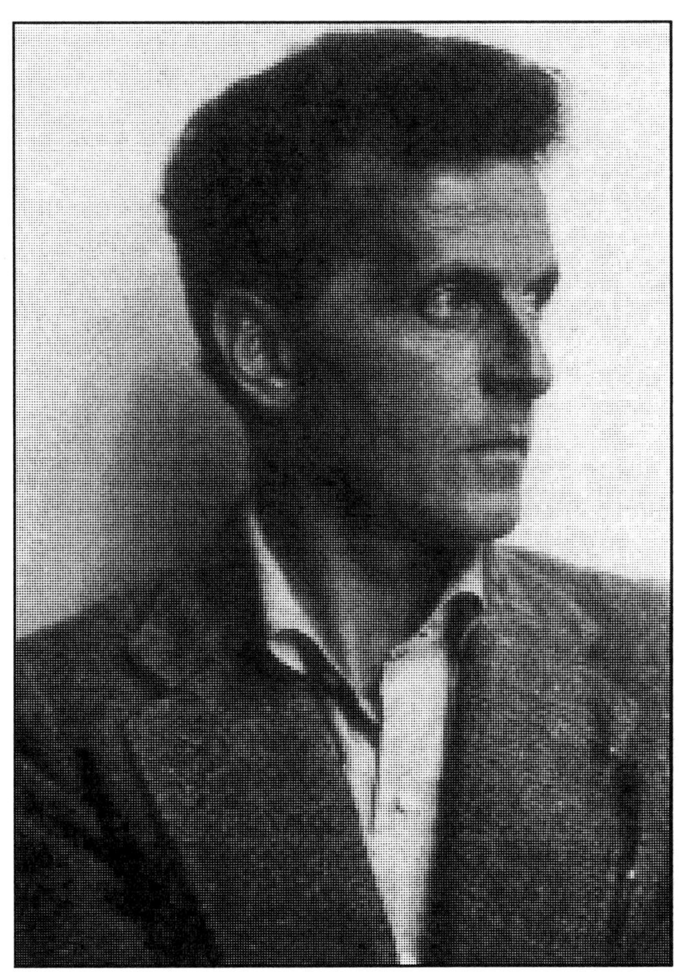

At some point one has to pass from explanation to mere description.

Wittgenstein

Chapter 24
20th Century Philosophy

Wittgenstein was enraged! How dare a journal accuse him of keeping his work a secret! Since 1930, for seventeen years, he had given lectures almost every year at Cambridge. Surely that was not the behavior of a man trying to keep a secret! It was true that his **Tractatus Logico-Philosophicus** was the only thing he had ever published. But he had never felt satisfied with any of his later work.

Showing the accusing article to some of his friends, Wittgenstein asked them to publish a reply. When they refused, saying they did not know how to answer the criticism, Wittgenstein became even angrier. Feeling forsaken and unfairly attacked, he considered having the manuscripts of the Philosophical Investigations published. That would prove that he was not trying to hide anything. But was he ready for that? Having rejected his earlier "picture" theory of language, how he could retain the distinction between factual language and religious and ethical language? How could he keep religious and ethical language safe from analysis? Given these reservations, Wittgenstein wondered whether or not he should publish.

Austria-Hungary

In the nineteenth century, Austria-Hungary was one of the most powerful countries in the world. Its solid constitution, history of stability, and large territory, made it one of the leaders of Europe. Its music and art were unrivaled throughout the world. Its industrial might was second only to that of the British Empire.

But as the nineteenth century came to an end and the twentieth century began, Vienna, the capital city of Austria-Hungary was faced with serious problems. The constitution that had remained solid throughout the nationalist struggles of the Czechs, Rumanians, and Slavs now proved inflexible. Rapid economic growth and continued racial turmoil shook the nation. A series of scandals left the population without trust in their leaders. The values of the past century were being discarded with nothing left to replace them. In music, people such as Arnold Schönberg were discarding the musical forms of the past. In art and architecture, conventional ornamentation was being replaced by bizarre decoration. In ethics, there was no recognized common ground for the discussion of personal or social morality.

Early Life

It was into this period of decline that Wittgenstein was born in 1889. Wittgenstein's family was, in many ways, a reflection of the Austro-Hungarian society. His father, Karl Wittgenstein, was a stern, unbending man who had become a millionaire in the Austro-Hungarian steel industry. In addition to his keen business sense, Karl also had a deep love and appreciation for music. Johannes Brahms, Gustaf Mahler, and Pablo Casals were frequent houseguests of the Wittgensteins.

Despite his love of music, Karl insisted that his five sons follow him into the business world. When his eldest son, Hans, asked that he be allowed to pursue a career in music, Karl refused. Following a prolonged argument over the matter, Hans fled to North America and finally killed himself. Karl's second son Rudi, made a similar request; and receiving the same answer, he too committed suicide.

In 1913, Karl died of cancer. His third son, Kurt, took his own life in World War I, preferring death to capture. Karl's fourth son, Paul, despite losing his right arm, became a successful concert pianist. Maurice Ravel's famous "Concerto for the Left Hand" was written specifically for Paul.

The women in the Wittgenstein family were equally as gifted (and equally as strong-willed) as the men. Ludwig's mother, Leopoldine, was an accomplished pianist. His eldest sister, Hermine, was an excellent painter. The youngest of his three sisters, Margarete, was the rebel of the family. A close friend of Sigmund Freud, she helped Freud escape from Austria when Hitler took over.[184]

The Wittgenstein family, with all its talents and conflicts, had an especially strong influence on the young Ludwig. Because Karl was a firm believer in private tutoring, Ludwig was educated at home. It was not until he was fourteen years of age that Ludwig spent much time away from the family residence.

Having shown great promise in the field of engineering (at age ten, he built a working sewing machine out of matchsticks), Wittgenstein was enrolled in the Linz Realschule in 1904. He arrived at the school at about the same time that another Austro-Hungarian was leaving: Adolf Hitler. Although he primarily studied engineering, Wittgenstein's course of study led him into philosophical and ethical questions. In the Austria-Hungary of that time, many educated people discussed philosophy as it related to their own particular fields.

Wittgenstein did not have any "formal training" in the classical problems of philosophy, although he was very impressed with the writing of Søren Kierkegaard. But the culture in which he lived provided him with a set of problems and a conception of philosophy which he continued to explore for the rest of his life.

After leaving Linz in 1906, Wittgenstein spent two years studying in Berlin. In 1908, he went to the University of Manchester in England to study aerodynamics.

While designing a propeller, Wittgenstein became interested in mathematics and eventually went to Cambridge in 1911 to study the subject under Bertrand Russell. Russell recalled one of his early encounters with Wittgenstein:

> At the end of his first term at Cambridge he came to me and said, "Will you please tell me whether I am a complete idiot or not?" I replied, "My dear fellow, I don't know. Why are you asking me?" He said, "Because if I am a complete idiot, I shall become an aeronaut; but, if not, I shall become a philosopher." I told him, to write me something during the vacation on some philosophical subject and I would then tell him whether he was a complete idiot or not. At the beginning of the following term he brought me the fulfillment of this suggestion. After reading only one sentence, I said to him, "No, you must not become an aeronaut."[185]

Following two years at Cambridge, Wittgenstein went to a remote region of Norway. He remained there, living in isolation until 1914 when war broke out. He enlisted as a volunteer in the Austrian artillery. While serving on the eastern front, he kept notebooks on various philosophical issues. These notebooks formed the basis for the *Tractatus Logico-Philosophicus.* Following his capture by the Italian army in 1917, Wittgenstein managed to complete the work. While still a prisoner of war, he had a copy of the *Tractatus* sent to Russell, who received it enthusiastically. The work was finally published in 1921.

Tractatus: Theory of Language

In the *Tractatus*, Wittgenstein portrayed philosophy as an activity, not a set of theories. In the nineteenth century, philosophers such as Kant and Hegel had tried to present systems that would account for all of reality. But these systems were often contradictory and antiscientific. According to Wittgenstein, most of the problems of philosophy could be traced to a misuse of language. As he put it in one of his early notebooks, "Philosophy gives no pictures of reality and can neither conform nor confute scientific investigations. Philosophy teaches us the logical form of propositions: that is its fundamental task."[186]

Throughout his life, Wittgenstein continued to hold on to this conception of philosophy. Thirty years later he wrote, "Philosophy is a battle against the bewitchment of our intelligence by means of language."[187]

Because most problems in philosophy were related to language, the greater part of the Tractatus was devoted to language; its nature and relation to the world. Wittgenstein presented this relationship in terms of a "picture theory of meaning." According to Wittgenstein, language consisted of statements or propositions that picture the world. Just as a picture had something in common with that which is pictured, language had a logical form in common with the world it pictured. This logical form was obscured by ordinary language. The job of philosophy was to clear up this obscure language and ultimately to develop a language that more perfectly pictured the world.

This "clearing up" of ordinary language was done by analysis. Propositions were made up of names (which stand for objects) and a logical form. Together, these names and the logical form created a picture. This picture was the meaning of the proposition.

The job of analysis was to find these names and clearly show the logical form. So, for example, the proper way to analyze the proposition "John is going to the store" was to discover what objects the names *John* and *the store* stood for and clearly show the logical form of "__________ is going to ____________."

Tractatus: Religious and Ethical Language

This method of analysis allowed Wittgenstein to make a sharp distinction between factual language, on the one hand, and religious and ethical language, on the other. Factual propositions were those, which could be analyzed, because they "pictured" a state of affairs in the world. Religious propositions, however, did not "picture" anything in the world. Terms such as *God* or Being were not really names. They did not point to anything. Wittgenstein explained "God does not reveal himself in the world."[188] Similarly, ethical assertions could not be analyzed. "The nature of the Good has nothing to do with the facts, and so cannot be explained by a proposition."[189] Wittgenstein wrote.

The separation of religious and ethical issues from philosophical analysis was fundamental for Wittgenstein. Living in a culture where values were constantly being attacked, he felt the need to remove values from the realm of criticism. Following in the footsteps of Kierkegaard, he made religion and ethics a matter of "wordless faith."[190] No longer were religious and ethical concerns subject to analysis. According to Wittgenstein, one could not even ask religious or ethical questions about the problems of life. As he stated near the end of the *Tractatus*,

> When the answer cannot be put into words, neither can the question be put into words. The riddle does not exist…The solution of the problem of life is seen in the vanishing of the question.[191]

But what about the propositions in the *Tractatus* itself? The book claimed that one could not use language to talk about the nature of reality. But to say that was to make a statement about the nature of reality! Wittgenstein was aware of this problem. He said,

> My propositions serve as elucidations in the following way: anyone who unders tands me eventually recognizes them as nonsensical, when he has used them--as steps--to climb up beyond them.[192]

He likened his work to a "ladder" that was discarded or kicked away once it had been used to climb to a correct picture of the world. Still, Wittgenstein felt that his book presented "on all essential points, the final solution of the problems."[193] However, he also felt that these solutions did not accomplish much. As he put it, "The value of this work consists [in showing] how little is achieved when these problems are solved."[194]

In 1919, following the war, Wittgenstein gave up philosophy, gave away his inheritance, and went to work teaching children in Upper Austria. Having given the "final solution" to the problems of philosophy, he believed that his philosophical work was completed.

Logical Positivism

The end of World War I destroyed the Austro-Hungarian Empire. The only remaining vestige of its former greatness was it music, art, and learning. In this period of political and social anarchy, a group of scientists and philosophers began to hold regular discussions. Later known as the "**Vienna Circle**" the group sought an account of science that would include both mathematics and sensory experience. **Ernst Mach**, **Moritz Schlick**, **Rudolf Carnap**, **Kurt Godel**, and **Friedrich Waismann** were all members of the group. The Vienna Circle developed a philosophy called "**logical positivism**" based on the thinking of David Hume and Ludwig Wittgenstein. The positivists began by using Hume's "empirical criterion of meaning." Hume had said that ideas only had meaning if they were copies of sense impressions. The positivists took this criterion and, using Wittgenstein, modified it slightly, developing the "verification criterion of meaning."

The positivists claimed that the "meaning of a proposition is its method of verification." To find the meaning of the proposition "That cow is brown," one had to discover how to verify it. Presumably one could verify it by going out into the pasture and looking to see if the cow was, in fact, brown. The proposition, then, meant something about physical cows and the color, brown. The appropriate kind of scientist should then verify the truth of the statement. The philosopher's task was simply to identify whether the proposition was meaningful; that is, whether there was a means by which it could be verified.

According to the positivists, there were two general types of propositions that were meaningful; propositions such as "That cow is brown," which could be verified empirically, and propositions such as "All unmarried men are bachelors," which were logically necessary. This was similar to Wittgenstein's picture theory of meaning. Like Wittgenstein, the logical positivists looked for names and logical form. They attempted to develop a perfect language that would clearly reflect the world. They also excluded religious and ethical propositions, maintaining that propositions about God, being, the good, and so on were meaningless because they were neither logically necessary nor empirically verifiable.

The logical positivists were similar to Wittgenstein in another way, as well. Like the propositions in the *Tractatus*, the propositions the logical positivists used to describe their philosophy did not meet their own criterion. Their basic assumption, "All meaningful statements must be either empirically verifiable or logically necessary," was itself neither "empirically verifiable" nor "logically necessary." The standard that they set up for meaningful propositions was not itself a meaningful proposition.

The Return to Philosophy

While working as a schoolteacher, Wittgenstein discovered that the ordinary language of his students was more rich and complex than he had previously realized. Without knowing anything about the logical form of propositions, his students were quite capable of communicating clearly.

Following six years as a schoolteacher, Wittgenstein resumed his studies in philosophy. In 1926, while working on a house that he had designed for his sister he attended the meetings of the Vienna Circle. New questions about language began to fascinate him. In 1929, he returned to Cambridge and, after submitting the already famous *Tractatus* as a doctoral dissertation, he became a research fellow.

For the rest of his life, Wittgenstein gave lectures almost yearly at Cambridge. One of his students gave the following account of those lectures:

> He nearly always held them in his own room or in the college rooms of a friend. He had no manuscript of notes. He thought before the class. The impression was of tremendous concentration. The exposition usually led to a question, to which the audience was supposed to suggest an answer. The answers in turn became starting points for new thoughts leading to new questions. It depended on the audience, to a great extent, whether the discussion became fruitful and whether the connecting thread was kept in sight from beginning to end of a lecture and from one lecture to another.[195]

After these intense sessions, Wittgenstein would often go to the movies. He insisted that Westerns were the only movies worth seeing because they portrayed the struggle of good versus evil in such a clear and simple way. He also enjoyed reading detective stories. Once he remarked that he could not understand how anyone who enjoyed detective stories could stand to read the philosophical journal *Mind*.

In general, Wittgenstein disliked professional philosophy. He once said to a friend,

> What is the use of studying philosophy if all that it does for you is to enable you to talk with some plausibility about some abstruse questions of logic, etc, and if it does not improve your thinking about the important questions of everyday life.[196]

During the early 1930s, Wittgenstein wrote a lot but did not publish. By this time, he had ceased to believe in a picture theory of language and was no longer interested in finding a perfect language hidden in the obscurity of ordinary usage. In place of thinking about language and pictures, he began to explore the relationship between language and games. In 1935, he returned to Norway and lived in isolation while working on the ***Philosophical Investigations***.

Philosophical Investigations: Theory of Language

The basic thesis of the Investigations was that meaningful language occurred in the life of human beings as they did the things that human beings do. The meaning of a given word was no longer to be found by showing how it was a part of a proposition that pictured the world. Rather, "the meaning of a word is its use in the language."[197]

The various situations of "**forms of Life**" in which human beings use language provided the context for what Wittgenstein called "**language games**." Just as there was no one characteristic that was common to all games, so also there was no theory that could explain all the uses of language. Wittgenstein explained,

> Instead of producing something common to all that we call language, I am saying that these phenomena have no one thing in common which makes us use the same word for all, but that they are related to one another in many different ways. And it is because of this relationship, or these relationships, that we call them all "language."
>
> Consider for example the proceeding that we call "games." I mean board-games, card-games, ball-games, Olympic games, and so on. What is common to them all? -Don't say: "There had to be something in common, or they would not be called 'games'"-but *look and see* whether there is anything common to all. For if you look at them you will not see something that is common to all, but similarities, relationships, and a whole series of them at that.[198]

For example, the proposition "that cow is brown" must be analyzed in its context. Was the proposition intended to make a scientific observation, or was it simply being used to distinguish one cow from the next? In the first case, what might be called the "language game of twentieth century zoology," there was a need for precision and accuracy not necessary in the second case, "the language game of farming." Although the proposition remained formally (structurally) the same in both cases, and the means of verifying the proposition were the same, it was clear that the zoologist meant something

quite different from the farmhand. The two uses of the proposition arose out of different contexts, different "forms of life."

Wittgenstein also maintained in the *Investigations* that there was no need for a "perfect" language. Rather than trying to sift out the names and logical form of language, one should examine the forms of life out of which language arose. All language was suited to the particular needs it served, so no sifting or perfecting process was needed, ordinary language was already perfectly suited to express the ideas people wanted to express. Wittgenstein declared,

> We are not striving after an ideal, as if our ordinary vague sentences had not yet got a quite unexceptionable sense, and a perfect language awaited construction by us. On the other hand it seems clear that where there is sense there must be perfect order. So there must be perfect order even in the vaguest sentence.[199]

The only time problems arose was when propositions were taken out of their particular language game and applied to a context for which they were not intended. For instance, when mathematical precision was called for in history or sociology, problems were bound to arise. Mathematical precision was part of the language game of the natural sciences but not of the liberal arts; consequently liberal arts could not be judged with the same precision by the standards of another language game. The rules of basketball could not be judged by the rules of chess, yet both were valid games with proper rules.

Philosophical Investigations: Religious and Ethical Language

The "game" theory of language left Wittgenstein with a major problem. The "picture" theory of the *Tractatus* had made a complete distinction between religious and ethical language on the one hand and factual language on the other hand. Because religious and ethical words did not picture anything in the world, they were without meaning. They were outside the world of facts, and hence, outside the world of analysis and critique.

But what happened to this distinction in the "game" theory of the *Philosophical Investigations*? The fact that at least some people apparently understood the use of words such as *God* and *good* seemed to indicate that they were a meaningful part of language. Such words seemed to belong to the "language games" of religion and ethics. Religious and ethical terms did not need to be "purged" in order to form a more perfect language.

What then was to become of the original absolute distinction? Wittgenstein attempted to deal with this problem by claiming that religious and ethical propositions were usually taken out of their contexts. In fact, religious and ethical propositions were usually so far removed from their respective contexts or language games that they were meaningless. As Wittgenstein explained,

> Suppose someone said: "What do you believe, Wittgenstein? Are you a skep tic? Do you know whether you will survive death?" I would really, this is a fact, say, "I can't say. I don't know," because I haven't any clear idea what I'm say ing when I'm saying, "I don't cease to exist," etc.[200]

(For a comparison of the basic ideas of the *Tractatus* and the *Investigations*, see the table at the end of this chapter)

The Return to Cambridge

Wittgenstein returned to Cambridge in 1937 and was appointed a full professor in 1939. But before he could begin teaching World War II began. Wittgenstein volunteered to work as a hospital orderly in London and later in Newcastle-upon-Tyne.

Following the war, Wittgenstein returned to his teaching post. He soon became depressed over his students' continual misunderstanding of his lectures. When he taught that words were to be understood in their context apart from "fixed" meanings, many students took it as an excuse for sloppiness in their own thinking. Furthermore, Wittgenstein was distressed about the *Philosophical Investigations*. Although he was close to completion, he still pondered the use of religious and ethical language. As he wrote to a friend in 1945, "My book is gradually nearing its final form…and the truth is: It's pretty lousy. (Not that I could improve on it essentially if I had tried for another 100 years.)" [201]

The Decision

In the winter of 1947, a literary and critical journal published an article giving a popular account of current British philosophers. In the article, Wittgenstein's later work was said to be basically unknown.

The insinuation that he kept his work a secret angered Wittgenstein. He considered his yearly lectures to be a kind of publication. As he reread the article, Wittgenstein considered the possible responses. He could immediately publish his *Philosophical Investigations*, but the problems of religious and ethical language still bothered him. He could continue to work on the manuscript and ignore the article, but would more time really help? What should he do?

Comparison of Wittgenstein's Early and Later Work

1. Similarities
   - a. Philosophy is an activity, not a set of theories.
   - b. Object of philosophy is to remove problems.
   - c. Primary interest is with the nature of language and its relation to philosophy.
   - d. Philosophy is concerned to show the separation between religious and ethical language on the one hand and factual language on the other.

2. Differences

		Tractatus (early) (1918-approx. 1930)	Investigations (later) (approx. 1930-1951)
a.	ultimate data	Names (which stand for objects) and logical forms	Forms of life in which games are embedded
b.	meaningful propositions	Only those which picture a state of affairs in the world	Those which arise out of the ordinary uses of words
c.	Religious And ethical Propositions	Meaningless because they are not pictures of states	Not completely clear: apparently to be understood in the context in which they are used

STUDY QUESTIONS & EXERCISES

I. Trace the development of Wittgenstein's views of language to his life situation and relationship with people. Illustrate your answer.

II. Outline the main principles contained in Wittgenstein's Tractatus Logico-Philosophicus and contrast them with Wittgenstein's later ideas concerning language found in Philosophical Investigations.

III. Discuss Wittgenstein's attitude towards metaphysics in both his earlier and later work.

IV. What is the meaning of the word game? Give examples. Divide the class into two teams and have one team define game according to Tractatus and the other team defend the view of game found in Philosophical Investigations.

V. Put yourself in the place of a logical positivist who has gone into a church and hear a minister preach that "God is Love." How would you the positivist react? Do the same simulation using a linguistic analyst as the hearer. How do you personally respond when you hear such proclamations as "God is love?"

Chapter 25
20th Century Philosophy

D. Jean Paul Sartre (1905-1980)

There are two kinds of existentialists, first, those who are Christian...and on the other hand the atheistic existentialists, among whom...I class myself. What they have in common is that they think that existence precedes essence, or, if you prefer, that subjectivity must be the turning point.

Sartre

Chapter 25
20th Century Philosophy

Existentialism

Sartre was one of those writers for whom a certain philosophical position was at the centre of their artistic being. Drawn from many sources, for example, Husserl's idea of a free, fully intentional consciousness and Heidegger's existentialism, the existentialism Sartre formulated and popularized is profoundly original. Its popularity and that of its author reached a climax in the forties, and Sartre's theoretical writings as well as his novels and plays constitute one of the main inspirational sources of modern literature. In his philosophical view atheism is taken for granted; the "loss of God" is not mourned. Life is absurd. Man is condemned to be free, a freedom from all authority, which he may seek to evade, distort, and deny but which he will have to face if he is to become a moral being. The meaning of man's life is not established before his existence. Once the terrible freedom is acknowledged, man has to make this meaning himself, has to commit himself to a role in this world, he has to commit his freedom. And this attempt to make oneself is futile without the "camaraderie" of others.

Early years

Jean-Paul Sartre was born June 21, 1905 in Paris, the only child of Jean-Baptiste and Anne-Marie Sartre, two individuals from distinguished families. Jean-Baptiste Sartre was the son of Dr. Eymard Sartre, a noted country doctor in the Dordogne region of France. Eymard had written several medical texts; he published his first work in his early twenties. Sartre's mother was the first cousin of Albert Schweitzer, the famous German missionary.

At the age of eight, Sartre received some puppets from his mother. These gifts inspired Sartre to write scripts and stage shows. He slowly gained a small group of friends, or at least children willing to tolerate him in return for entertainment. Sartre enjoyed the attention associated with his shows; he had learned that people like a performer.

Germany declared war in August 1914. Sartre, like most French citizens, was caught up in the frenzy of nationalism. In October of 1914, Sartre even wrote a short story about a young French private who captures the Kaiser. To prove he is superior to the German, the young Frenchman challenges the Kaiser to a fistfight and wins. Jean-Paul was writing constantly; he felt a sense of power and control while writing.

In the fall of 1915, Jean-Paul enrolled at Lycée Henri IV, a well-regarded school. At the school, Sartre demonstrated an abundance of wit. One instructor noted that Sartre possessed an excellent mind, but lacked mental discipline; Jean-Paul did not refine his thoughts. This criticism mirrors that of scholars who now study Sartre's works, they claim this is clearly a personality trait Sartre never outgrew. His mind would race from topic to topic, never focused long enough to refine a thought.

Sartre, after receiving a doctorate in philosophy, went on to teach at LeHavre, Lyon and Paris. During WWII he was active in the French resistance, and at the first of the war he was taken prisoner for nine months. He gave up teaching after the war and devoted all his time to writing. In 1964 he declined the Nobel Prize for Literature. He emerged as the leading light of the left wing, the supporters of which could be found at the *Cafe de Flore* on the left bank. (Sartre eventually broke with the communists.)

He was probably the most famous representative of existentialism, along with Camus and de Beauvoir. Existentialism is a philosophical approach that emphasizes, among other things, the ultimacy of human freedom. In his later writings, however, Sartre attempted to combine the individualism of his existentialist work with a form of Marxism, which stresses the collective aspects of human existence.

As Sartre explained in his autobiography, (1963; Eng. trans., 1964), his career as an author was a response to his childhood experiences of rejection. He was short and eye sided and because of this "others" usually rejected him. By the time he graduated from the Ecole Normal Superieure, Paris, in 1929, he had met Simone de Beauvoir, who became his lifelong companion as well as his intellectual associate. Sartre taught in various secondary schools, until 1945, after which time he devoted himself exclusively to writing and editing the journal Les Temps Modernes (Modern Times). He was a key figure among the French intellectuals who resisted the Nazi occupation.

The Mind of Sartre

Sartre conceives that it is very distressing that God does not exist, because all possibility of finding values in a heaven of ideas disappears along with Him; there can no longer be a priori of God, since there is no infinite and perfect consciousness to think it. Nowhere is it written that the Good exists, that we must be honest, that we must not lie, because the fact is that we are on a plane where there are only men. Dostoyevsky said, "If God didn't exist, everything would be possible." That is the very starting point of existentialism. Indeed, Sartre believed that everything is permissible if God does not exist, and as a result man is forlorn, because neither within him nor without does he find anything to cling to.

Basic Existensialism

Jean Paul Sartre

Humankind is the only known animal, according to earth-bound existentialists, that defines itself through the act of living. In other words, first a man or woman exists, and then the individual spends a lifetime changing his or her essence. Without life there can be no meaning; the search for meaning in existentialism is the search for self. In other words, we define ourselves by living; suicide would indicate one have chosen to have no meaning. Existentialists believe in living and in fact fighting for life. Camus, Sartre, and even Nietzsche were involved in various wars because they believed so passionately in fighting for the survival of their nations and peoples.

According to Sartre, it is our sad fate to find ourselves trapped in a world that makes no sense. Whether we like it or not, this is a fact and it's inescapable. We try to make sense of the world to the best of our abilities. Yet, the world does not make sense. The world is simply as it is. There is no explanation we can encounter to uncover for its existence or nature.

The next question would be: What should we do? We are aware that we are free to do what we like, anything at all. The world then, is arbitrary and senseless. It does not matter what we do, for what real difference could it make? The only reality we have is the fact that we are free to make choices, but can find no way to decide what to do. There are no guides, or certainties in this absurd world into which we have been thrust.

Yet, we must choose, we must choose, for not to do so is to remain forever in the "nausea of existence." We must take the risk and choose and act. Even though our choices might prove to be disastrous. However, no other path exists to an "authentic" life and existence.

In a world where there is no God, nothing more can be done than to make one's own decisions and heroically live by them. Any other life is no life at all. Some critics have said about this kind of existentialism: "They have abandoned philosophy for literature." Philosophy has always been marked by careful, logical analysis. In the writings of Sartre, we find emotion, exhortation, passion, pessimism, and even traces of nihilism. Yet, in this passion we find a very real world. A common property of existentialists is the concept of the absurd. This feeling follows from the realization that we inhabit a world devoid of human values. A world in which things simply are without having sufficient reason for being as they are, a world we try to make sense out of it.

Sartre is quoted to have said: "The sense of the world must lie outside the world. Everything in the world is accidental, arbitrary, and beyond good and evil. It is impossible for there to be propositions of ethics."

Sartre believed that there is no grand design to the world and no meaning to it. It has no special plan or destiny. The same is true for humanity. Existence precceeds essence. Instead of this fact defeating us, we should make the most of what there is, trusting in ourselves.

Existentialism and Humanism

Jean Paul Sartre

What is this that we call existentialism? … Actually it is the least shocking doctrine, and the most austere; it is intended strictly for technicians, and philosophers. However, it can easily be defined. What makes the matter complicated is that there are two kinds of existentialists; the first who are Christian, and among whom I will include Jaspers and Gabriel Marcel, of the Catholic faith; and also, the atheistic existentialists among whom we must include Heidegger, and also the French existentialists, and myself. What they have in common is simply the fact that they think that existence precedes essence, or, if you wish, that we must start from subjectivity....

What does it mean here that existence precedes essence? It means that man exists first, experiences himself, spring up in the world, and that he defines himself afterwards. If man, as the existentialist conceives him, is not definable, it is because he is nothing at first. He will only be [something] afterwards, and he will be as he will have made himself. So, there is no human nature, since there is no God to think it. Man simply is, not only as he conceives himself, but as he determines himself, and as he conceives himself after existing, as he determines himself after this impulse toward existence; man is nothing than that what he makes himself. This is the first principle of existentialism. It is also what we call subjectivity.... Man is at first a project which lives subjectively, instead of being a moss, a decaying thing, or cauliflower; nothing exists prior to this project; nothing is intelligible in the heavens, and man will at first be what he has planned to be. Not what he may wish to be.... If existence really precedes essence, man is responsible for what he is. Thus, the first step of existentialism is to show every man [to be] in control of what he is and to make him assume total responsibility for his existence. And, when we say that man is responsible to himself, we do not [only] mean that man is responsible for his precise individuality, but that he is responsible for all men.... When we say that man determines himself, we understand that each of us chooses himself, but by that we mean also that in choosing himself he chooses all men. Indeed, there is not one of our actions which, increasing the man we wish to be, does not [also] create at the same time and image of the man we think we ought to be. To choose to be this or that, is to affirm at the sum time the value of what we choose, for we can never choose level; what we choose is always the good, and nothing can be good of us without [also] being [good] for all....

This enables us to understand what some rather lofty words, like anguish, abandonment, despair mean. As you will see, it is quite simple. First, what do we mean by anguish? The existentialist readily declares that man is [in] anguish. That means this: the man who comits himself and who realizes that it is not only himself that he chooses, but [that] he is also a lawgiver choosing at the same time [for] all mankind, would not know how to escape the feeling of his total and profound responsibility. Certainly, many men are not anxious; but we claim that they are hiding their anguish, that they are fleeing from it; certainly, many men believe [that] in acting [they] commit only themselves, and when one says to them: "what if everyone acted like that?" they shrug their shoulder and reply: "everyone does not act like that." But really, one should always ask himself: "what would happen if everyone did the same?" and we cannot escape this troubling thought except by a kind of bad faith. The man who lies and who excuses himself by declaring: "everyone does not act like that," is someone who is ill at east with his conscience, because the act of lying implies a universal value attributed to the lie. Even when it conceals itself, anguish appears….

And when we speak of abandonment, an expression dear to Heidegger, we mean only that God does not exist, and that we must draw out the consequences of this to the very end…. The existentialist, on the contrary, thinks that it is very troubling that God does not exist, for with him disappears every possibility of finding values in an intelligible heaven; there can no longer be any good a priori, since there is no infinite and perfect consciousness to think it; it is not written anywhere that the good exists, that we must be honest, that we must not lie, since precisely we exist in a context where there are only men. Dostoyevsky has written, "If God did not exist, everything would be allowed." This is the point of departure for existentialism. Indeed, everything is allowed if God does not exist, and consequently man is abandoned, because neither in himself nor beyond himself does he find any possibility of clinging on [to something]. At the start, he finds no excuses. If, indeed, existence precedes essence, we will never be able to give an explanation by reference to human nature [which is] given and give; in other words, there is no determinism, and is free, man is freedom. Moreover, if God does not exist, we do not find before us any values or orders which will justify our conduct. Some we have neither behind us nor before us is the luminous realm of values, any justifications or excuses. We are alone, without excuses. It is what I will express by saying that man is condemned to be free. Condemned, because has not created himself, and nevertheless, in other respects [he is] free, because one [he is] cast into the world, he is responsible for everything that he does…

To give you an example which [will] allow [you] to understand abandonment better, I will cite the case of one of my students who came to see me in the following circumstances. His father was on bad terms with his mother, and moreover, was inclined to be a collaborator. His older brother had been killed in the German offensive of 1940, and this young man, with feelings somewhat primitive but generous, wanted to avenge him. His mother lived alone with him, quite distressed by the semi betrayal of his father and by the death of her eldest son, and found consolation only in him. This young man had the choice, at that time, between leaving for England and enlisting in the Free French Forces—that is to say, to forsake his mother—or to stay near his mother and help her [to] live. He fully realizes that this woman lived only for him and that his disappearance—and perhaps his death—would cast her into despair. He also realized that, in reality, [and] concretely, each action that the performed with regard to his mother had its surety in the sense that the was helping her to live, whereas each action that he might perform in order to leave and fight was an ambiguous action which could be lost in the stands, to answer no purpose. For example, leaving for England, he might remain indefinitely in a Spanish camp, while passing through Spain he might arrive in England or in Algiers and be placed in the office to keep records. Consequently, he found himself facing two very different kinds of action: one concrete, immediate, but applying only to on individual; or else an action which applied to a whole [group] infinitely vaster, a national community but which was by that reason ambiguous, and which could be interrupted on the way. And, at the same time, he hesitated between two kinds of ethics. On the one hand, an ethic of sympathy, of individual devotion; and on the other hand a wider ethic but whose effectiveness was more questionable. He had to choose between the two. Who could help him choose? Christian doctrine? No. Christian doctrine says? "be charitable, love you neighbor, devote yourself to others, choose the hardest way, etc…." But which is the hardest ways? Whom must we love as our brother, the soldier or the mother? Which has the greatest utility, the one [which is] definite, to help a definite individual to live? Who can decide it a priori? No one. No written ethic can tell him. The Kantian ethic says: "never treat others as [a] means, but as [an] end." Very well; if I remain near [with] my mother I will treat her as an end and not as means, but by this same action, I risk treating those who fight around me as a means; and conversely if I go to rejoin those who are fighting I will treat them as an end, and by this action I risk treating my mother as a means.

If these values are vague, and if they are still too broad for the specific and concrete case that we are considering, it remains for us only to rely on our instincts. This is what this young man tried to do; and when I saw him, he said: "Basically, what counts is the sentiment; I ought to choose that which actually pushes me in a certain directions. If I feel that I love my mother enough to sacrifice everything else for her—my desire for vengeance, my desire for action, my desire for adventures—I [will] stay near her. If, on the contrary, I feel that my love for my mother is not sufficient, I [will] leave." But how [do we] judge the weight of the feeling? What constituted the worth of his feeling for his mothers? Precisely the fact that he stayed for her. I may say, I love the friend enough to sacrifice such [a certain] sum of money for him; I can say it, only if I have done it. I may say: I love my mother enough to remain with her, if I have remained with her. I can determine the worth of this affection only if, precisely, I have performed an action which confirms and denies it. Now, as I require this affection to justify my action. I find myself caught in a vicious circle.

Further, Gide has said very well, that a feeling which is acting and a feeling which is real are two nearly indiscernible things: to decide that I love my mother by remaining near her, or to act a part which will make me stray for my mother, is nearly the same thing. In other words, the feeling is constituted by the actions that we perform: I cannot then consult it in order to guide myself according to it. What that means is that I can neither seek for in myself the authentic state which will push me to act, honor demands from an ethic the concepts which will allow me to act. At least, you say, he went to see a professor to ask his advice. But, if you seek advice from a priest, for example, you have chose this priest, you already knew, after all, more or less, what he as going to advise you. In other words, to choose the adviser is still to commit yourself. The proof of it is what you will say, if you are a Christian: consult a priest. But there are priests who are collaborators, priests who wait for the tide to run, and priests who belong to the resistance. Which [should you] choose? And if the young man choose a priest who is a member of the resistance, or a priest who is a collaborator, he has already decided [on] the kind of advice he will receive. Thus, in coming to see me, he knew the reply that I was going to make too him and I had only on reply to make: you are free, choose, that is to say, invent. No general ethic can show you what there is to do; there is no sign in the world. The Catholics will reply; "but there are signs." Let's admit it: it is myself in any case who chooses the meaning that they have.

Abandonment implies that we ourselves choose our being. Abandonment goes with anguish. As for despair, this expression has a very simple meaning. It means that we will restrict ourselves to a reliance upon that which depends on our will, or on the set of probabilities which make our action possible…. From the moment when the possiblities that I am considering are not strictly involved by my action, I must take no futher interest in them, because no God, no design can adjust the world and its possibility to my will…. Quietism is the attitude of men who say: "others can do what I cannot do." The doctrine that I am present to you is exactly opposite to quietism, since it claims: "there is reality only in action." It goes futher [than this] besides, since it adds: "man is nothing other than his project, he exists only in so far as he realizes himself, thus he is no other other than whole of his actions, no other other than his life." According to this, we can understand why our doctrine horrifies a good many men. Because often they have only way of enduring their misery. Is to think; "circumstances have been against me, I was worth much more than what I have been; to be sure, I have not had a great love, or a great friendship, but it is because I have not met a man or woman who was worthy of it I have not written very good books because I have not had the leisure to do it. I have not had children to whom to devote myself because I did not find a person with I could have made my life. [There] remains, then, in me, unusued and wholly feasible a multitude of dispositon, inclinations, possibilities which give me a worth that the simple set of my actions does not allow [one] to infer." Now, in reality, for the existentialist there is no lover other than that which is made, there is no possibility of a lover other than that which manifests itself in a love; there is no genius other that which expresses itself in works of art. The genius of Proust is the totality of Proust's works; the genius of Racine is the set of his tragedies, beyond that there is nothing. Why [should] we attribute to Racine the possibility of writing a new tragedy, since precisely he did not write it? In his life a man commits himself, draws his own figure, and beyond this figure there is nothing. Obviously this thought may seem harsh to someone who has not had a successful life. But, on the other hand, it prepares men to understand that only reality counts, that the dreams, the expectations, the hopes allow [us] only to define a man as [a] disappointed dream, as miscarried hopes, as useless expectations; that is to say that that defines them negatively and not positively. However, when we say "you are nothing other than your life," that does not imply that the artist will be judged only be his artworks, for thousand other things also contribute to define him. What we mean is that man is nothing other than a set of understakings, that he is the sum, the organization, the whole of the relations which make up these undertakings.

STUDY QUESTIONS & EXERCISES

I. Why is the philosophy of Sartre considered to be an extremely pessimistic philosophy?

II. In his essay entitled Existentialism and Humanism, how does he define existensia lism?

III. Write a summary of the life of Jean Paul Sartre?

IV. Do you believe life sometimes does not make sense? Why or why not?

V. Sartre lived in very difficult times. Do you believe one existence can be influenced by the circumstances he/she lives? Why or why not?

Chapter 26
20th Century Philosophy

E. Albert Camus

You will never be happy if you continue to search for what happiness consists of. You will never live if you are looking for the meaning of life.

Albert Camus

Chapter 26
20th Century Philosophy

His Life

Albert Camus, son of a working-class family, was born in Mondovi, Algeria on November 7, 1913. He spent the early years of his life in North Africa. In primary school, Camus was fortunate enough to cross paths with a teacher, Louis Germain, who recognized the young boy's intellectual potential and encouraged him in his studies. By the time Camus received his baccalauréat in 1930, he was reading the likes of Gide, Montherlant and Malraux.

He worked a various jobs--in the weather bureau, in an automobile-accessory firm, in a shipping company. He was paying for his courses at the University of Algiers. He then turned to journalism as a career. His report on the unhappy state of the Muslims of the Kabylie region aroused the Algerian government to action and brought him public notice.

During World War II he was one of the leading writers of the French Resistance. He was editor of ***Combat***, then an important underground newspaper. After the war, however, he gave up politics and journalism and devoted himself to writing. He soon established an international reputation with such works as **The Stranger** (1946), **The Plague**

(1948), **The Rebel** (1954) and **The Myth of Sisyphus** (1955). In these last two works, Camus illuminates the problems of the human conscience in our times.

Camus was always very active in the theater. From 1935 to 1938 he ran the Theatre de l'Equipe. It was a theatrical company that produced plays by **Malraux**, **Gide**, **Synge**, **Dostoevski**, and others. Several of his plays have been published and produced. For example, the two most important of Camus' plays are ***Caligula*** (performed 1945, written 1938) and ***Cross Purpose*** (1944). In *Caligula*, a young Roman emperor comes face to face with the terrible lack of meaning in the universe after the senseless death of his beloved sister Drusilla. In order to teach the world the true nature of life, Caligula goes on a murder-spree, killing his subjects indiscriminately. After this act of rebellion fails, he chooses to court his own assassination. The plays of Camus have assured him of a preeminent position in modern French letters.

In 1957 Camus was awarded the Nobel Prize for Literature. He responded with characteristic humility, insisting that he would have voted for Malraux.

On January 4, 1960, Camus was killed in an automobile accident while returning to Paris with his friend and publisher Michel Gallimard. He was only forty-six years old and had written as recently as 1958, "I continue to be convinced that my work hasn't even been begun." Adding to the tragedy was the fact that Camus disliked cars and had intended to return to Paris by train until Gallimard convinced him to change his mind. The return half of a rail ticket was found unused in his pocket. His sudden death cut short the career of one of the most important literary figures of the Western. He died when he was at the very summit of his powers.

Life is absurd

Although it encompasses atheism and agnosticism, existentialism has had a profound influence on the 20th-century. It is addressing such issues as transcendence and the limits of human experience, as well as a personal sense of authenticity and commitment. Existentialism has been a vital movement in literature, particularly in the works of Russian novelist **Fyodor Dostoyevsky**, Austrian writer **Franz Kafka**, and of course, French writer Albert Camus.

Camus principle thesis is that life the way we find it is totally absurd. The notion of absurdity implies there is no reason for things to be the way they are. This means life is unjust it frustrates human needs. This in turn, gives rise to what is called **existential**

predicament. Camus believes that the world does not provide the basis for absolute or necessary values. Therefore, we are just alive, living in this existentialistic predicament.

These tendencies are also prominent in the **theater of the absurd**, notably in the plays of Irish-born writer **Samuel Beckett**. ***Waiting for Godot*** is one of the best-known plays by Samuel Beckett. In this play two tramps **Vladimir** and **Estragon**, wait for Godot. He never arrives. Beckett's play addresses the absurdity of, and the human need for hope. This performance pictured above was in February 1965, at the Schiller Theater in Berlin.

For Camus, "absurdity" is the given premise of all modern experience, an uneasy feeling, a sense of contradiction. It is only the begining of a perception of life, its meaning and consequences. Unlike the German philosopher Friedrich Nietzsche, Camus does not need to declare God "dead." God, or any kind of divine "unmoved mover" or guiding hand for human life, does not even come into the picture.

According to Camus, in this senseless world, the basic needs of human kind are two: the need for clarity or understanding and the need for social warmth and contact. However, since the world makes no sense, these basic human needs are not meet.

Camus focused his concern on the grotesque inhumanity and cruelty of a world torn by war and Nazism. He believed that civilization certainly with some justification, is suffering from a "plague" of epidemic proportions, a plague that kills many and sickens all (from here perhaps his most famous work The *Plague*). In such a world, one finds oneself committing violent acts merely to survive. Camus viewed the world as, in effect, sponsoring an ongoing competition in murder, as a place in which it is difficult to raise a finger without killing somebody. He wrote: one cannot always live on murders and violence." By living out the values of the lowest animals, the individual is delivered up to the merciless power of despair and cynicism. Camus despised the absolute cynicism of his time, he implied that modern society drove humans to desperation and prevented them "from taking responsibility for their own life."

The Myth of Sisyphus

Albert Camus

Of whom and of what indeed can I say: "I know that!" This heart within me I can feel, and I judge that it exists. This world I can touch and I likewise judge that it exists. There ends all my knowledge and the rest is construction. For if I try to seize this self of which I feel sure, if I try to define and to summarize it, it is nothing but water slipping through my fingers. I can sketch one by one all the aspects is able to assume, all those likewise that have been attributed to it, this upbringing, this origin, this ardor or these silences, this nobility or this vileness. But aspects cannot be added up. This very heart which is mine will forever remain indefinable to me. Between the certainty I have of my existence and the content I try to give to that assurance, the gap will never be filled. Forever I shall be a strange to myself. In psychology as in logic, there are truths but no truth. Socrates' "Know thyself" has as much value as the "Be virtuous" of our confessionals. They reveal nostalgia at the same time as ignorance. They are sterile exercise on great subjects. They are legitimate only in precisely so far as they are approximate.

And here are trees and I know their gnarled surface, water and I feel its taste. These scents of grass and stars at night, certain evening when the heart relaxes—how shall I negate this world whose power and strength I feel? Yet all the knowledge on earth will give me nothing to assure me that this world is mine. You describe it to me and you teach me to classify it. You enumerate its laws and in my thirst for knowledge I admit that they are true. You take apart it mechanism and my hope increases. At the final stage you teach me that this wondrous and multicolored universe can be reduced to the atom and that the atom itself can be reduce to the electron. All this is good and I wait for you to continue. But you tell me of an invisible planetary system in which electrons gravitate around a nucleus. You explain this world to me with an image. I realize then that you have been reduced to poetry: I shall never know. Have I the time to become indignant? You have already changed theories. So that science that was to teach me everything ends up in a hypothesis, that lucidity founders in metaphor, that uncertainty is resolved in a work of art. What need had I of so many efforts? The soft line of these hills and the hand of evening on this troubled heart teach me much more. I have returned to my beginning. I realize that if through science I can seize phenomena and enumerate them, I cannot, for all that, apprehend the world. Were I to trace its entire relief with my finger, I should not know any more. And you give me the choice between the description that is sure but that teaches me nothing and hypotheses that claim to teach me but that are not sure. A stranger to myself and to the world, armed solely with a thought that negates itself as soon as it asserts, what is this condition in which I can have peace only by refusing to know and to live, in which the appetite for conquest bumps into walls that defy its assaults? To will is to stir up paradoxes. Everything is ordered in such a way as to bring into being that poisoned peace produced by thoughtlessness, lack of heart, or fatal renunciations.

Hence the intelligence, too, tells me in its way that this world is absurd. Its contrary, blind reason may well claim that all is clear; I was waiting for proof and longing for it to be right. But despite so many pretentious centuries and over the head of so many eloquent and persuasive men, I know that is false. On this plane, at least, there is no happiness if I cannot know. That universal reason, practical or ethical, that determinism, those categories that explain everything are enough to make a decent man laugh. They have nothing to do with the mind. They negate its profound truth, which is to be enchained. In this unintelligible and limited universe, man's fate henceforth assumes its meaning. A horde of irrationals has sprung up and surrounds him until his ultimate end. In this recovered and now studied lucidity, the feeling of the absurd becomes clear and definite. I said that the world is absurd, but I was too hasty. This world in itself is not reasonable, that is all that can be said. But what is absurd is the confrontation of this irrational and the wild longing for clarity whose call echoes in the human heart. The absurd depends as much on man as on the world. For the moment it is all that links them together. It binds them one to the other as only hatred can weld two creatures together. This is all I can discern clearly in this measureless universe where my adventure takes place.

STUDY QUESTIONS & EXERCISES

I. How does Camus present the idea that life is absurd in his essay The Myth of Sisyphus?

II. The play Waiting for Godot illustrates the idea of the absurd. How?

III. Go to the Encyclopedia of Philosophy find the name Camus, read the article and then write a summary of it.

IV. What are some of the names identified with existentialism and the idea of the absurd?

V. Mention at this point, your favorite three philosophers and give the reasons for it.

Endnotes

[1]Before the Common Era, it replaces the locution B.C.

[2]The word myth comes from the Greek μύθος . It implies tale, story, legend, community. In a literal sense it means "what they say." Therefore, a myth belongs to the community from which it comes from. The word can be highly regarded when it is taken to express a total view of things or to have the dignity of supreme religious value. Basic here is the opinion that life can be expressed in terms of myth.

[3]This is known in Greek mythology as "The Judgment of Paris."

[4]Troy was located in the western part of what is now Turkey. The ruins were discovered in the 19th century.

[5]In classical mythology, this apple had written in it "For the Fairest."

[6]An ancient Greek city-state.

[7]Homer, *The Iliad*, trans. Robert Fitzgerald (New York: Anchor Books, 1975).

[8]An ancient Greek historian, often called the father of history. His history of the invasion of Greece by the Persians became the first attempt at narrative history and was the beginning of all Western history writing.

[9]From A.E. Taylor, *Aristotle and His Predecessors* (La Salle, Ill.: Open Court, 1962; first printed in 1907).

[10]*Ibid.*

[11]Philosopher and author born in Wales. He was awarded the Nobel Prize for Literature in 1950.

[12]Bertrand Russell. *A History of Western Philosophy.* New York: Simon & Schuster, 1977.

[13]All Biblical quotations are taken from the Revised Standard Version.

[14]Based on John Burnet's *Early Greek Philosophy* (1892), with minor emendations by Daniel Kolak.

[15]Daniel Kolak, *The Mayfield Anthology of Western Philosophy*, Mountain View, California: Mayfield Publishing Company, 1998.

[16]Based on John Burnet's *Early Greek Philosophy* (1892), with minor emendations by Daniel Kolak.

[17]Dr. Daniel Farhey (Jacob Caspi Lodge), "Pythagoras and Mystic Science."

[18]Heraclitus, frag. 30 quoted in W.K.C. Guthrie, *The History of Greek Philosophy* (Cambridge, England: Cambridge University Press, 1962), vol. 1, p. 454.

[19]Parmenides, frag. 2, quoted in Guthrie, vol. 2, pp. 13-15.

[20]Ibid.

[21]Parmenides, frag. 6, quoted in Guthrie, vol. 1, p. 20.

[22]It should be noted that many of the ideas the authors have attributed to Socrates may actually have been developed by Plato and put in the mouth of Socrates. For our purposes, however, we will credit Socrates at this point.

[23]This is called in the *Dialogues of Plato:* "What is"

[24]Plato, *Apology*, 38A, quoted in *The Encyclopedia of Philosophy*, s.v. "Socrates."

[25]Plato, Phaedo, quoted in Romano Guardini, *The Death of Socrates* (New York: Sheed and Ward, 1948), p. 102.

[26]Plato, *The Republic*, trans. B. Jowettt (New York: Random House, n.d.), 473 CD.

[27]Aristotle, *Metaphysics*, 1072 b 19, cited in *Encyclopedia of Philosophy*, s.v. "Aristotle."

[28]Aristotle, *The Nicomachean Ethics of Aristotle, trans.* With introduction by David Ross (London: Oxford University Press, 1925), pp. 275-276.

[29]Ibid., p. 262.

[30]Ibid.

[31]Ibid., p. 263.

[32]Ibid., p. 268.

[33]Ibid., p. 274.

[34]Ibid., p. 289.

[35]Augustine, *Letters*, Library of Christian Classics, vol. 7, trans. Albert C. Outler (Philadelphia: Westminster Press, 1955), p. 348.
[36]Augustine, *Confessions*, trans. Albert C. Outler (Philadelphia: Westminster Press, 1955), pp. 103-104.
[37]Ibid., p. 150.
[38]Ibid., p. 176.
[39]Ibid., p. 176.
[40]Augustine, *The Trinity*, trans. Stephen Mckenna, *The Fathers of the Church* (Washington, D.C.: Catholic University of America Press, 1963), vol. 45, p. 440.
[41]Augustine, *Confessions*, p. 93.
[42]Augustine, *The Trinity*, p. 432 (Scripture passage is from Job 28:28).
[43]Anselm, Proslogion, chap. 1, in M.J. Charlesworth, *St. Anselm's* Proslogion (Oxford, England: Clarendon Press, 1965), p. 115.
[44]Ibid., preface, p. 103.
[45]Ibid., chap 2, p. 117.
[46]Ibid.
[47]Thomas Aquinas, *Summa Theologica*, from Basic *Writings of St. Thomas Aquinas*, ed. Anton C. Pegis (New York: Random House, 1945), as quoted in *Classical and Contemporary Readings in the Philosophy of Religion*, 2nd ed., ed. John Hick (Englewood Cliffs, N.J.: Prentice Hall, 1970), p. 40.
[48]Ibid., p. 39.
[49]Ibid., p. 41.
[50]Thomas Aquinas, *Summa Theologica* Contra Gentiles, from *Basic Writings, as quoted* in Josef Pieper, *Guide to Thomas Aquinas*, trans. Richard and Clara Winston (New York: Pantheon Books, 1962), p. 100.
[51]Summa Theologica, p. 42.
[52]Ibid.
[53]Ibid.
[54]Ibid.
[55]Ibid.
[56]Ibid., p. 43.
[57]Ibid.
[58]Ibid.
[59]Ibid.
[60]Ibid.
[61]See Maynard Mack and others, *World Masterpieces* (New York: Norton, 1965), vol 1, pp. 1141-1143.
[62]Cited in Peter Gay, *Age of Enlightenment*, Great Ages of Man (New York: Time-Life, 1966), p. 19.
[63]Ibid., p. 18.
[64]René Descartes, *Oeures*, ed. Cherks Adam and Paul Tannery (Paris: Cerf, 1897-1913, Finnovembre 1633), 13 vols., pp. 241-242, trans. Jack Rochford Vrooman in RenJ *Descartes: A Biography* (New York: Putnam's, 1970), p. 84.
[65]René Descartes, *Discourses on Method*, from *Descartes's Philosophical Writings*, trans. Norman Kemp Smith (New York: Random House, 1958), p. 95.
[66]Ibid., p. 97.
[67]Ibid., p. 99.

[68]René Descartes, Rules for the Guidance of Our Native Powers, from *Descartes' Philosophical Writings,* pp. 8-21.
[69]Descartes, *Discourse*, pp. 118-119.
[70]René Descartes, *Meditations on First Philosophy*, from Descartes' Philosophical Writings, pp. 177-182.
[71]Descartes, *Discourse*, pp. 118-119.
[72]Descartes, *Meditations*, p. 186.
[73]Descartes, *Discourse*, p. 120.
[74]Descartes, *Meditations*, p. 212.
[75]Ibid., p. 185.
[76]Ibid., 188.
[77]S. V. Keeling, *Descartes*, rev. ed. (London: Oxford University Press, 1968), p. 113.
[78]René Descartes, *Philosophical Works of Descartes*, trans. E. S. Haldane and G. R. T. Ross (Cambridge: University Press, 1931-1934), pp. 347-350.
[79]David Hume, quoted in Ernest Mossner, *The Life of David Hume* (Oxford, England: Clarendon Press, 1954), p. 26.
[80]Ibid., p. 40.
[81]Ibid., p. 52.
[82]David Hume, A *Treatise of Human Nature*, ed. With an introduction by D.G.C. Macnabb (Cleveland: World, 1962), p. 7.
[83]Ibid., p. 46.
[84]Ibid., p. 51.
[85]Ibid., 54.
[86]Ibid., 54-55.
[87]Ibid., 55.
[88]David Hume, *An Enquiry Concerning the Human Understanding*, ed. L.A. Selby-Bigge (Oxford, England: Clarendon Press, 1902), p. 24.
[89]Ibid., pp. 63-74.
[90]*Treatise*, p. 59
[91]Ibid., p. 301.
[92]Ibid., p. 302.
[93]For a very interesting proposition see John Hick, *An Interpretation of Religion.*
[94]Immanuel Kant, *Critique of Pure Reason*, trans. Norman Kemp Smith (New York: St: St. Martin's Press, 1929), p. 22.
[95]Ibid.
[96]Ibid., p. 170.
[97]Ibid., p. 67.
[98]Ibid., p. 71.
[99]Ibid., p. 77.
[100]Ibid., p. 323.
[101]Ibid., p. 560.
[102]Immanuel Kant, *Fundamental Principles of the Metaphysics of Morals*, trans. T.K. Abbot (New York: Longmans, Green, 1909), cited in Robert F. Davidson, ed. *The Search for Meaning in Life. Readings in Philosophy* (New York: Holt, Rinehart and Winston, 1962), pp. 309, 311.
[103]Immanuel Kant, *Religion Within the Limits of Reason Alone*, trans. Theodore M. Greene and Hoyt H. Hudson (New York: Harper & Row, 1960), pp. 5-6.

[104]Kant, *Critique of Pure Reason*, p. 29.

[105]Søren Kierkegaard, quoted in Walter Lowrie, *Kierkegaard* (London: Oxford University Press, 1938), p. 22.

[106]Søren Kierkegaard, *The Journals of Søren Kierkegaard*, A Selection, ed. and trans. Alexander Dru (London: Oxford University Press, 1938), p. 8.

[107]Ibid., p. 27.

[108]Ibid., p. 59.

[109]Søren Kierkegaard, *Concluding Unscientific Postscript*, trans. David Swenson and Walter Lowrie, with introduction and notes by Walter Lowrie (Princeton, N.J.: Princeton University Press, 1944), p. 49.

[110]Lowrie, pp. 570-571.

[111]Søren Kierkegaard, *Fear and Trembling*, trans. With introduction and notes by Walter Lowrie (Princeton, N.J.: Princeton University Press, 1945), pp. 51-52.

[112]Ibid., p. 57.

[113]Ibid., p. 55-56.

[114]Ibid., p. 56.

[115]Ibid., p. 53.

[116]Ibid., pp. 21-23.

[117]Ibid., p. 38.

[118]Ibid., p. 47.

[119]Lowrie, p. 197.

[120]Kierkegaard, *Journals*, p. 92.

[121] Ibid., pp. 92-93.

[122]Heinrich to Karl Marx, Karl Marx and Friedrich Engels, *Werke*, quoted in David McLellan, *Karl Marx: His Life and Thought* (New York: Harper & Row, 1973), p. 33.

[123]Ludwig Feuerbach, *The Essence of Christianity*, trans. M. Evans, 2nd ed. (London: Kegan Paul, Trench, Trübner, 1890), pp. viii-ix.

[124]Karl Marx, Writings of Young Marx on Philosophy and Society, ed. and trans. L. Easton and K. Guddat (New York: Doubleday, 1967), pp. 289-290.

[125]Ibid., p. 294.

[126]Ibid., p. 305.

[127]Ibid., p. 302.

[128]Ibid., p. 314.

[129]Engels, Werke, quoted in McLellan, Karl Marx, p. 140.

[130]Karl Marx and Friedrich Engels, *The German Ideology*, ed. C.J. Arthur, (New York: International Publishers, 1970), p. 64.

[131]Ibid., p. 60.

[132]Marx, Writings, p. 402.

[133]Marx, German Ideology, p. 60.

[134]Karl Marx, *Capital*, ed. Friedrich Engels (Chicago: Encyclopedia Brittanica, Great Books of the Western World, 1952), p. 355.

[135]Ibid., p. 378.

[136]Karl Marx, *The Civil War in France* (New York: International Publishers, 1940), p. 34.

[137]Ibid., p. 86.
[138]Ibid., p. 85.
[139] See, for example, C.S. Burchell et al, *Age of Progress*, Great Ages of Man (New York: Time Life, 1966).
[140]Richard L. Schoenwald, ed., *Nineteenth-Century Thought: The Discovery of Change* (Englewood Cliffs, N.J. Prentice-Hall, 1965), p. 1.
[141]Karl Marx, *Writings of the Young Marx on Philosophy and Society*, ed. and trans. L. Easton and K. Guddat (Garden City, N.J. Doubleday, 1967), p. 402.
[142]Victor Lowe, "The Development of Whitehead's Philosophy," in Paul Arthur Schilpp, ed., *The Philosophy of Alfred North Whitehead*, The Library of Living Philosophers, 2nd ed. (New York: Tudor, 1951), p. 124.
[143]Alfred North Whitehead, "Mathematics and the Good," in Paul Arthur Schilpp, ed., *The Philosophy of Alfred North Whitehead*, The Library of Living Philosophers, 2nd ed. (New York: Tudor, 1951), p. 681
[144]William James, quoted in Ralph Barton Perry, *The Thought and Character of William James* (New York: Braziller, 1954), p. 121.
[145]William James, *The Literary Remains of the Late Henry James* (Boston: Osgood, 1885), pp. 59-60.
[146]Leon J. Edel, *Henry James* (Philadelphia: Lippincott, 1953), p. 45.
[147]Perry, p. 78.
[148]Melvin Marx and William Hillix, *Systems and Theories of Psychology* (New York: McGraw Hill, 1963), p.146.
[149]William James, *Essays in Pragmatism*, ed. Alburey Castell (New York: Hafner, 1955), p.142.
[150]William James, *Principles of Psychology*, vol. 2 (New York: Dover, 1950), p. 450.
[151]Edward C. Moore, *William James* (New York: Washington Square Press, 1966), p. 80.
[152]Ibid., p. 92.
[153]Ibid., p. 7.
[154]William James, *The Will to Believe and Other Essays in Popular Philosophy* (New York: Dover, 1956), pp. 146-147.
[155]Moore, p. 61.
[156]Alfred North Whitehead, *Essays in Science and Philosophy* (New York: Philosophical Library, 1947), p. 4, hereafter cited as Essays.
[157]Nathaniel Lawrence, *Alfred North Whitehead: A Primer of His Philosophy* (New York: Twayne, 1974), pp. 13-14.
[158]Whitehead, Essays, p. 5.
[159]Ibid., p. 32.
[160]Ibid., p. 37.
[161]Quoted in Lawrence, p. 17.
[162]Lucien Price, *Dialogues of Alfred North Whitehead* (Boston: Little, Brown, 1954), pp. 6-7.
[163]Whitehead, *Essays*, pp. 8-9.
[164]Price, p. 10.
[165]Ibid., p. 11.
[166]Ibid., p. 11.
[167]Alfred North Whitehead, *Science and the Modern World* (New York: Macmillan, 1925), p. 111, hereafter cited as *Science*. See Victor Lowe, *Understanding Whitehead* (Baltimore: Johns Hopkins University Press, 1962), p. 13.
[168]Whitehead, *Science*, p. 270.
[169]Alfred North Whitehead, *Religion in the Making* (Cleveland: World, 1960), p. 55, hereafter cited *as Religion*.
[170]Alfred North Whitehead, *Process and Reality* (New York: Macmillan, 1929), p. 31, hereafter cited as Process, quoted

in Donald W. Sherburne, ed., *A Key to Whitehead's Process and Reality* (New York: Macmillan, 1966), p. 218. We are indebted to Sherburne's careful work for the analysis of this term and others that follow. Words underlined are technical terms in Whitehead's thought.

[171]Alfred North Whitehead, *Modes of Thought* (New York: Macmillan, 1938), pp. 205-206, hereafter cited as *Modes*. See the helpful glossary of terms in F.S.C. Northrop and Mason W. Gross, eds., *Alfred North Whitehead; An Anthology* (New York: Macmillan, 1961), pp. 925-928.

[172]Whitehead, *Process*, p. 28, quoted in Sherburne, p. 225.

[173]Whitehead, *Process*, p. 521, quoted in Sherburne, pp. 225-226. It is clear that Whitehead did not believe that God was a male, nor even a person. However, in accordance with the conventions of his time, Whitehead regularly refers to God with the masculine pronoun.

[174]Whitehead, *Process*, p. 73, quoted in Sherburne, p. 226.

[175]Whitehead, *Process*, p. 525, quoted in Randolph Crump Miller, *The American Spirit in Theology* (Philadelphia: United Church Press, 1974), p. 154.

[176]Whitehead, *Modes,* p. 140. See Northrop and Gross, p. 926

[177]Whitehead, *Religion*, p.105. See the helpful treatment in Miller, p. 155.

[178]Ibid., p. 92.

[179]Ibid., p. 149. See Miller, p. 155.

[180]Whitehead, *Process*, p. 526, quoted in Miller, p. 156.

[181]Whitehead, *Science*, p. 276.

[182]Whitehead, *Process*, p. 520, quoted in Sherburne, p. 244.

[183]Price, pp. 370-371. See the treatment of this passage in Norman Pittenger, *Alfred North Whitehead* (Richmond, Va.: John Knox Press, 1969), pp.ix-xx, and also David Ray Griffin, *God*, *Power, and Evil* (Philadelphia: Westminster Press, 1976).

[184]For more information on Austria-Hungary and the Wittgenstein family, see Allen Janik and Stephen Toulmin, *Wittgenstein's Vienna* (New York; Simon & Schuster, 1973).

[185]Bertrand Russell, *Portraits from Memory* (London: Allen & Unwin, 1957), pp. 26-27.

[186]Ludwig Wittgenstein, *Notebooks* 1914-1916 (London: Basil Blackwell, 1961), p. 93.

[187]Ludwig Wittgenstein, *Philosophical Investigations* (New York: Macmillan, 1958), no. 109, p. 47.

[188]Ludwig Wittgenstein, *Tractatus Logico-Philiosophicus* (London: Routledge & Kegan Paul, 1922), 6.432, p. 149.

[189]From Friedrich Waismann, *Ludwig Wittgenstein und der Wiener Kreis*, p.115, cited in Janik and Toulmin, p. 233.

[190]Janik and Toulmin, *Wittgenstein*, p. 24.

[191]*Tractatus*, 6.5-6.521, p. 149.

[192]Ibid., 6.54, p. 151.

[193]Ibid., preface, p. 5.

[194]Ibid.

[195]Ibid., preface, p. 5.

[196]Ibid.

[197]Norman Malcolm, *Ludwig Wittgenstein: A Memoir* (London: Oxford University Press, 1958), pp. 16-17.

[198]Malcolm, p. 39.

[199]Wittgenstein, *Investigations*, no.43, p. 20.

[200]Ibid., nos. 65-66, p. 31.

[201]Ibid., no. 98, p. 45.

Index

D

E

R

S

T

BIBLIOGRAPHY

Adler, Mortimer. *Aristotle for Everyone: Difficult Thought Made Easy*. New York: Macmillan, 1978.

Anscombe, G. E. M., and Geach, Peter. *Three Philosophers*. Oxford, England: Oxford University Press, 1961.

Anselm. *St. Anselm*, Basic *Writings*. Translated by S. N. Deane. 2nd ed. LaSalle, Ill.: Open Court, 1974.

Aquinas Thomas. *Basic Writings of St. Thomas Aquinas*. Edited by Anton C. Pegis. New York: Random House, 1955.

Aristotle. The Basic Works of Aristotle. Edited by Richard McKeon. New York: Random House, 1941.

Augustine. *Augustine: Confessions and Enchiridion.* Translated and edited by Albert C. Outler. Philadelphia: Wesminster Press, 1955.

Augustine. *The City of God*. New York: Doubleday, 1958.

Barrett, William. *Irrational Man.* New York: Doubleday, 1958.

Battenhouse, Roy W. A *Companion to the Study of St. Augustine*. New York: Oxford University Press, 1955.

Berlin, Isaiah. *Karl Marx: His Life and Environment*. New York: Oxford University Press, 1959.

Brumbaugh, R.S. *Plato for the Modern Age*. New York: Macmillan, 1964.

Campbell, Keith. *Body and Mind*. New York: Doubleday, 1970.

Carnell, Edward John. *The Burden of Søren Kierkegaard*. Grand Rapids, Mich.: Eerdmans, 1965.

Charlesworth, M.J. St. Anselm's Proslogion. Oxford, England: Clarendon Press, 1965.

Chesterton, G. K. *St. Thomas Aquinas*. New York: Doubleday, 1936.

Chroust, Anton-Hermon. *Aristotle*. Notre Dame: University of Notre Dame Press, 1973.

Cobb, John B., Jr., and Griffen, David Ray. Process Theology: An Introductory *Exposition*. Philadelphia: Westminster Press, 1976.

Copleston, Frederick. *Aquinas.* Baltimore: Penguin, 1955.

D'Arcy, M. C. and others. *St. Augustine: His Age, Life, and Thought*. New York: World Publishing, 1957.

Davis, Stephen T. *Faith, Skepticism and Evidence*. Lewisburg, Pa.: Bucknell University Press, 1977.

Descartes, René. *Descartes Philosophical Writings.* Selected and Translated by Norman Kemp Smith. New York: Random House, 1958.

Ewing, A. C. *A Short Commenatry on Kant's Critique of Pure Reason.* London: Methuen, 1950.

Fann, K. T. *Wittgenstein's Conception of Philosophy.* Berkeley: University of California Press, 1969.

Field, G. C. *Plato and His Contemporaries.* London: Methuen, 1930.

Friedlander, Paul. *Plato* New York: Harper & Row, 1958.

Gibson, A. B. *The Philosophy of Descartes.* London: Russell and Russell, 1932.

Gill, Jerry H. ed. *Essays on Kierkegaard.* Minneapolis: Burgess, 1969.

Gilson, Etienne. *The Christian Philosophy of Saint Augustine.* Translated by L. E. M. Lynch. New York: Random House, 1960.

Gilson, Etienne. *The Christian Philosophy of St. Thomas.* New York: Random House, 1956.

Grabmann, M. *Thomas Aquinas: His Personality and Thought.* New York: Longmans, Green, 1928.

Green, Majorie. *A Portrait of Aristotle.* Chicago: University of Chicago Press, 1963.

Guardini, Romano. *The Conversion of Augustine.* Translated by Elinor Briefs. Westminster, Md.: Newman Press, 1960.

Guardini, Romano. *The Death of Socrates. An Interpretation of the Platonic Dialogues: Euthyphro, Apology, Crito, and Phaedo.* New York: Sheed and Ward, 1948.

Guthrie, W. K. L. *The History of Greek Philosophy.* Cambridge, England: Cambridge University Press, 1962-1978. Five vols.

Haldane, E. S. *Descartes: His Life and Times.* New York: Dutton, 1905.

Hendel, Charles W. *Studies in the Philosophy of David Hume.* New York: Liberal Arts Press, 1963.

Hendel, Charles W. , ed. *The Philosophy of Kant and Our Modern World.* New York: Liberal Arts Press, 1957.

Holmes, Arthur. "Christian Philosophy." *Encyclopedia Britannica.* 15th ed.

Hook, Sidney. *Towards the Understanding of Karl Marx.* New York, Day, 1933.

Hopkins, Jasper. *A Companion to the Study of St. Anselm*. Minneapolis: University of Minnesota Press, 1972.

Hume, David. *A Treatise of Human Nature*. Edited with an introduction by D. G. C. Macnabb. Cleveland: World Publishing, 1962.

James, William. *Pragmatism*. London: Longmans, Green, 1928.

James, William. *Varieties of Religious Experience*. New York: University Books, 1963.

Janik, Allen, and Toulmin, Stephen. *Wittgenstein's* Vienna. New York: Simon & Schuster, 1973.

Kamenka, Eugene. *Marxims and Ethics*. New York: St. Martin's Press, 1969.

Kant, Immanuel. *Critique of Pure Reason*. Translated by Norman Kemp Smith. New York: St. Martin's Press, 1929.

Kant, Immanuel. *Religion Within the Limits of Reason Alone*. Translated by Theodore M. Green and Hoyt H. Hudson. New York: Harper & Row, 1963.

Kaufmmann, Walter. *From Shakespeare to Existentialism*. New York: Doubleday, 1960.

Keeling, S.V. *Descartes*. Rev. ed. London: Oxford University Press, 1968.

Kenny, Anthony. *Descartes: A Study of His Philosophy*. New York: Random House, 1968.

Kenny, Anthony. *Wittgenstein*. Cambridge, Mass.: Harvard University Press, 1973.

Kierkegaard, Søren. A *Kierkegaard Anthology*. Edited by Robert Bretall. New York: Modern Library, 1936.

Koerner, S. *Kant*. Baltimore: Penguin Books, 1955.

Kuklick, Bruce. *The Rise of American Philosophy*. New Haven, Conn.: Yale University Press, 1977.

Laird, John. *Hume's Philosophy of Human Nature*. London: Methuen, 1932.

Lawrence, Nathaniel. *Alfred North Whitehead: A Primer of His Philosophy*. New York: Twayne, 1974.

Leclerc, Ivor. *Whitehead's Metaphysics*. New York: Macmillan, 1958.

Lichtheim, George. *Marxism: An Historical and Critical Study*. New York: Praeger, 1961.

Lowe, Victor. *Understanding Whitehead*. Baltimore: Johns Hopkins University Press, 1962.

Lowrie, Walter. *Kierkegaard: A Life*. New York: Harper & Row, 1962. Two vols.

Malcolm, Norman. *Ludwig Wittgenstein: A Memoir.* London: Oxford University Press, 1958.

Marx, Karl, and Engels, Friedrich. *The Communist Manifesto.* New York: Appleton -Century-Crofts, 1955.

Marx, Karl. *Capital.* Edited by Friedrich Engels. Chicago: Encyclopedia Britannica (Great Books of the Western World), 1952.

Mays, W. *The Philosophy of Whitehead.* New York: Crowell-Collier, 1962.

McLellan, David. Karl Marx: *His Life and Thought.* New York: Harper & Row, 1973.

Mossner, Ernest. *The Life of David Hume.* Oxford, England: Clarendon Press, 1954.

Nash, Ronald H. *The Light of the Mind: St. Augustine's Theory of Knowledge.* Lexington, Ky.: University Press of Kentucky, 1969.

Paulson, Friedrich. *Immanuel Kant: His Life and Doctrine.* Translated by J. E. Creighton and Albert LeFerre. New York: Ungar, 1963.

Pears, David. *Ludwig Wittgenstein.* New York: Penguin, 1969.

Perry, Ralph Barton. *The Thought and Character of William James.* New York: Braziller, 1954.

Pitcher, G. *The Philosophy of Wittgenstein.* Englewood Cliffs, N.J.: Prentice-Hall, 1964.

Plato. *The Collected Dialogues of Plato.* Edited by Edith Hamilton and Huntington Cairs. Princeton, N.J.: Princenton University Press, 1961.

Price, Lucien. *Dialogues of Alfred North Whitehead's Process and Reality.* Boston: Little Brown, 1954.

Randall, J.H., *Jr. Aristotle.* New York: Columbia University Press, 1960.

Ross, W. D. *Aristotle.* New York: Meridian Books, 1959.

Roth, John K. *Freedom and the Moral Life: The Ethics of William James.* Philadelphia: Wesminster Press, 1969.

Schilpp. Paul Arthur. Ed. *The Philosophy of Alfred North Whitehead.* The Library of Living Philosophers. New York: Tudor, 1941.

Sherburne, Donald W., ed. *A Key to Whitehead's's* Process and Reality. New York: Macmillan, 1966.

Shorey, P. *What Plato Said.* Chicago: University of Chicago Press, 1933.

Smith, John E. *Purpose and Thought: The Meaning of Pragmatism.* New Haven, Conn.: Yale University Press, 1978.

The Other It was printed in January 2003. The edition and publishing process were under the supervision of Manuel

Smith, Norman Kemp. *A Commentary to Kant's Critique of Pure Reason*. London: Macmillan, 1930.

Smith, Norman Kemp. *New Studies in the Philosophy of Descartes*. London: Russell and Russell, 1952.

Smith, Norman Kemp. *The Philosophy of David Hume*. New York: St. Martin's Press, 1941.

Southern, R. W. *Saint Anselm and His Biographer*. Cambridge, England: Cambridge University Press, 1963.

Taylot, A.E. *Plato, the Man and His Work*. New York: Barnes and Noble, 1966.

Thompson, Josiah. *Kierkegaard*. New York: Doubleday, 1972.

Tucker, R. C. *Philosophy and Myth in Karl Marx*. New York: Cambridge University Press, 1961.

Van Der Meer, F. *Augustine the Bishop*. Translated by Brian Battershaw and G. R. Lamb. London: Sheed and Ward, 1961.

Whitehead, Alfred North. *Process and Reality*. New York: Macmillan, 1929.

Whitehead. Alfred North. *Essays in Science and Philosophy*. New York: Philosophical Library, 1947.

Wild, John. *The Radical Empiricism of William James*. New York: Doubleday, 1969.

Wittgenstein, Ludwig. *Philosophical Investigations*. New York: Macmillan, 1958.

Wittgenstein, Ludwig. *Tractatus. Logico-Philosophicus*. London: Routledge & Kegan Paul, 1922.

Zabech, F. *Hume: Precursor of Modern Empiricism*. New York: Humanities Press, 1960.

The Other
It was printed in January 2003. The edition and publishing process were under the supervision of Manuel Murrieta, Ph.D. , editor in chief of *Editorial Orbis Press*

To order this book for academic institutions and bookstores please contact:
Editorial Orbis Press
4000. N. 7th Street-suite 102
Phoenix, Arizona 85014
USA

Phone (602) 264-5011
Fax (419) 821-5046
editor@orbispress.com
www.orbispress.com